Hope at Sea

. . . .

Possible Ecologies in Oceanic Literature

Teresa Shewry

University of Minnesota Press
Minneapolis
London

An earlier version of chapter 2 was published as "In Search of Changed Climates: Water, Weather, and Sociality in Gary Pak's 'Language of the Geckos,'" *Interventions: International Journal of Postcolonial Studies* 13, no. 4 (2011): 627–39. Published by Taylor and Francis, www. tandfonline.com/doi/abs/ 10.1080/1369801x.2011.628149.

An earlier version of chapter 3 was published as "Pathways to the Sea: Involvement and the Commons in Works by Ralph Hotere, Cilla McQueen, Hone Tuwhare, and Ian Wedde," in *Environmental Criticism for the Twenty-First Century*, edited by Stephanie LeMenager, Teresa Shewry, and Ken Hiltner (New York: Routledge, 2011).

Poetry by Cathy Song was originally published in Cathy Song, *Picture Bride* (New Haven: Yale University Press, 1983); copyright 1983 by Yale University Press. Reprinted with permission.

"Kākā Point" by Hone Tuwhare was originally published in Hone Tuwhare, *Shape-Shifter* (Wellington, New Zealand: Steele Roberts, 1997). "Friend" by Hone Tuwhare was originally published in *No Ordinary Sun* (Auckland, New Zealand: Blackwood & Janet Paul Ltd., 1964). These poems are now available in Hone Tuwhare, *Small Holes in the Silence: Collected Works* (Auckland, New Zealand: Random House, 2011); copyright 2011 by the Estate of Hone Tuwhare. honetuwharepoetry@gmail .com. Reprinted with permission.

"Letter to Peter McLeavey: After Basho" by Ian Wedde was originally published in Ian Wedde, *Three Regrets and a Hymn to Beauty* (Auckland, New Zealand: Auckland University Press, 2005); reprinted by permission of Auckland University Press and Ian Wedde.

Poetry from "L(o)osing the Edge" by Teresia K. Teaiwa was originally published in *The Contemporary Pacific* 13, no. 2 (2001): 343–57. Published by the University of Hawai'i Press. Reprinted by permission of Teresia K. Teaiwa.

Published by the University of Minnesota Press
111 Third Avenue South, Suite 290
Minneapolis, MN 55401-2520
www.upress.umn.edu

Library of Congress Cataloging-in-Publication Data
Shewry, Teresa.
    Hope at sea: possible ecologies in oceanic literature / Teresa Shewry.
    Includes bibliographical references and index.
    ISBN 978-0-8166-9157-9 (hc) ISBN 978-0-8166-9158-6 (pb)
    1. Pacific Island literature (English)—History and criticism. 2. Ecology in literature.
    3. Ecocriticism. 4. Oceania—Climate. I. Title.
    PR9645.S54 2015
    820.9'99—dc23   2014043034

Printed in the United States of America on acid-free paper

The University of Minnesota is an equal-opportunity educator and employer.

21 20 19 18 17 16 15   10 9 8 7 6 5 4 3 2 1

For Mum and Dad
For Ben and Tamie

Contents

Hope in the Shadow of Sorrow

Ecology in Oceanic Literatures

The conscious field is so narrow, and on all sides it shades off into darker edges and dissolves.

Ernst Bloch, The Principle of Hope, Volume 1

What is the right colour for incredulity, anger, determination, indignation? And within these, what is the colour for hope that must persist? Surely, it is black.

Rob Garrett, "Ralph Hotere, Towards Aramoana, 1982"

SHARKS EMERGE AT NIGHT, cutting their way through black waters onto land. All night, they play in the coastal world from which they have been displaced for tourism and where they are tormented by pollutants that move with the ocean and with fish into their bodies. As dawn begins to transform the ocean once again, they glide silently away on canoes, stirring the water into wake "like fires to light the coming day" (McPherson 1998, 318).

This story, told in Hawaiian writer Michael McPherson's poem "The Waking Stone," mourns a colonial history that exposed sharks to stress on their "ancient" social and political bonds with Hawaiians, to hunts to eliminate them from coastal areas important to tourism in Hawai'i, and to oceanic poisons such as mercury (McPherson 1998, 318). But it also offers readers hope by imagining a present world that—in the survival of sharks and of Hawaiian relationships with them—evokes an open, promising future. McPherson describes the sharks as "spirit warriors," referencing Hawaiian cultural approaches in which sharks may shape-shift between human and shark form and may be 'aumākua or ancestral family guardians (318). Efforts to revitalize relationships between people and sharks are underway as part in struggles for Hawaiian forms of environmental life that support both human and nonhuman beings.[1] These emergent forms of life are "like fires to light the coming day" (318). They allow a relationship with a future that is not yet fully determined and that could in some way be good, because they are actual realities—a collection of life forms, practices, memories, and aspirations—that might enable further creativity in the environmental life shared by people and sharks. In keeping people awake to such realities, as well as in gesturing toward an environmental life that could be, "The Waking Stone" is crafted to animate hope, an awareness of the future in terms of openness and promise.

McPherson locates the sources of hope not only in Hawaiian relationships with sharks and the ocean but inseparably also in the agencies of nonhuman beings, here in sharks' persistent return to coastal waters. Hope might seem more like disengagement or denial than attunement to the bleak contexts of contemporary environmental life. The term perhaps evokes a pitiful retreat down bolt holes that time and time again fail, obliterated by the rushing melt water of glaciers, with each scientific report of a rise in sea level. But hope is also capable of animating the fear that it is all too alive and well today, a powerfully blinding experience that turns people away from environmental realities to a "castle on the clouds."

In this book, I develop a different possibility for understanding hope, drawn from my engagements with literature, theory, and film from Australia, Aotearoa New Zealand, and Hawai'i, among other sites. Hope, as animated in many contemporary literary works from the Pacific, is a relationship with the future that involves attunement to environmental change and more specifically to the ocean, nonhuman beings such as sharks, people, and deep, irreversible loss. This book makes an argument for the relevance of hope as a creative and critical engagement with present and past environmental constraints, including myriad forms of loss. It also reflects on the critical approaches that hope as an analytic category opens up for the study of environmental literature. Through this category, I develop a method for reading literary works as creative engagements with present and past life that might allow for a relationship with the future that includes hope.

Cultural production from the Pacific draws readers into varied contexts in which sweeping environmental changes have reshaped life possibilities. In this part of the world, people live closely with rivers that no longer reach the sea, with dwindling animals such as sharks and squid, and in the labyrinthine, animated spaces of cities. These are stories of loss and struggle. But they are also crafted to animate hope, or to support an awareness of a future that is partly open and promising. The term *hope* refers to a psychic, political, and social mode of engaging the future in terms of specific aspirations and imagined pathways. But the futures apprehended in hope are partly open, or multiple and subject to uncertainty, rather than are fully determined and locked into one pathway in advance, since they are shaped by unsettling present world struggles such as people's efforts to transform relationships with sharks. Such futures are promising, not only because they could be good in some measure but also because they are suggested by the struggles of the present world. Literary writers evoke hopeful futures through their stories of existing beings, commitments, struggles, and imaginaries. In the short story "Language of the Geckos" (Pak 2005a), for example, Hawai'i writer Gary Pak represents a community's struggle for the restoration of water to a river, many decades since water was first diverted out of most Hawaiian rivers to sugar plantations. The resources of this struggle—such as people's reinhabitation of an ordinary life involving water through the cultivation of taro—suggest that a river could well support the life of both nonhuman and human beings in this area and more broadly that the future is a site of possibility. In political discourses, the term *hope* is sometimes invoked to offer a vaguely promising and easily deferrable future without commitments to actual change. Literary writers such as Pak offer a more reflexive approach to the concept of hope, sharply connecting awareness of a promising, open future to present world capacities and struggles and to specific pathways and imaginaries of what could or should be.

In Pak's "Language of the Geckos," a hopeful relationship with the future is nourished not only by people's activities, aspirations, and achievements but also by water's enduring patterns of return to the mountains in the hydrologic cycle, and by the riverine beings, such as the fish, who still hang onto life at the threshold of extinction. Here and in all the literary works engaged in this book, hope is not simply a human or individual experience. It relies on other beings, human and nonhuman. A shark, a river, a forest, a community, a memory, or an imaginary are all agents that may allow people an awareness of future openness and promise. Hope is not simply given to people by the broader world, however; it is enabled by their connections with that world, including by how they see, feel, act, and imagine. Consequently this book explores literary writings that are crafted to support particular interactions between readers and the world.

"Language of the Geckos," for example, reminds people of histories involving the appropriation of river water but also encourages them to see people's struggles to return water to rivers and the alternative forms of environmental life that these struggles might yet foster.

In addition to examining how literary writings are formally crafted to animate hope, this book explores their search for words that could convey what hope might mean and how hope might feel in conditions of severe environmental upheaval. *Hope* is a term that appears frequently in contemporary literary writing as well as environmental journalism from varied places in the Pacific Ocean. How does hope emerge in contexts where environments are already damaged and where futures are also being damaged or denied? Does hope involve imaginatively drifting away from the bleak environmental conditions of the world in which we live? Could hope be a mode of facing rather than of mollifying or forgetting environmental loss? Is hope a way of devaluing and deferring life in the name of a better world to come?

The topic of hope does not simply lead us into places and forms of life that feel "good." In Australian writer Richard Flanagan's *Gould's Book of Fish: A Novel in Twelve Fish* (2001), which I engage more closely in chapter 4, hope will take us toward an early nineteenth-century penal settlement in Tasmania. Here a convict named William Buelow Gould bargains for his life by painting fish for a settlement administrator who acquires the paintings for science. Painting the fish allows Gould hope, an awareness of the future that includes multiple possibilities and that more specifically includes the potential of survival rather than only of execution. But Gould's hope is locked into the resource-extractive economy of the penal colony, specifically into the continued deaths of fish so that they can be painted. As Gould gets to know and becomes attached to the fish, it becomes impossible to clearly separate his hope from loss. Hope emerges within the turbulent environmental life of militarized global capitalism, rather than is simply resistant or situated outside. Many of the literary works I read in this book address the violent environmental relationships in which hope takes part. They imaginatively explore how such relationships, which may give hope to some and mean destruction for others, might be reshaped to better support varied lives. In *Gould's Book of Fish*, Gould increasingly comes to associate a promising future with his efforts to halt the excessive destruction of fish rather than simply with his own survival. He tells us that he is "smuggling hope," or using his paintings to push hope through time to future viewers who might be able to intervene in the decline of fish (386).

Hope will always be troubling in its intimacies with the lives of others and with environmental change, just as it will always be somewhat unreliable in its grasp of any futures that might eventually unfold. But in my estimation, hope is important as a mode of engagement in environmental struggles in the Pacific and elsewhere. Some of the most powerful stories that are told in the contemporary world insist on inevitable futures in which there are no alternatives to the unjust environments that are being created in global, militarized capitalism.[2] Anna Lowenhaupt Tsing argues that intellectuals are sometimes complicit in narratives of inevitable futures, outlining a struggle in which people in South Kalimantan, Indonesia, forced a timber company to stop removing trees from the lands of a local village and established a community-managed forest. Intellectuals, in their resignation to the predicted trajectories of globalization and environmental degradation, may denigrate and undermine such people who still fight for entities like a forest that can support the life of humans and nonhumans. To elide the potential of such struggles is "not just pessimistic; it is also historically misleading" (Tsing 2005, 266). Tsing suggests that scholars tell critical stories that allow for hope by recognizing the passions, struggles, and dreams of justice that, in the violent contexts of capitalist resource extraction, force uncertainties into what might yet come (269). Hope, as a relationship with a future that is in some measure indeterminate, supports people's struggles for more viable forms of environmental life, suggesting that not all is already given and so that such struggles are relevant.[3]

As Tsing suggests, hope involves orientation of the critical eye to what in the present world might otherwise escape notice; such an orientation allows a relationship with an uncertain, promising future. As such, hope is important not only because it involves awareness of the future, but also as attunement to existing environmental life. In Pak's short story, "Language of the Geckos," living people, ancestors, geckos, land forms, atmosphere, and water, among other forces, draw a rainstorm to a site where water was long ago appropriated. These activities might allow hope, awareness that the life people share with water is a site of possibility. As in this story, literary writers offer hope through a critical, creative, and uncertain look into the present world rather than by turning away from it. They apprehend upheaval and loss, as well as the tenacious ways in which human and nonhuman beings have sought to live well with the ocean, from people's continuing struggles for the recovery of ecosystems blasted by nuclear weapons, to community efforts to reanimate their ways of engaging with threatened ecosystems such as springs and rivers, to the social movements that have forged linkages across archipelagoes and ocean. The material impacts of these struggles can be traced back across decades and even centuries in the Pacific. But they often appear nowhere in contemporary accounts of marine environmental change. Hope does not involve drifting away onto a "castle on the clouds." It is part in a sharp and confrontational, although limited, perspective on this world.

One of my broad aims in this book is to explore stories about the hope that is entangled in the environmental life of the ocean and that has never been theorized in a direct, sustained way in ecocriticism. This book brings ecocriticism into dialogue with theories of hope that have been developed in literary studies and other disciplines over many years. Hope is not the only mode of engagement in environmental life that matters, but it is relevant as an attunement to existing environmental life and to promising, open futures. Nonfiction writers who engage the ocean often express unease regarding the topic of hope. In *Sea Sick: The Global Ocean in Crisis,* Canadian journalist Alanna Mitchell ponders hope at a time of evident, momentous environmental disaster. Although hope is not naïve and depends on engagement with actual contexts of environment degradation, she argues, it involves orienting from such contexts toward the future through reliance on the irrational and the unexpected rather than on logic (2010, 190). Its existence is a "mystery" (190). This book does not settle the discomfort that flickers and flares around hope, but it does offer the possibility that hope is not entirely mysterious, if we are attentive to the damage *and* the struggles in this world.

A second aim here is to explore creative thought about environmental change in literature as well as theory, art, and film from the Pacific. These archives situate the sea as interconnected with life on land, and so their engagements with the ocean not only take us across and below the waters but span rapidly growing cities, the fragmentary remainders of forests that were carried away on logging trucks, and rivers that run with silt or that no longer reach the sea. In engaging cultures that situate people as part of the ocean, this book builds on the work of scholars who seek to complicate the heavy focus on U.S. and British archives in some ecocritical scholarship. The remaining sections of this introduction further outline my engagement with literary thought about hope in the context of the Pacific

Ocean, elaborate some of the controversies that surround hope, and introduce the book's literary and theoretical archive.

Hope in a Sea of Change

The ocean—falling around 11,000 meters and taking up most of the available space for life on Earth—was largely inaccessible to humans until the late nineteenth century. "The ocean is strange," writes Stefan Helmreich: "For those of us settled in down-to-earth common sense and facts-on-the-ground science, the ocean symbolizes the wildest kind of nature there is" (2009, ix).[4] In countless ways and across varied historical contexts, writers have envisioned alternative worlds that might be possible in the malleable imaginative spaces of the sea. The Pacific, or the peaceful sea *(Mare Pacificum)*, has been framed by visiting writers as a site of aspirational life ways, deeply wild nature, and isolated islands.[5] Early European explorers sometimes associated oceanic peoples and nature with a possible escape from the corruptions of civilization through return to the ancient golden age or devolution to a state of nature. These explorers endlessly collected, drew, engraved, carried away—and were carried away by—the natures of the Pacific.

The literary history of the Pacific Ocean is dotted with utopias, including the first utopia, Thomas More's *Utopia* (1999 [1516]), set in the ocean between Ceylon (Sri Lanka) and America, and Francis Bacon's *New Atlantis* (1999 [1627]), located in the South Sea. The ocean is also a recurring site in twentieth-century science fiction, from the poignant human interactions with an alien ocean in Stanisław Lem's *Solaris* (1970 [1961]), made into a film by Andrei Tarkovsky (2002 [1972]), to Jacques-Yves Cousteau's *Le Monde sans Soleil [World without Sun]* (2010 [1964]), which documents efforts to create a livable environment for humans—Continental Shelf Station Two—in the Red Sea. The deep waters and their life are apparently so strange that in *Avatar* (2009) filmmaker James Cameron models the terrestrial beings and ecology of the alien and utopian world Pandora in part on the oceanic world, on creatures such as jellyfish and hammerhead sharks. As Ernst Bloch writes of the utopian legacies of the ocean, "The genuine fairy-tale aura of a wild kind originates here. The Stevenson world 'heat and cold, storms and winds, of ships, islands, different types of adventures, or marooned people, treasures and pirates'" (1988, 183).

There are impossible fault lines between historical imaginaries of livable and desirable oceanic worlds and conditions of life in the ocean today: its fish, dwindling through industrial fishing and other impacts; its radioactive or vaporized nuclear bomb ecosystems; its "garbage patches," which are vast fields of plastics and other debris held together by the spiraling currents of gyres. The concepts of the environment and ecology designate these entanglements among human and nonhuman forces, processes, and beings, which we can never pull cleanly apart.[6] The environmental legacies of imperialism and global capitalism are revealed in the ocean, in waters thick with plastic debris, on atolls where radioactive sludge lies buried, in the patterns of marine life that flourishes and that disappears.

In this book, I read literatures from the Pacific as imaginative accounts of present life and futures that might allow for hope, among other relationships with the ocean. My approach here draws on Sophia A. McClennen's analysis of "aesthetics of hope" in the literary works of Chilean writer Ariel Dorfman (McClennen 2010). McClennen argues that Dorfman's writings work toward "provoking the reader to have hope for a different future," including by exploring collective life as important to change (63). As experimental stories of present worlds, Pacific literatures traverse environmental destruction but also describe alternative environmental processes that evoke still promising places where life might go. Michael McPherson's poem "The Waking Stone," with which I began, opens out into a world where sharks swim in a living sea "stained" by runoff and where effluents "open like brown dark flowers" (1998, 318). The sharks are ghostly, displaced figures who, by night, reinhabit coastal areas covered in tourism developments (318). "The Waking Stone" is a sharp critique of environmental destruction in an enduringly colonial context. But the poem is also crafted to be a waking stone, keeping readers alive to a world that includes different, persistent realities and potentials of people–shark relationships on Hawaiian terms of kinship, loyalty, and "ancient ways" (318). McPherson emphasizes a porous border between people and sharks in describing the "grey swimmers" variously as sharks, spirit warriors, and as traveling by canoe (318). This collection of life forms, relationships, and imaginaries suggests the possibility of revitalizing relationships between sharks and people and for recovery from the colonial situation in which they are caught up: as the sharks-canoeists cross the waves, they leave wake of "long white phosphors" to illuminate the emerging day (318). In this book, I understand literary texts as registering environmental change in a creative way. Such texts suggest new ways to apprehend the present world and offer imaginaries of what might be, not as blueprints but to clear space for a relationship with a present world and future that includes possibility and experimentation. As Hawaiʻi writer Gary Pak writes in the preface to his short story collection, *Language of the Geckos and Other Stories*, "I am writing my impressions of life, my visions of what I feel should be. . . . I offer *Language of the Geckos and Other Stories* as a look into a world that I don't know completely but one in which I live and am learning more and more about every day. I offer these stories as interpretations of my continuing activism and commitment to 'this earth of humankind,' to paraphrase the title of the remarkable novel by Indonesian writer Pramoedya Ananta Toer, with the hope that they may help to make this a better, more humanistic world" (Pak 2005b, xvi).

Literary writings evoke hopeful futures by making claims on present world struggles and specific trajectories and future scenarios, but they are not stories of certainty about what the future will involve.[7] Hope involves apprehension of the future in terms the openness, or uncertainty, without which hope would not be required. Although the concept of hope has not been engaged in a sustained way in ecocriticism, it is closely related to common temporal frameworks in the field. Imaginaries of risk, as theorized in ecocriticism by Ursula K. Heise, are particularly tightly entangled with hope, because both hope and risk involve awareness of the openness of the future. Heise observes that narratives of risk often stretch to desired, potential futures. Apprehensions of such futures cannot entirely eliminate risks, in other words, the potential for incurring damages and losses (Heise 2008, 142). Indeed, the literary texts read here often describe characters as precariously holding onto hope alongside much bleaker relationships with the future. In *Meḷaḷ: A Novel of the Pacific* (2002), a work I read in more depth in chapter 5, Hawaiʻi-based writer Robert Barclay describes a character's experience of the precariousness of his hope, in a distressed social world shaped by U.S. military activities in the Republic of the Marshall Islands. Ṇoniep, a figure of the spirit world, dreams of intervening in the economic, environmental, and health problems faced by his community. He has "a plan, a hope, a small and unrealistic chance of stopping what looms like a monstrous wave risen to a precarious height" (14). Ṇoniep's hope involves specific aspirations but it does not involve a sense of the certainty or even of the likelihood of a good outcome. He experiences his hope as on the verge of obliteration by powerful forces of the spirit world in their entanglement with U.S. militarism. N̦oniep's hope is a critical reminder of potential for the revitalization of life in this place—potential that Barclay imaginatively sketches out in terms that include an adequate hospital, new sewage and freshwater systems, and power plant repairs (92). It is also a reflection on how efforts to actualize such potential are made precarious in the contingent economic and political conditions of this place that has seen multiple colonialisms and military occupations.

The literatures read in this book situate hope as a relationship with the future that is sparked not only by the agencies of people but also by nonhuman beings. Many Pacific literatures emerge in cultural contexts that take entities such as mountains, rivers, birds, buildings, and the ocean as vital, animated protagonists. These literatures represent a person's or community's hope as entangled with a broader environmental world. For example, Hawai'i poet Cathy Song, whose work I engage in more depth in chapter 2, situates water and atmospheric conditions as a force in the activation of a character's relationship with a promising, uncertain future. In the poem "Easter: Wahiawa, 1959," Song describes the processes of water and atmosphere—"the storm that threatened / to break"—as shaping a character's sense that a disruption might open up in the claustrophobic social order in which she lives (1983, 7). In its cyclical but stormy return to land, water orients people toward an unsettling present world and to the open, promising futures evoked by such a world.

My approach here is also drawn from theorists who connect hope with worlds in which it takes form. Mary Zournazi, for example, suggests that hope is affected by creative social relationships but also by powerful messages regarding "what life is 'meant to be,'" in Australia particularly encompassing personal financial success and national security (2002, 15). She argues that we "explore hope through the societies we live in" (16). The socially uneven distributions of health, technology, media attention, money, and physical and political power can enable or undermine a hopeful relationship with the future. Julianne A. Hazlewood also links hope to lived experience, writing of Chachi, Afro-Ecuadorian, and Awá peoples whose lands are now surrounded by oil palm plantations. These vast seas of oil palms fuel climate change mitigation efforts in the Global North but in the Ecuadorian Pacific mean the destruction of native forests and peatlands, species loss, the contamination of waterways, and the disturbance and displacement of life worlds. Hazlewood describes how affected peoples forge social linkages among each others' territories and maintain alternative agro-ecosystems attuned to human and nonhuman well-being. These activities form a material and imaginative "basis" for hope (2012, 140).

People do not passively receive hope from a broader environmental world; hope emerges through their interactions with the world. In this book, I understand hope as a mode of engagement that involves awareness of the future in thoughts as well as in other physical experiences. Hope involves interactions among thoughts, emotions, and actions.[8] The English language figures hope as involving a person's agency as well as his or her connections with others: if a person is given hope, inseparably he or she hopes and is hopeful. Hope is unique to an individual and cannot simply be conflated with the experiences of others, then, but inseparably it is a way of being affected by activities that may have been carried out over many years and be extended across other beings, objects, and processes.

Hope's Controversies

Ernst Bloch observes that philosophers have largely ignored hope, so much so that he likens it "to a place in the world which is as inhabited as the best civilized land and as unexplored as the Antarctic" (1986, 6). When hope does draw attention, it sometimes stirs up controversy. By some accounts, hope is an alluring but dangerous mode of existence, cutting against the grain of bleak pictures that could be made of current life and its futures, or involving optimism without any effort to actually change the world.[9] Although I begin a discussion of some of these concerns here, they cannot be resolved in an absolute way because the concept of hope is an uncertain attempt to understand experiences that are unstable, always being reworked by the living.

We might start with histories in which severe environmental upheaval—the displacement of Indigenous peoples from their territories in colonialism; nuclear weapons testing on people's homelands—was discursively associated with promising, and sometimes open, futures, most infamously with progress and utopia. The utopian literary form generally involves the imagining of a different world, often in which almost every aspect of the present world has been transformed or replaced. Fátima Vieira observes of nineteenth-century political utopia: "The vision of a completely different future" is often "based on the annihilation of the present" (2010, 22). From certain critical angles, this literary form intensely devalues the people and other beings not needed nor wanted in the new world.[10] Although such a reading of utopia is not inevitable, these concerns do draw us into the thick of empire in nineteenth-century New Zealand, where utopia came to be conceptualized as a blueprint and linked to the obliteration or improvement of others. Some settlers used the language of utopia to frame their efforts to make neo-European ecosystems and communities. Suggesting just how little already existing places and life forms mattered within these new worlds, English politician Edward Gibbon Wakefield, who directed the New Zealand Company, an organization for promoting colonization in the archipelago, created plans for a perfect colony before he had even seen New Zealand. "Wakefield and his supporters' self confidence and zeal were as high as their knowledge of Maori and New Zealand was low," observes the Waitangi Tribunal, the organization that makes recommendations to the government about breaches of the Treaty of Waitangi, signed by the Crown and Māori in 1840 (Waitangi Tribunal 1991, 5.4.2). To make a better world, settlers burned and cut down forests, drained swamps, appropriated land, and waged war against Indigenous peoples. Persistence within such conditions was difficult, or impossible, for some individuals and social groups.

We might assume that writers would draw on concepts such as improvement, transformation, and new worlds in evoking promising futures, but these concepts failed to support environmental protection and justice and instead call up histories of violence. "My haunting," writes New Zealand ecologist Geoff Park, "derives from knowing what I now do about the life and life forces of indigenous New Zealand before my own culture got to it with its 'improving' urge and what James Cook called 'better plants'" (2006, 10–11). In addressing contexts of deliberately instituted environmental loss, many contemporary writers from New Zealand associate hopeful futures with strong continuities between the past, present, and future, particularly with endurance. They insist that not everything on the planet needs to be improved, and advocate for the relative stability of certain environmental processes, such as the temperature zone within which the planet exists.[11] Rather than designating an impossible and troubling aspiration to maintain the world just as it is, attention to endurance cuts across the imaginative divide that sometimes opens up between change and continuity. In order to position people, nonhuman animals, and processes such as the water cycle to survive, activists attempt to change dangerous environmental conditions. For example, they may block a factory from dumping waste into a river or force a government to regulate carbon dioxide emissions. Along with people, nonhumans and ecosystems endure their potentials, which are embodied and exist in the actual world and might one day support the emergence of new forms of life.[12]

In the first chapter of this book, I explore how writers formally associate promising, open futures with endurance by emphasizing a porous border between the actual world and a world that might one day exist, instead of setting up the rupture between two worlds that characterizes utopian literary form. I do not use the concept of utopia to characterize the literary works read in this book, partly because of these often striking structural differences and colonial histories.[13] Fredric Jameson differentiates utopia, with its sharp structural politics, from hope, a weak mode of engagement that presumably can be drawn from just about anything at all (2005, 3). In my estimation, utopian literatures do allow hope in encouraging readers to see their ordinary world from a strange vantage point and so in blasting notions of that world as moving in inevitable direction. As Jameson suggests, however, utopias illuminate hope only through structural engagements with economy and social life. These inherent structural concerns may be lost in other literary forms, but such a loss is not inevitable. Most of the literary writers engaged in this book struggle to negotiate complex dilemmas that early utopian writers did not face when they thought about structural change, including the issue of the survival of the living and the tight ways in which that survival may be both woven into and threatened by hegemonic existing structures such as economy. Hope is a concept vulnerable to all manner of mobilizations, not all of which are compelling. Literary writers offer a politicized approach to hope as a mode of engagement, contesting the present world realities and futures that come to be linked to hope.

At this time when people have to navigate brutal forms of environmental damage, hope could perhaps be interpreted as willful blindness to reality. In my estimation, however, hope is not well understood simply as the loss of awareness of reality—which in itself is a complex, context-specific form of being—or as entirely distinct from sorrow, despair, and other experiences.[14] Hope does not entail a complete grasp on reality, and no other kind of awareness does either. But, in the literary stories told in this book, hope is offered through attunements to present world struggles to enliven environmental relationships that have been lost or damaged. Such hope contingently responds to a world characterized by injury and loss. As such, it is never alone; it always exists intimately with experiences such as sorrow.[15] For example, in the novel *Black Rainbow* (1995 [1992]), which I read more closely in chapter 5, Samoan writer Albert Wendt evokes complex relations between hope and loss in contemporary environmental life. He imagines a marginalized people named the Tangata Moni, who exist in subterranean infrastructures beneath a militarized utopia where they face exploitation and deprivation, as have their ancestors. The Tangata Moni exist in tension with the utopians, including in remembering the dead despite the utopians' ban on history. They maintain ways of life that hold potential for addressing the violence of the utopia, and that allow a relationship with the future that includes openness and promise. But if Wendt's narrative is crafted to emphasize hope, it also suggests that such hope cannot be cleanly separated from loss, including in describing how the Tangata Moni's unsettling mode of life brings further wrath from the utopians, who secure their world by seeking to destroy or hurt those people who live differently. I see little risk in the literatures read in this book that hope could somehow be a way of masking the hurt, indignity, and uncertainty faced by many Pacific communities and individuals over the years. Hope may even intensify sorrow at loss, since attunement to the many possibilities inhering in the world leads writers toward what could have been.

The Pacific Ocean may more readily evoke images of retreat to blue expanses of water, sparkling beaches, and tranquil rainforests than of militarism and environmental destruction. This ocean—perhaps more than any other ocean on Earth—has provoked narratives of "good feeling," like hope, peace, love, and happiness, to borrow from Sara Ahmed (2010, 30).[16] These narratives can be tracked through many years and across countless tourism advertisements, Hollywood films, travel writings, and other materials that seek to take people beyond the desolate spaces of industrialization and urbanization. They evoke a promising, open future by offering viewers a retreat from the worlds in which they ordinarily live. In contrast, literary works such as *Black Rainbow* connect hope, however limited and compromised, to ordinary people and nonhuman beings who live in places damaged by nuclear weapons and other processes, rather than evoke hope by turning away to an entirely alternative world.

Environmental loss is not just a dimension of the past and present world. It heavily occupies the futures projected in scientific research and other sites. If the waters of the Pacific Ocean continue to warm up and acidify rapidly, many of its creatures will not survive. This could become an "ocean of ghosts," suggests Michael V. McGinnis, adding that this already is in many ways such an ocean (2011, n.p.). Hope is always inseparable from awareness of risk, or of potential dangers, because it involves recognition of the openness of the future. A politics of a future that is shaped and yet not determined in the present, and even of the "right to a non-projected future," has been important for many scholars and activists, given that telling people that their future is inevitable has long been a tactic of domination (Hirschman 1971, 37).[17] Scientists at work in the Pacific and elsewhere sometimes head in the direction of inevitability, however. They suggest that certain future trajectories have already been set in motion and cannot be halted, although they can be mitigated and their full consequences are unknown. This understanding of time is often present in narratives about climate change. Because of the ocean's thermal inertia, or the slow pace at which atmospheric heat and carbon dioxide are distributed through the deep ocean, scientists understand the ocean's response to the accumulation of greenhouse gases in the atmosphere, or its "commitment" to warming, as achieved already and yet as still playing out (Donner 2009). Even if all carbon dioxide emissions into the atmosphere are radically curbed, the ocean will continue to warm and rise (Wigley 2005, 1766). The pathways and implications of climate change remain surrounded in uncertainty, however.

Onlookers sometimes speak of hope as if it excludes such ways of relating to the present world and future, such that if someone lives with hope, they could not also feel depressed or have an idea that the future could or will be disastrous. But the writers and filmmakers I engage in this book cannot always represent the future as such a homogenous entity. In engaging likely or inevitable environmental upheaval, such as the undermining of life on low-lying atolls in the context of sea-level rise, they also explore peoples' efforts to allow maneuverability in relation to such upheaval. These efforts include advocacy for reductions in greenhouse gas emissions, attempts to establish pathways for migrations to higher ground, and dogged persistence in maintaining research on climate change. In U.S. director Elizabeth Pollock's *Atlantis Approaching* (2006), Tuvaluan Minister Suamalie Iosefa says, "We have long visions, you know, looking into the future and preparing our people to accept the consequences. People now seem to realize the effect of global warming. And as a consequence out of that threat, now people have decided within their families that they need a safer place." Pollock situates Tuvaluans as living in relation to a future that is in certain ways already achieved, in which life within certain parameters has been foreclosed. Yet she also suggests that this future is in many ways incredibly uncertain. People engage and alter these experiences of time in tangible if small ways, including through migration. They may face hostile receptions and many life changes in the places lying across the ocean. While migration or other efforts at mitigation may allow a relation with the future that includes promise, to some extent, a number of people interviewed in the documentary films identify climate migration as a site where their lives, and many of their hopes, are being set adrift from the narrow worlds of well-being made possible by the dominant architectures of the capitalist economy and ecology. Even when writers and filmmakers address climate change as an actual process that is altering life in the ocean now and portending further upheavals, then, their narratives may continue to illuminate hope, and hope does not necessarily signal an effort or ability to undermine bleak narratives.

Oceanic Literatures

As the films about climate change suggest, life is connected to the ocean in ways that have not always been apprehended, even in some environmentalist writing.[18] The ocean composes around 99 percent of the space available for life in the biosphere, produces most of the oxygen we breathe, and modulates the climate by taking up carbon dioxide and heat from the atmosphere. It is also a crucial source of food and other materials. Human activities have been diminishing the complex, exuberant worlds below water, and in consequence, those above water too. The sea has so far absorbed about half of the carbon dioxide that people have flooded into the atmosphere (Wood, Spicer, and Widdicombe 2008, 1767). It has also taken up most of the extra heat that has been generated in climate change. The ocean's acidity, salinity, temperature, ice cover, and volume, relationship to carbon and oxygen cycles, and perhaps the dynamics of its currents, are changing in connection with the climate (Mitchell 2010, 12). In addition to these disturbances, industrial fishing "as if there were no tomorrow" continues in the ocean, even though many commercially fished species are in decline or endangered (Ellis 2003, 13).

At this moment, when forces such as climate change and commercial overfishing are reshaping the ocean in precarious ways, many environmental activists and academics alike frame this as a setting on which

people have turned their backs, usually on the basis of European and
Euro-American archives: "Our general obliviousness to the gigantic bodies of water surrounding islands and continents is astonishing," writes
Patricia Yaeger in introducing a special issue of the journal *PMLA* on
oceanic literatures (2010, 525). Similar stories mark some activists' accounts of the ocean. Faced with trawlers scraping up everything in their
path on the seafloor, with corporations carrying out precarious "frontier
drilling" in ever deeper waters, and with fisher-people hacking the fins off
still-living sharks, the oceanic environmental organization Sea Shepherd
Conservation Society flies a pirate flag on its ships, marking its habitat as
a no-man's-land abandoned to intensive economic exploitation through
institutions' and peoples' failures to adequately care for marine life.

These narratives provide important ways to understand marine environmental change. But in this book, I tell a different story, drawing on
intensely vibrant literary, theoretical, and activist writing that is engaged
with peoples' struggles to live well with the ocean in their everyday practices, in the creative projects of art, and in the multitude of social movements that exist in the Pacific, including social movements oriented
toward action on climate change, a nuclear-free ocean, moderation in
fishing, restoration of reefs, rivers and wetlands, and alternatives to deep
sea oil drilling. Such struggles are unfolding not only in the most recognizable forums of environmental activism but also in cultures such as
surfing, diving, agriculture, and fishing. Attending to a different archive
reveals textures in people's relationships with the sea. Many intellectuals
have written about the environment in varied contexts of imperialism and
economic globalization in the Pacific, understanding environmental concerns as inseparable from concerns for social and economic well-being,
cultural recognition, political autonomy, and justice.[19] Their archives include not only literature but also statements and reports, press releases, essays, and websites, among other materials. For example, in an NGO statement to The Treaty on the Non-Proliferation of Nuclear Weapons (NPT)
Review Conference Preparatory Committee in New York in 2002, Palauan
(Belauan) intellectual Richard Salvador illuminates the interconnection
of struggles for a nuclear-free ocean and for political independence, since
colonial occupations paved the way for nuclear testing programs: "There
is little that we meaningfully distinguish between uranium mining and its
draconian practices, testing of nuclear weapons AND colonialism" (2002,
7). Engaging nonfiction theoretical writings, rather than only literature,

from the Pacific is vital to my project of doing ecocriticism beyond its common focus on American and British archives. Scholarly work at the intersection of ecocriticism and postcolonial studies has also shaped my attention to fractures and inequalities among stories about the ocean.[20] This work complicates tendencies to centralize European and Euro-American archives in some strands of ecocriticism. Engaging varied cultures globally, it understands environmental thought beyond a focus on writing about nature or wilderness and beyond what Rob Nixon calls "antihuman environmentalism," in which green concerns fall away from struggles for human health, livelihood, and political participation (2011, 5).

Literary writers and theorists from the Pacific usually situate the ocean in a framework of daily life and in connection with the land rather than take it as a primary, singular setting. They describe the ocean as a place of livelihoods such as fishing, of varied ancestors and spirits, like the shark 'aumākua (ancestors and protectors) known to some Hawaiian peoples, and of Indigenous territorial claims on expanses of the seabed, fishing grounds, and surf and coastal zones. As Isaiah Helekunihi Walker writes in his history of surfing in Hawai'i: "The ocean has been a place of autonomy, resistance, and survival for many Pacific Islanders" (2008, 91). These relationships between people and the ocean are not simply a product of the rise of global environmentalism in the late twentieth century. They emerge from the long durations in which Indigenous peoples developed environmental protocol and knowledge in the wake of the great migrations through which the first people inhabited the Pacific, as well as from colonial economic contexts that saw intensive marine environmental change. For example, nineteenth- and early twentieth-century archives show that a number of people, Māori and European, apprehended environmental changes brought about by colonial fishing, whaling, and sealing economies in New Zealand. In a 1903 petition to the parliamentary speaker, Rewi Maaka "and twenty nine others" observe heavy fishing around Rangitoto Island, asking that the *iwi* or tribe Ngāti Koata be allowed to impose a *rāhui* (restriction, embargo) as a way to maintain the fish populations and their livelihood:

> But this petition prays that the ships and boats of the Europeans who kill the fish be shut out, as they (the fish) will presently be very scarce, seeing that there is but one small portion of the sea for people residing at these places. . . .

> *Therefore your petitioners have decided to petition that this sea be duly set apart, and that the sea of Rangitoto Island, as a separate reserve for the tribe of Ngati Koata and their relatives who are living close to, or together with them.*
>
> *And that the said tribe, Ngati Koata may (hereby) be able to make sacred the said seas, so that the fish be not killed, whenever they know that here are no fish in the said sea, (and that) they shall be able to reserve (them) for two or three years in accordance with Maori custom of former days.* (qtd. in Young 2004, 113)

Such struggles have slowly but visibly reshaped the political life of the sea in New Zealand, producing material changes such as *mātaitai* reserves, which give local Māori greater access to and guardianship of marine areas, and the Treaty of Waitangi (Fisheries Claims) Settlement Act 1992, which engages Māori rights regarding commercial fishing.

Environmentalists' silence on these oceanic struggles can be understood partly in the context of the long-standing marginality of Indigenous peoples' perspectives on history and on viable futures.[21] Rather than recognizing that Indigenous peoples are capable of imagining and shaping the future, European writers historically have often framed them as having no future. For example, in 1913 *My Magazine* published an image of Māori hunter with a moa, a large, extinct bird that was endemic to New Zealand. The caption reads: "THE GREAT MOA OF NEW ZEALAND, WHICH HAS PERISHED FROM THE EARTH WITHIN THE MEMORY OF THE MAORI RACE—A RARE EXAMPLE OF A DYING RACE OF MEN HUNTING A DYING RACE OF BIRDS" (qtd. in Park 2006, 221). Stories of absent or highly limited futures are recalibrated in some contemporary forums about the Pacific, particularly in governmental and corporate discourses about the economic hopelessness of the island nations.[22]

In this book, I move in a different direction, exploring hope in this time of environmental uncertainty and loss in the Pacific. In the literary and theoretical works I engage, people's connections with the ocean and its life can allow for, as well as diminish, hope. In an essay titled "Reservoir of Hope," D. Māhealani Dudoit associates hope with long-standing Native Hawaiian and local community struggles to restore water to streams in Waiāhole Valley on Oʻahu. The water, which was diverted to sugar plantations in the late nineteenth and early twentieth centuries, would support existing and future social projects related to *kalo* (taro) cultivation, allow native riverine life to flourish, and support the life of Kāneʻohe Bay. This struggle "is about the integrity of the land: *ka pono o ka ʻāina*. It is about the kind of life we can still have in Hawaiʻi and about what these islands will look like in the future. In the fortitude of the valley residents lies a reservoir of hope from which we can all draw strength to set aright the course of our lives as a community in this ʻāina of generous, but limited, resources" (Dudoit 1997, 163). Dudoit suggests that hope is a force that energizes these struggles, but inseparably is a mode of engagement allowed by the "fortitude" of the people, calling up the long histories in which people have sought to actualize alternative social relationships with rivers in this part of the world. Dudoit connects such fortitude to people's direct re-inhabitation of an everyday life in relation to water by planting taro, removing weeds, swimming, and fishing: "We are on our way to a clearer understanding of the kinds of dreams still possible in our islands" (161). She also connects hope with the native streamlife ʻoʻopu and ʻōpae, noting that they can be seen more often since a temporary agreement has allowed increased water to run down the river.

If hope is a relationship with the future supported partly by nonhuman beings like the rain that brings water to a river, or the native fish and invertebrates that provide food, such hope is reliant not only on a local place but on expansive processes such as water's migrations through land, ocean, and atmosphere. Many early European and Euro-American archives situate the Pacific Ocean as home to primitive peoples lost to time on remote islands—peoples who could not apprehend, let alone live in relation to, the world over the horizon. But Pacific peoples have long apprehended and engaged the wide-ranging currents as well as the fractures that shape life in the ocean. Recent examples of such engagements include petitions to colonial governments, cases at the International Court of Justice, and oceanic coalitions such as the Nuclear-Free and Independent Pacific movement and Moana Nui Action Alliance. Global-scale concepts such as freedom, peace, sustainability, and decolonization have often been important in anticolonial and environmental struggles. But they have not always supported well-being or even survival. For example, the U.S. military narrated its nuclear weapons testing program in the Pacific in terms of global peace. In 1946, the U.S. military governor to the Marshall Islands told the people of Bikini Atoll that they would have to be temporarily relocated so that a new bomb could be tested for "the good of mankind and to end all world wars" and "for the welfare of all men" (qtd. in Alexander 1994, 21). This abstract future draws us far away from the lived experiences of people in the Marshall Islands at that time. There is no regard here for Marshallese interpretations of welfare and peace; nor is there concern for nonhuman animals and ecosystems. The places that were caught in the fallout of nuclear weapons fell away from the world that such weapons were said to be making possible, as Robert Stone poignantly illustrates in *Radio Bikini* (1987), a documentary film about the U.S. nuclear tests in the Marshall Islands. He incorporates desolate footage of people who were exposed to radioactive fallout and of goats who were placed on ships near bomb sites and filmed during the explosions.

People's struggles for alternative forms of environmental life have been made difficult by conditions of great physical and economic disparity and by both mundane corrosion and spectacular upheaval in the Pacific: militarized state violence against protestors; the difficulty of gaining access to land in a world divided up into property; the profound asymmetries in international media attention, in which the marginality of the intimate oceanic hinterland of more visible locations of war elsewhere takes form. In order to rework the power disparities in relation to which environmental projects emerge and must survive in the Pacific, social movements sometimes connect struggles across the ocean. They emphasize that meaningful forms of transnational interdependence must be woven together with rights to self-determination. For example, the Nuclear-Free and Independent Pacific movement, an expansive oceanic coalition that emerged in the 1970s and 1980s, framed their collective struggle for a nuclear-free ocean as supporting, and supported by, a multitude of independence struggles (Firth 2005, 361–62). Strong connections among peoples throughout the ocean, and concerns for peoples' active participation in the shaping of their environmental realities, make it more difficult to ignore places that get caught in the fallout of utopian visions, such as the places of nuclear weapons testing.

Most of the literary writers engaged in this book imagine or are directly involved in social movements, and suggest that these movements' efforts to resist predatory environmental practices allow for hope, along with other relationships with the ocean. Rather than persistently evoking hope, their narratives are broken by many points at which their ability to construct a relationship between their present world and a future—let alone a promising future—is abruptly crushed or slowly beaten down. In the novel *Ocean Roads*, New Zealand Māori writer James George describes a family who have been deeply affected by nuclear weapons development, writing that these weapons made a "hole in the future" (2006, 254). Such a chasm opened up in the present and its futures during the 1952 U.S. "Ivy Mike" hydrogen bomb test, when Elugelab Island in Enewetak (Eniwetok) Atoll, the Marshall Islands, was vaporized. In Pacific literary texts, relationships with futures fall apart in the face of particularly brutal forms of economic practice or militarism, but also in the moments when nonhuman forces unexpectedly and devastatingly break into ordinary spaces and times. In the so-called Pacific Ring of Fire, people seek to live in some of the most geologically active parts of the planet, including with earthquakes, volcanic eruptions, tsunami, floods, and typhoons. Hope, as a relationship with a future that is always in certain ways ungraspable, is closely attuned to this unsettling world.

The Chapters

My aim in this book is not a comprehensive overview of literary thought about environmental change in the Pacific, but rather to bring together selected texts so as to develop a discussion of the connections among environment, hope, and the creative projects of literature. Some ecocritics have framed the task of literature as "inscribing the materiality of the natural world onto the materiality of the printed page" (Ingram et al. 2007, 8). The possibility—or impossibility—of such a literature has been debated in and beyond the field.[23] If the task of literature is to inscribe the materiality of nature, what can we make of literatures about natures that do not materially exist in full and indeed that will never entirely exist as such?

Literary writers have long, in disparate ways, explored "the possibility of a better life through models for the renovation of an establishment that is rotten, old, and out of luck," as Indonesian writer Pramoedya Ananta Toer puts it (2007, n.p.). Throughout this book, I explore literary works that evoke futures in terms of openness and promise. Some of their imaginative work lies in putting words and narratives to recognized and unrecognized realities. But they also contribute to this world their stories about seas, forests, rivers, and cities that should or could be. Rather than read these stories as blueprints, I understand them as encouraging thought regarding existing environmental life and that yet to come. Each chapter focuses on a different way in which writers evoke and reflect on hope in relation to the life of the ocean, from the stories of endurance that animate hope in much writing after the environmental violence of imperialism, to the entanglements between hope and water, transnational spaces, and nonhuman animals, to the troubled relationships between hope and loss. Chapter 1 explores writers' struggles to illuminate hope as these struggles become interlocked with the precarious endurance of human and nonhuman beings in a context of prolonged and severe environmental upheaval. Focusing on English writer Samuel Butler's utopian novel *Erewhon* (1970 [1872]), I trace how sweeping disregard for human and nonhuman lives is figured as improvement, transformation, and new worlds in a number of European New Zealand colonial archives. Turning to *The Bone People,* first published in 1984 by Keri Hulme, a writer of Māori (Ngāi Tahu) and European heritage, I examine a language of endurance and survival that animates Hulme's and numerous contemporary writers' reading of actual conditions as well as the hope that they evoke (Hulme 1986). Such language complicates utopian writers' emphasis on alternative worlds, improvement, and transformation, providing a way of selectively directing care toward both the living and the futures that they might shape. Writers' concerns for endurance turn this book toward literary forms that insist on a porous, murky border between the present world and promising, imagined futures.

In the Pacific, a profoundly amphibious expanse of the planet, early European utopian writers heavily mapped potential human well-being onto islands. Yet, they also drew on water and its migratory dynamics for navigation, waste disposal, scientific experiments, and security. The importance attributed to water in these early texts anticipates later colonial projects in which governments and capitalists would profoundly alter water regimes through infrastructures like dams and ditches. In chapter 2, I examine how writers from Hawai'i associate hope with water. In Hawai'i from the late nineteenth century onward, the agricultural industry diverted water from rivers and other sources to sugar plantations in particular. The recent collapse of the sugar industry fueled struggles for the restoration of water. Gary Pak's short stories represent the return of water to places and peoples from which it was taken for sugar plantations, anticipating a promising, open future through engagement with the migratory spaces and temporal uncertainties of water. Poet Cathy Song provides a different perspective, writing about people who live and work on the plantations to which water was diverted. In exploring the gendered and racialized labor arrangements woven together with water in these sites and beyond, she recognizes alternative social practices and potentials in the everyday, mundane, and yet creative interactions between migrant workers and water.

In chapter 3, I focus more directly on literary works that illuminate open, promising futures in relation to the transnational forces that shape life in the ocean. New Zealand poets Hone Tuwhare, Cilla McQueen, and Ian Wedde critically explore the relationships of human and nonhuman beings across long distances, including over national borders, in processes of capitalist resource extraction and production. They connect hope with concern for the exuberant differences that characterize the life of the ocean but also with the ability to speak regarding people, places, beings, and institutions in spaces that stretch well into and beyond the ocean. Yet their works are almost always conversational in form, speaking with rather than simply about others. They associate hope with differences as well as with the conversations that are enlivened by such differences.

Scholars almost always focus on human relations with hope. But most of the beings who make a home in the ocean are not human. In chapter 4, I explore a story about hope that takes form through the connections between human and nonhuman beings, specifically fish, against the backdrop of the rapid loss of fish through excesses in fishing in a nineteenth century penal colony. The chapter moves to an archipelago at the border of the Pacific Ocean, Tasmania, and to Australian writer Richard Flanagan's novels *Gould's Book of Fish: A Novel in Twelve Fish* (2001) and *The Unknown Terrorist* (2006). In reading these novels, I come to understand hope as a relation with the present world and future that is accessible only to particular characters and yet that always exists within a broader ecology involving intimacies between people, fish, and the ocean. I reflect on the catastrophic material realities that sometimes come to be apprehended in terms of hope, including empire, incarceration, and fishing. Although such realities may evoke a future involving survival for some, they mean devastation for others. In Flanagan's writings, people's passionate interactions with each other and with fish spark new hopes, based on struggles for a communal life better defined by the expressions of nonhuman beings.

In an ocean that has seen so much environmental loss, hope might seem naïve or even to involve willful ignorance. In chapter 5, I engage literary writing about oceanic places heavily affected by nuclear weapons testing programs, some of the most brutally damaged living places on Earth. France, the United Kingdom, and the United States exploded hundreds of nuclear bombs in the Pacific between 1946 and 1996, while China, the

United States, and the Soviet Union shot nuclear missiles into the ocean (Teaiwa 1994, 87–88). Samoan writer Albert Wendt's novel *Black Rainbow* (1995 [1992]) and Hawaiʻi writer Robert Barclay's *Meļaļ: A Novel of the Pacific* (2002) link hope to places where people and nonhuman beings have struggled with the loss of life, home, environmental well-being, economic viability, health, and political autonomy. These literary texts evoke intimate relationships between hope and loss. They make claims on limited future possibility by imagining efforts to address the dead and injured. Such efforts are heavily shaped by the contingencies of a world involving nuclear weapons and other forms of violence.

In the conclusion, I briefly reflect on hope in the context of climate change, which is shaping new forms of precariousness as well as struggles for justice in the Pacific. Hope might be understood as a passive or weak way of interacting with climate change. In the stories told by filmmakers, activists, and others, however, hope is connected with the world in which it emerges, including with people's efforts to address climate change through collective action.

Tim Winton, an environmental activist and one of Australia's most important contemporary writers, describes the importance of hope in a struggle to prevent the development of tourism infrastructures at Ningaloo Reef, a fringing coral reef off Australia's west coast. He describes the recent World Heritage designation of this reef—in "a world where the forests are falling and species disappearing"—as an affirmation of those "*who never lost hope*" (Winton 2003, n.p.; Winton qtd. in Australian Marine Conservation Society 2011, n.p.). This book tells a story about hope in this sea of disappearing species and falling forests. I see hope, in the troubled but still promising worlds of the Pacific Ocean, as a limited but relevant site through which we can think about economy, history, aesthetics, and environment. Hope is a mode of engagement that turns us toward the creativity and struggles that exist in the world and the environments that they might yet enable.

CHAPTER 1

Endurance, Ecology, Empire

We are not trying to become something different. We are instead trying
to extend something over space and time that has no viable language
outside this iteration of its persistence. We are trying to be within a
social imaginary in which the substance of human life is cosubstantial
with geological/geographic life. . . . We are not trying to become otherwise,
we are trying to be the same, and this is enough for us.

Elizabeth Povinelli, *Economies of Abandonment:*
Social Belonging and Endurance in Late Liberalism

"WE CAN ENDURE ANYTHING," says Joe toward the end of New
Zealand writer Keri Hulme's *The Bone People* (1986 [1984]). The
novel tells the story of three characters—Kerewin, Joe, and Simon—who
persist through experiences that include intense violence from others
as well as against each other, pervasive economic hardship, imprisonment, and sickness. To endure is to exist "without giving way" (Oxford
Dictionaries n.d.). It implies that some form of continuity stretches over
the fissure between what is and what has been. Joe uses the term to evoke
his own persistence into the present, as well as that of Kerewin and Simon.
But the words are also spoken here to allow hope, by suggesting that these
people can continue into the future.

Classical European utopian literatures are little concerned with endurance, at least on the surface. They formally involve the imagining of
promising worlds that are different from the actual world. Immersed in
these new worlds, visitors might look back at their own world from a
different and critical vantage point, a reading process known in utopian
studies as estrangement.[1] In order to open up a fault line between the utopian world and the actual world, utopian writers imaginatively jettison all
manner of existing beings, ecosystems, and ways of life. Their emphasis
on imagining different worlds may seem to involve the diminishment and
dismissal of existing people and ecology, to be "a negation or a deferral

of life" rather than to be "on the side of life," to draw from an observation made by Ghassan Hage of a history of the term *hope* (Hage and Zournazi 2002, 151).[2]

Imagining a radically different world is not inevitably a way of devaluing everything that exists, and we need not assume that a reader will take an imagined world as a blueprint.[3] Yet, if we turn toward colonial contexts, we quickly come up against histories in which existing life was brutally negated in association with utopian thought. In nineteenth-century New Zealand, the Crown and settlers sought to create new, neo-European ecosystems and societies, including by draining swamps, cutting and burning forests, and waging war against Māori who sought to hold onto their land and sovereignty. Large numbers of utopian literary and political writings attended settlers' efforts at making a country that they were coming to know as New Zealand. The modes of life that had already taken form and had accrued relative stability in the archipelago mattered very little to some of the powerful people and institutions involved in the shaping of these utopian projects. Edward Gibbon Wakefield, an English politician and director of the New Zealand Company, planned and promoted colonization before he had ever laid eyes on the land and the people of Aotearoa. He sent out a surveyor to divide the land into rational, sellable blocks, "without a thought of checking the place out first" (Park 2006, 38).[4] Many beings did not survive these projects of making a better and alternative world. In the South Island, where *The Bone People* is set, the Crown and settlers bought up virtually all the land and converted much of it into sheep and cattle farms. Ngāi Tahu, the iwi or tribe whose territories stretch through this land, were left without adequate resources to maintain an effective economic life. It is not surprising that in *The Bone People,* Hulme, a Ngāi Tahu writer, is concerned for endurance as well as for the socially uneven distribution of this potential, in the time after European settlement.

Several literary critics have characterized *The Bone People* in terms of utopian themes (Williams 1990, 104; Wittmann 2002, 102). Hulme does not structure the novel in the way of a classical utopia, however. In other words, she does not structure *The Bone People* through a distinctive spatial or temporal divide between a utopian world and a narrator's world. She sketches an indistinct border between what already exists and what could exist. This aesthetic reflects Hulme's concern for endurance, for people who might persist, along with marginalized ways of relating to the land and sea, including forms of social life that extend between human and nonhuman beings and a relationship with the land that is not based on capital accumulation. *The Bone People* is about seams—human and nonhuman—that have persisted amid and beyond the colonial environmental projects that were crafted to replace them with something better. For many writers concerned for environmental politics in the aftermath of imperial histories, it is all too obvious that endurance—not only of life forms and ecosystems, but also of commitments, practices, understandings, and memories—allows awareness of future promise and openness. It is also clear that such hope is shadowed by immense insecurity. Tracking many forms of environmental loss—an entire forest carted away on boats or going up in smoke; a "dying" glacier; the extinction of a species—and struggling to maintain the existence of the beings that are now precariously situated on the threshold of disappearance, writers insist that not everything in this world needs to be made into something better and that making entirely new worlds is not possible nor desirable. It would be unusual to find the language of a better world or even of improvement in environmental writings from New Zealand today. But we readily encounter apparently more muted terms like *survival* and *endurance*. In *Ngā Uruora: The Groves of Life: Ecology and History in a New Zealand Landscape*, ecologist Geoff Park writes about the remaining fragments of floodplain forests that were almost entirely eliminated by European settlers. He concludes the work with the words: "We have exploited these islands' richest ecosystems with all the violence that modern science and technology could summon. We will need more than that to keep their survivors alive" (1995, 332).

In this chapter, I consider how writers link hope to actual and potential endurance in the face of deliberate, sweeping, and prolonged histories of environmental transformation. I use the terms *endurance* and *survival* interchangeably here, but I prefer *endurance* because it more readily evokes not only the living but also materials and beings that are often considered nonsentient.[5] Endurance, a term through which writers seem to insist on animating hope through practices of some measure of continuity, or on enabling some beings to extend through time, may raise the specter of impossible and problematic efforts to maintain the world just as it is. Some environmental activists and writers have been criticized for aspiring to a secure world without the pain of loss or the strangeness of emergence. They have associated nature with stillness and human life with restlessness.[6] The ocean, trees, rivers, cities, people, and indeed all entities are always on the move. In the words of Timothy Morton, "Species and individual members of a species are like the flowing flames of flowers discovered in time-lapse animation" (2010, 43). But in this dynamic world, relative stability takes shape and sediments in forms, structures, and processes, at least for a while. The acid-alkaline balance or pH of the ocean has remained within fairly steady parameters for around 20 million years, for example (Mitchell 2010, 30). Arturo Escobar suggests that "life entails the creation of form (difference, morphogenesis) out of the dynamics of matter and energy" (2012, xxvii). He argues that the emergence, stability, alteration, or destruction of practices and structures—whether these are recognized as forests, trees, concepts, or economic systems—can be explored, in part, as a matter of power and imagination. Environmental writers today emphasize the loss of much precious stability, including that of the temperature zone in which the planet exists. Their stories are heavily oriented toward tracking the processes by which environmental difference emerges across time, or "watching the world change," as journalist Elizabeth Kolbert frames her work, *Field Notes from a Catastrophe: Man, Nature, and Climate Change* (2009, 2).

In this chapter, I suggest that environmental writers do not inevitably set up a divide between continuity and change through their imaginative experiments in connecting hope with endurance. Their concern for endurance stretches from actual beings to the "spaces of potentiality" that also form part of their existence, to draw from Elizabeth Povinelli (2011b, 113). Tracing the endurance of people and objects in varied late liberal sites of impoverishment, abandonment, and exhaustion, from Indigenous Australian social projects to radical U.S. environmental activism, Povinelli observes that every human and nonhuman entity is stretched between actual and potential modes of being, between what it is and what it could do and be one day, should the conditions arrive. For example, a social group may know how to support a forest that would benefit people as well as nonhuman beings, but they may not be able to actualize this project if they have been dispossessed of land and economically marginalized and so have little agency to shape or access a forest in the world in which they live. Concern for endurance—whether of a forest, an idea, a memory, or of a people—does not mean struggling to maintain the world just as it is. It marks a struggle to allow a being, as well as its potentials, to exist across time, including by selectively changing certain conditions of that existence; it is also a struggle to open up the question of what and who can persist long enough to shape the future, either from one moment to the next or into the long term. In what follows, I first bring into focus nineteenth-century imperial projects that place utopia in sites already long inhabited and position the life of such sites as disposable, particularly through a reading of Samuel Butler's *Erewhon* (1970 [1872]). I then explore how a contemporary literary writer—Keri Hulme in *The Bone People*— illuminates hope in a context of severe environmental loss following colonial settlement. *The Bone People* offers readers hope by imagining a present world that—in the survival of certain individuals and of struggles to support forms of life such as forests—evokes an open, promising future. In formally and thematically associating such a future with endurance, Hulme complicates but does not simply break with utopian writers' transformative aspirations.

In the Direction of Destruction

It is 1868 when our anonymous narrator, a twenty-two-year-old man, travels from England to a new colony and begins work at a sheep station. He will not tell us the location of the colony, he says, presumably because we may seek to profit from the places and peoples he has discovered. He eventually sets out into mountainous and riverine country beyond the settlement, hoping to find land that will bring him wealth and fame. His hope is interrupted when he stumbles into an already existing utopia. This expanse of villages, towns, and cultivated landscapes, aesthetically crafted in a way that the narrator likens to a strange version of Europe, momentarily appears to reflect an ideal world. Yet, its status becomes more and more uncertain. The utopians have experimented with vegetarianism, but this experiment has fallen apart in tragic circumstances. They have eliminated machines such as trains from their world but remain insecure about a possible resurgence of these disturbing entities, imprisoning the narrator when he is found with a watch in his possession.

English writer Samuel Butler tells this ambivalent story of utopia in *Erewhon*. Born in 1835 in Nottinghamshire, Butler lived in Canterbury Settlement in New Zealand between 1860 and 1864. *Erewhon* took form through articles that Butler published in the New Zealand newspaper *The Press* during that time (Mudford 1970, 7). *Erewhon* was released in book form in 1872. In the preface, Butler writes that *Erewhon*'s first chapters, in which the narrator arrives at a settler colony dedicated to sheep farming and then travels into the unknown country beyond, are modeled on Canterbury in the South Island of New Zealand (Butler 1970, 33). Butler explored the Rakaia, Rangitata, and Waimakariri rivers in this huge expanse of plains and braided rivers, which runs into the Southern Alps to the west and the ocean to the east. He accumulated land that became known as Mesopotamia Sheep Station. The highly recognizable utopia of Erewhon, into which Butler's narrator stumbles after leaving the settler colony and traveling through the mountains, has attracted much critical attention, but here I explore utopian thought through the interactions between three environmental zones that structure *Erewhon*: the utopia, the sheep farming settlement, and the mountains that lie between.

Some settlers and colonial administrators directly articulated the British colonization of New Zealand in the language of utopia (Sargent 2010, 209–10; Zemka 2002). Butler would have been confronted with efforts to actualize a utopian society in Canterbury, a settlement designed as a utopia in which settlers would eliminate the expanse between the very poor and the very rich that existed in Britain (Sargent 2010, 209).[7] The founder of Canterbury Settlement, John Robert Godley (1814–61), writes that he first imagined Canterbury "in the colours of a Utopia" but that the "unreality" of that vision became apparent with experience (qtd. in Sargisson and Sargent 2004, 13).

A gap may have opened up between actual experience and the "colours of a Utopia," but settlers' efforts to remake the archipelago saw profound environmental upheaval. The landscapes of green grass, wooden houses, hedges, and sheep that now form a patchwork across much of Aotearoa New Zealand reflect histories of immense environmental change. By the time Europeans came to Canterbury, the iwi or tribe Ngāi Tahu had acquired massive territories that stretched throughout the South Island. Soon after the Treaty of Waitangi was signed by the Crown and Māori in 1840, the Crown began heavily buying Ngāi Tahu land, eventually taking from them over half of New Zealand, or 34.5 million acres, and leaving them with just 35,757 acres (Waitangi Tribunal 1991, 24.1). The economic and political marginalization of Ngāi Tahu took form through the immense diminishment of their environmental base, as settlers fired forests and drained wetlands for sheep farms, introduced new plants and animals, and diverted water from rivers. Ngāi Tahu did not have the land and start-up capital required to participate in the new sheep farming economy, while their *mahinga kai*, the areas where they gathered and produced food, were depleted or destroyed (Waitangi Tribunal 1991, 18.3.7, 18.4.3, 2.12).

How could this time of momentous upheaval have been characterized by the production of so many literary and political utopias, of archives with titles such as *The Happy Colony* (Pemberton 1985 [1854]), *New Zealand: An Earthly Paradise* (Union Steam Ship Company of New Zealand 1889), and *The Islands of the Blest* (Union Steam Ship Company of New Zealand 1914)? Some utopian writers simply ignored the people and ecosystems that already existed in the sites to be turned into utopias. Lyman Tower Sargent observes that in *The Happy Colony* Robert Pemberton represents the establishment of a settler community "in an area of New Zealand that was heavily populated by Maori as if there was no one there at all" (2010, 205). Other settler writers framed Māori as a dying people and suggested that they underutilized their territories.[8] Butler observes such imaginative maneuvers in "Waste Lands," the first chapter of *Erewhon*. Here, the narrator announces his plan of "finding, or even perhaps purchasing, waste crown-land suitable for cattle or sheep farming" (Butler 1970, 39). The concept of "waste lands" suggests that Europeans can ethically and legally settle on land that in their eyes is not well used, regardless of Indigenous peoples' claims on that land. Some nineteenth-century onlookers denounced the concept as a thin imaginative veneer over the appropriation of land owned by Indigenous peoples.[9]

As well as undermining the relationship between Indigenous people and land, the term *waste lands* elides a range of nonhuman beings and forces. The possibility of such diminishment is evident in a nineteenth-century archive, the newspaper of the King Movement or the Kīngitanga, as historian David Young notes (Young 2004, 74). Based in the Waikato-Waitomo region of the North Island, the movement emerged when Māori established a Māori king amid their struggles to retain land and sovereignty during the 1850s. From the 1860s to the 1880s the movement maintained Te Rohe Pōtae, or the King Country, as a relatively autonomous space beyond the reach of the settler state and military. Europeans were blocked from the area unless they received permission to enter from the Māori king.[10] In the newspaper, a writer advocates that "lest there be no trees for our descendents *[sic]*. Do not either set fire to the scrub on the waste lands lest the manuka and the eel-weirs be destroyed and the land spoilt" (qtd. in Young 2004, 74). The newspaper takes up the language of "waste lands," but poignantly here this area does not designate empty space but rather an important site that supports interconnected human and nonhuman life.[11]

In implying that land could be well used in the future, even though it is not used as such now, the concept of waste lands orients people not only in space but also in time. In the nineteenth century, utopian literary writers began to craft developmental narratives that relocated utopia from space into time (Ahmad 2009, 22–23; Bloch and Adorno 1988, 3). They moved the site of utopia from empty spaces that might be discovered on the Earth to an improved, future version of the worlds in which they lived. The shift from spatial to temporal utopias reflected the increasingly unmistakable impossibility of discovering unclaimed lands on the Earth. Butler reflects on the intense orientation of colonial life toward a futuristic, economic frontier in *Erewhon*, relentlessly using the languages of capacity, potential, and speculation. The first page of the novel takes us into the thick of a world oriented toward "fortunes," "profit," "pecuniary advantage," and "money" (Butler 1970, 39). Our narrator "could not help speculating upon what might lie farther up the river and behind the second range" (43). He primarily views the world around and within him in terms of promise. An "unknown world," in which mountains, rivers, and weather obstruct movement and vision, and where the Indigenous man Chowbok is secretive about what lies beyond the mountains, is a frontier for imaginative and material incorporation that drives our narrator onward (57). While Butler's use of speculative language is satirical, it reflects more seriously intended sources from that time. On arriving in Cook Strait, New Zealand, as a representative of the New Zealand Company in 1839, William Wakefield wrote, "The first appearance of the coast . . . is extremely unpromising" (qtd. in Park 2006, 38). In this way of seeing, the existing life of the archipelago matters little, and largely not at all; such life is situated only in terms of the future into which it could, or could not, be made. All manner of beings are disposable in this relentless momentum toward promising futures. In *Erewhon*, indeed, settler projects of environmental transformation seep together with destruction. Butler provides a sharp picture of ecosystems that are being incinerated to make way for better worlds when he describes the mountainous expanses between the settler colony and Erewhon, which as yet are beyond the reach of the settler-farmers. Accompanied by Chowbok, the narrator leaves the colony and follows a river into the mountains, hoping to find country that would "secure me a position such as has not been attained by more than some fifteen or sixteen persons, since the creation of the universe" (Butler 1970, 39). His transition from settler colony into the mountains is visually jarring, revealing the extensive environmental transformations that have accompanied settler colonialism in the former. The mountainside, which has been burned to create pastoral land, is "deliciously green and rich," while the terrain beyond is "rank and coarse" (42).

While our narrator affirms, rather than is alarmed by, such environmental change, he cannot always experience and imagine this place and Chowbok as disposable frontiers to be transformed into profit. He begins to appreciate the mountain and river country in ways not simply based on its possible financial value, affirming the ranges, river gorge, valley, and forest for beauty that "cannot be conveyed in language" (49). His relationship with Chowbok also changes in this section of Erewhon. Earlier in the novel, he frames Chowbok as an object for demonization and for financial and spiritual speculation, making repeated swipes about Chowbok's stupidity and ugliness. But once beyond the immediate reach of the familiar infrastructures of European settlement, he acknowledges that Chowbok's labor and knowledge is important to his survival. When Chowbok runs away, he feels "in great want, having had an insufficient diet from the time that Chowbok left me" (63). He also apprehends that Chowbok knows his way around and has "traditions" of these lands, complicating his earlier framing of this place as a frontier for the settler colony, a framing based on the extent of European cultivation and exploration rather than on Indigenous peoples' territories (45). The narrator is drawn into strange, unsettled modes of being in engaging with others in conditions where his dominance is not assured. These interactions disturb his familiar ways of experiencing the world, particularly his sense of a hierarchical order between himself (and Europeans more broadly), Indigenous peoples, and nonhuman life forms onto which competence, creativity, intelligence, and the potential of survival can be mapped. He experiences this imaginative disorder in terms of misery and near madness. Making his way through the difficult terrain of a river gorge, he feels, "I had completely lost my head" (58). Later, he suggests, "Solitude had unmanned me" (67). He is wildly affected by the mountain and riverine country: in just two pages, he describes his experience of this country in terms that include "sombre," "subdued," "exhilarating," "delightful," "peace," and "contentment" (50–51).

If utopian fiction is crafted to enable estrangement from a known and assumed world, and if such a position of exile may support critical and aspirational thought regarding that world, here Butler perhaps slyly situates a near-utopian experience in the liminal zone between the settler colony and the utopia known as Erewhon, with which the narrator later collides.

Such an experience is unlikely to simply feel safe, pleasurable, or even survivable, as Leela Gandhi has suggested of the utopian social politics of radical groups in late nineteenth- and early twentieth-century Britain. She observes that such groups broke with dominant imperial mappings of social life along lines such as race, sexuality, and species. They experienced their exile from hegemonic social affiliations in terms of "profound psychic derangement" (2006, 7). Suggesting that such experiences may not only be psychic, our narrator in *Erewhon* fears that he may not be able to physically endure in the mountains once Chowbok leaves. A life that is actually somewhat different from dominant forms of sociality and economy, and that in addition holds immense potential to be different, may mean a struggle to survive conditions of grinding poverty, social abandonment or persecution, and battering wear and tear on the body.[12] In *Erewhon*, Butler does not grapple with this issue in a sustained way because our narrator can eventually recover his familiar imaginative and material world. On finding no country that would support a viable sheep farm, he suggests that the mountains are "perfectly worthless" and the main range is "hopeless" (52). He can piece back together his familiar mapping of the world because a powerful material infrastructure supports it, from the legal status of this land as Crown waste land to the gathering military force behind the settler colony. The presence of the latter is evident at the end of *Erewhon,* when the narrator plans to return to Erewhon with a gunboat and transport the Erewhonians to work on plantations in Queensland (255–57).

In moments when the dominant narratives and material infrastructures through which the narrator engages other people and nonhumans are disturbed, however, Butler faintly imprints the possibility that the narrator need not interact with others by aggressively seeking to transform them. He evokes the violence of a place where European settlers primarily relate to Indigenous peoples and nonhuman beings as material to be wiped out or made otherwise, but he also delineates emergent, different, fragile forms of sociality. A measure of uncertainty and respect momentarily enters our narrator's story of Chowbok, as he admits Chowbok's competence in survival and contemporary and historical relationships with the land. He also appreciates the varied affective experiences allowed by his connections with nonhuman beings, beyond seeing those beings as speculative objects for economic profit. Butler barely formulates these emergent forms of life, and they do not complicate the narrator's intention of remaking this place if that would prove financially beneficial. These scenes simply suggest that Europeans had room to maneuver, and that indeed sometimes they did maneuver, beyond dominant ways of seeing and interacting with other peoples and nonhumans. Imperial projects of transformation do not simply destroy environmental continuities; inseparably, they destroy emergent forms of life and potentials for change driven by different configurations of agents. Endurance and change are interlocked processes: if Butler's emergent, marginal forms of life could survive and develop, they would profoundly challenge imperial ways of interacting with Indigenous peoples and nonhumans. But in *Erewhon*, these forms of life are destroyed shortly after they emerge.

Transformation

Contemporary New Zealand environmental writing is shadowed by these histories in which the destruction of long-standing and newly emergent forms of life came together with colonial practices of utopia, transformation, new worlds, and improvement. One writer pores over the last photograph that was ever taken of a now extinct wren; another traverses a farm landscape in search for surviving patches of forest and swamp. Their writings evoke not only the transformation but also the destruction of ecosystems and beings that they never had a chance to know. Faced with uncountable numbers of similar histories, some writers attempt to turn completely against deliberate, or even unintended, environmental transformation. Their narratives aim to separate people, as well as their axes and fires, from the last fragments of pristine nature.[13] Utopian writers, in contrast, have often expressed vivid, detailed dreams of technologically animated worlds. They have associated promising states of being with heightened human knowing, control, and reshaping of ecosystems, elaborating mechanisms to suppress nonhuman beings' differences from and disturbances to utopian life, from the domestication of animals to the securing of rivers. Sure enough, Butler repeatedly tells us that the ecosystems of Erewhon—the distinctive utopia for which he names the book and into which the narrator finally stumbles after his travels through the mountains—are "highly cultivated, every ledge being planted with chestnuts, walnuts, and apple-trees from which the apples were now gathering" (80). While enchantingly different, Erewhon is not troubling in the way of the wild territories through which the narrator has come. Its places and inhabitants are appealingly foreign and familiar, resembling varied, and particularly European, locales and beings, with a twist.

The association that Butler makes between utopia and ecosystems that are controlled and productive, at least according to European ways of seeing, recalls Thomas More's *Utopia*, which sharply differentiates the utopians' well-kept gardens from the unruly forests, towering mountains, and climatic extremes inhabited by the equally wild peoples, the Zapoletes: "They be hideous, savage, and fierce, dwelling in wild woods and high mountains where they were bred and brought up. They be of an hard nature, able to abide and sustain heat, cold, and labour, abhorring from all delicate dainties, occupying no husbandry nor tillage of the ground" (More 1999, 101). Francis Bacon's *New Atlantis* contains startling lists of transformative activities undertaken by a utopian people, who make flowers blossom at irregular times and combine species to create new ones (Bacon 1999). In another story of the utopian possibilities of environmental transformation, *The Theory of the Four Movements* (1996 [1808]), French intellectual Charles Fourier famously imagines that boreal citric acid dispersed into the sea will give it the flavor of lemonade, making it easier to transform into drinkable water for sailors (50). This will also fortuitously dispense of "the ghastly legions of sea-monsters which will be annihilated by the admixture of boreal fluid and the consequent changes in the the [sic] sea's structure" (50).

Today these imagined environments have taken on a distinctly less surreal and less utopian edge: ocean acidification is threatening the life of sea creatures; flowers are blooming at out-of-the-ordinary times. Concern for the violent realities and partly unpredictable consequences of deliberate environmental transformation, as well as for limits on dreams of controlling other beings, does not mean that we can place nature aside, as an object that is cleanly separated out from human creative activities.[14] We can rather seek some measure of agency within assemblages among varied forces, processes, and life forms. The spatial template through which Butler structures *Erewhon* may appear to set up an impossible divide between the anthropogenic utopian ecosystems of Erewhon and the wild mountainous country beyond, but Butler archives varied ways in which people are part of all the ecosystems of *Erewhon*. For example, his reference to Chowbok's peoples' "traditions" of the mountainous country between Erewhon and the settler colony suggests that Indigenous peoples' presence extends well beyond the border of the settlers' sheep farms (Butler 1970, 45). People are implicated in differing ways in all the spaces of *Erewhon*. Butler modeled the early chapters of *Erewhon* on Canterbury, a region woven together with Māori economies and cultures long before Europeans arrived, marked by the tracks of trading networks, quarries, cooking sites, rock drawings, and the archives of fires that may have been deliberately lit to clear expanses of forest.[15] "They claim and exercise ownership over the whole surface of the country, and there is no part of it, however lonely, of which they do not know the owners. Forests in the wildest part of the country have their claimants. . . . Forests are preserved for birds; swamps and streams for eel-weirs and fisheries," scientist William Swainson writes in 1859 (qtd. in Park 1995, 40).

Although Butler does not structure the environmental life of *Erewhon* in terms of a fissure between nature and utopia, the novel is marked by anxiety regarding particular human activities within this life, especially in observing upheaval brought about by colonial sheep farms.[16] Erewhon—the utopia in which the narrator makes his way after traveling up river and over a mountain pass—is an imaginary world through which Butler tinkers with, but does not ultimately think his way beyond, these anxieties. *Erewhon* is particularly striking for Butler's interest in the liveliness and character of nonhumans and for his questions about how people might coexist with them. The issue of how to live well with nonhuman animals has shaped the political life of Erewhon. Butler tells a story about the utopian government's failed efforts to establish and enforce vegetarianism. Magistrates began to police laws of vegetarianism after a prophet drew on evolutionary theory to argue that animals share much in common with humans and consequently that animals have rights. By the emergent laws, the utopians could only eat nonhumans who died a natural death. Suddenly, a flood of animals began to die such deaths: "Suicidal mania, again, which had hitherto been confined exclusively to donkies, became alarmingly prevalent even among such for the most part self-respecting creatures as sheep and cattle. It was astonishing how some of these unfortunate animals would scent out a butcher's knife if there was one within a mile of them, and run right up against it if the butcher did not get it out of their way in time" (Butler 1970, 230). The utopians' practices of vegetarianism would fall into abandonment over the years, but at times of crisis, such as outbreaks of pestilence, the laws against eating animals would be enlivened and "people were imprisoned by the thousand for illicitly selling and buying animal food" (235).

Through this story about vegetarianism, Butler expresses concern about directed social transformations that are imposed on people through the architectures of the state, the law, religion, and academic knowledge production. Discourses against meat eating would have been widely known in England by the early eighteenth century (Gandhi 2006, 75). Leela Gandhi suggests that vegetarian politics were moving on at least two distinctive pathways in the nineteenth century. The first involved legislative reform directed at animal welfare, so that violence against animals could be punished by the state. Animal welfare enabled increased government interference in the lives of working-class and colonized people and was directed at "self-regulative obedience" or governmentality (94, see also 67–114). In practicing an alternative form of vegetarian politics, people forged connections among animal welfare, working-class, and anticolonial struggles. In this radical "orientalist" form of vegetarianism, the "West" was conceptually linked to "anthropocentric brutality and carnage" while vegetarianism was linked to hospitality to outsiders, aliens, strangers, and foreigners (76, see also 97–114).

Butler condemns the potential growth in governmental power that was taking form through the enforcement of animal rights. He emphasizes that the policing of vegetarianism in Erewhon has tragic consequences, telling a "sad story" in which an amiable young man was told by a doctor that he must eat meat for health purposes (1970, 232). The man was faced with two conflicting voices: "Common Sense and Nature" versus "Duty" (233). One night he was caught with meat by an authority "who was always prowling about in search of law-breakers," and, with his life destroyed, the young man committed suicide (234). Butler does not imagine an alternative relationship between people and nonhuman beings, beyond suggesting that people will revert to meat eating through common sense (227). Efforts at organized social change may involve brutal, prying forms of power, but more important they will be hopelessly overrun through the irresistible trajectories of common sense. Butler does not account for heterogeneity, power, and conflict in the meanings of sense, or for the capacity to cultivate shared perspectives in ways that do not involve violence. For Butler, common sense is a phenomenon that is natural, albeit on the move in an evolutionary tide of life. As such, he leaves the issue of how people can live well with animals open, and perhaps, unapproachable. While provocatively setting the story of vegetarianism against the backdrop of a colonial economy directed at sheep and cattle farming, and so at killing animals, he does not connect vegetarianism with an anticolonial imaginary.

In conclusion, *Erewhon* emerges at a time of slippage between the radically different worlds imagined in classical utopian literature—complex and often unsubtly miserable places that are crafted to provoke critical thought and creativity—and the utopias of imperial projects in New Zealand, which were templates that people struggled to actualize. Butler suggests that human and nonhuman beings were little recognized, if they were recognized at all, in these utopian projects. Seen as unimportant to present life and its futures, they faced violence through activities that settlers presented as the making of a better world. What might *Erewhon* have looked like had it been told from the perspective of Chowbok, an Indigenous character living through such a time? By the turn of the twentieth century, some Europeans mistakenly thought that Māori were dying out (Park 2006, 88). Such a narrative made it easier to disengage from Māori claims regarding land, sovereignty, and unfulfilled promises made by the Crown. Ngāi Tahu sold much of their land to the Crown between 1844 and 1863, and in the years during and after these sales, they left many archives of their grievances and interpretations of what should be, including requests for payments for land rights, that Europeans stop using poisons on their lands, and for hospitals and schools that the Crown had promised to build within their territories (Tau 2009, n.p.; Waitangi Tribunal 1991, 18.2.4, 19.1). Ngāi Tahu pursued grievances at Parliament, to Queen Victoria, at the Native Land Court, at royal commissions, and at the Waitangi Tribunal (Tau 2009, n.p.). In the 1990s, they negotiated a settlement with the Crown regarding breaches of the Treaty of Waitangi. Writers who engage these histories and their reverberations in contemporary life come up against imagined, promising futures that advanced through violence in the present world and through the marginalization or destruction of other futures. Wary of linking hope to improvement, transformation, and alternative worlds, they may search for different concepts. Endurance and survival—of people, ecosystems, nonhuman beings, but also of commitments, ideas, and memories, as well as of their potentials—are terms that animate much contemporary environmental writing in New

Zealand. In turning to Hulme's novel *The Bone People* here, I explore one story about the endurance in the present world, as well as about the promising environmental futures that endurance may enable.

Ecologies of Hope after Colonial Settlement

The Bone People was first published almost a hundred years after *Erewhon*, quickly flying into controversy after it won the Pegasus Prize for Māori Literature. Literary critic C. K. Stead questioned whether Hulme could write the novel and win the prize as Māori, given her dual European and Māori heritage (Stead 1985).[17] Critics have also expressed concern that *The Bone People* reflects the utopian thought associated with colonialism. Mark Williams argues that Hulme projects "backwards into prehistory the familiar settler myth of New Zealand as a possible Eden. Eden, of course, is always located in the past, although promised in the future" (1990, 96). The recurring language of a new world in *The Bone People* perhaps recalls the utopian archives of settlement. On the first page of the novel, Hulme describes the emergence of a "New marae from the old marae, a beginning from the end" (Hulme 1986, 3). Later, she refers to "the possible new world, the impossible new world" (377).

This language resonates not only with nineteenth-century European literary and political archives, but also with Ngāi Tahu accounts of Te Ao Hou (the new world). Early in the novel, Hulme describes her main character, Kerewin, as taking "the glimmering road of the past / into Te Ao Hou" (91). In investigating Ngāi Tahu claims regarding breaches of the Treaty of Waitangi, the Waitangi Tribunal writes, "Te Ao Hou was described to us as the new world, the world after the adoption of Christianity and following the Treaty, and after the loss of the tribe's lands" (1991, 18.1). With their territories heavily diminished by land sales and without adequate startup capital, Ngāi Tahu were marginalized from the colonial farming economy but also struggled to maintain their existing economic modes of life: "Ngai Tahu's ability to cope with this change was severely checked by the Crown's failure to ensure that the tribe had a sizable stake in Te Ao Hou, the new world. Without that stake, Ngai Tahu were forced to deal with an alien culture stripped of the resources to ensure their survival" (Waitangi Tribunal 1991, 18.5).

Instead of reading *The Bone People* as a utopian novel, here I explore how Hulme illuminates hope through this framework of life after the loss of land and other upheavals of European settlement. The novel follows a child, Simon (Haimona, Himi), his father Joe, and Kerewin (Kere) as they meet and form a friendship or a new kind of family. Kerewin, who has Māori (Ngāi Tahu) and European ancestry, lives in an isolated tower on the coast, having fallen out with her family. She encounters Simon, and through him, Joe, a Māori (Ngāti Kahungunu) man who has unofficially adopted Simon after finding him washed up from the sea after a storm. Simon has very limited ability to speak and no one knows where he came from, although it seems that he has lived through immense violence and has connections to France and Scotland. He has "horror . . . at home in him" (1986, 73). Joe, who regularly gets drunk and batters Simon, is a factory worker ("I push levers") whose wife Hana and son Timote have died (131). He knows "the deep of despair" (6). After Kerewin allows Joe to beat Simon almost to death, the three are separated. Joe is sent to prison, Simon is taken to hospital and then on to welfare homes, and Kerewin, who is sick, retreats to the high country. In an interview, Hulme suggests that *The Bone People*'s characters include not only people but also the land and the sea (Alley 1992, 149). A storm of economic change is sweeping through the terrestrial and marine ecosystems of the novel, as trees, sand, fish, and stones are incorporated into the capitalist economy. Hulme takes pathways through the fallen forests and scarred lands of plantation agriculture, dams, road works, and other developmental schemes. *The Bone People*'s settings are likely modeled on the West Coast of the South Island, where Hulme lives, a patchwork of coast, forest, glaciers, mountains, clouds, and rain, dotted by few human settlements. The southern expanses of this coast form Te Wāhipounamu UNESCO world heritage site.

In contrast to the narrator of *Erewhon*, who associates extensive, deliberate environmental upheaval with the possibility of financial and spiritual success and with hope, the characters of *The Bone People* experience such upheaval as a largely negative or unimportant force in their lives. In an interview, Hulme suggests that hope is present among their experiences, nevertheless: "You have got some very damaged people there who remain damaged, but they do have one enormous hope and I wouldn't call it stronger than that" (Alley 1992, 149–50).

The characters of *The Bone People* live in somewhat different ways than through market-oriented plantation agriculture and other economic forces that are shaping inhospitable conditions for many nonhumans and humans in this part of the world. Through these activities, Hulme evokes the differing, unsettling textures that characterize present environmental life and some measure of openness in the futures that such life could shape, specifically imagining futures involving repair and regeneration rather than simply continued degradation of the life shared by human and non-human beings. Through subsistence practices, Kerewin maintains a position of limited difference in relation to plantation agriculture and other forms of market-oriented resource extraction.[18] She gathers coastal plants and animals, sharing the resulting food and materials with Simon and Joe. These activities provide sustenance and pleasure, but they also involve damage and loss. As Kerewin digs in the sand for pipi, cuts the shellfish from their shells, and eats them alive, Simon watches with "his mouth agape in horror" before asking if he can also try them (124). Kerewin is very aware of the upheaval of the ecology that supports her subsistence practices: "They'll be selling the air we breathe next. . . . First gold, then coal, then all the bush they could axe, and all the fish they could can. And now the very beach" (284). She perceives the land and sea as relatively autonomous beings that speak and act but also as physically inseparable from her life, as "deep in my heart and mind" and as "the blood of me" (166). In her claim on connection with the land and sea, Kerewin perhaps draws on the Māori framework of *whakapapa* or genealogy, "networks of interactive links between beings of different kinds," involving not only people but also entities such as mountains, rivers, and the sea (Salmond 1997, 32).[19] In contrast to Kerewin, Joe, a factory worker associated with industrial capitalism, feels alienated by, rather than connected to, this coast. He does not speak directly to the land and sea or imagine that they speak to him. Instead, they reflect his misery and loneliness:

> The rocks are black and jagged and wet. Not bare rocks: covered with life of all kinds, grapeweed and kelp, coralline paint and slow green snails. But the impression they give is desolation: black broken rocks, streaming seawater. I feel an intruder, he thinks. Unwelcome. As though this is ages past and people haven't lived yet. (Hulme 1986, 187)

Joe's feeling of being an intruder evokes his limited experience of such places, given that Hulme associates working-class life with an exhausting struggle to keep afloat. Kerewin describes her memories of such a life as involving "horrible jobs to earn enough money to buy food to eat in order to live to work at horrible jobs to earn enough" (28). Kerewin's subsistence practices involve a different economic life that supports more intimate relationships with the land and sea.

The association that Hulme makes between subsistence practices and rural areas in *The Bone People* may evoke often-criticized strands in environmental thought that take areas known as remote, rural, or wild as embodying and promising viable forms of environmental life. In such thought, these areas may support the establishment of more simple or natural modes of human life. For other onlookers, these rural places may appear as the pitiful and ghostlike remnants of a world long since vanished, or they may simply be overlooked, not important enough to warrant critical engagement. Cultural critics do not use the concept of the global rural as freely as they do that of the global city, for example. As Raymond Williams observes, however, the idea that the country stands for nature and the city for worldliness suppresses labor and economic transformation in the country, not only within national contexts but also within the global economy (1973, 46). Some European and Euro-American pastoral literature has missed this rural worldliness, involving all manner of tactics for imagining one's way out of working-class and imperial histories in rural areas.[20] Although these literary histories have no straightforward equivalent in New Zealand, European nationalist discourses heavily focus on the ancient and dramatic nature of the archipelago. A controversial government-sponsored international advertising campaign describes New Zealand as "100% Pure," for example (Tourism New Zealand 2011, n.p.). The tracks of such language can be followed to emergent concepts of a unique New Zealand nature in late nineteenth-century literature and science.[21] In certain contemporary forums, the mountains, alpine plateaus, shaggy rivers, and dense rainforests of New Zealand may be framed as the living remnants of an ancient and magical world, where one is more likely to encounter a hobbit or an ork than a colonist or a capitalist. Director Peter Jackson writes that he filmed *The Lord of the Rings* trilogy and *The Hobbit* in New Zealand because "Tolkien's world was one of deep hidden valleys, barren wastelands, remote mystical mountains and lush, low valleys, and we found all these places throughout New Zealand" (2003, 7).

Although Hulme suggests that rural places form vital homes for varied nonhumans and humans and for characters' alternative economic practices, she describes these places as economically and socially troubled rather than as pristine spaces of nature. Forests, beaches, the ocean, and small towns are sites through which Hulme recognizes and theorizes, rather than retreats from, economy. She situates rural life in the context of economic globalization and as "moving and present," to borrow from Raymond Williams (1973, 7). Postcolonial critics have often theorized socioeconomic contradictions related to colonialism by examining spaces that humans have clearly extensively altered, particularly cities, but such contradictions may be less easily seen in non-urban spaces. In *The Wretched of the Earth*, Frantz Fanon famously illuminates socioeconomic disparity by comparing a settler town that is well lit, strongly built of stone and steel, and has garbage cans, asphalt, and a "belly" that is "always full of good things," with the native town, a "hungry town" without lights and where huts are constructed on top of each other (1963, 39). In moving beyond the town, however, he finds that such fault lines are difficult to trace. In fact, the very appearance of calmness, continuity, and autonomy in non-urban spaces may be complicit with the very uncalm events of colonialism: "In this becalmed zone the sea has a smooth surface, the palm tree stirs gently in the breeze, the waves lap against the pebbles, and raw materials are ceaselessly transported, justifying the presence of the settler" (1963, 51). Hulme has similarly pointed out the difficulty of apprehending the human histories of the South Island's West Coast, where there are few traces of more than one thousand years of human presence: "The land sort of scrubs you out of the way quite quickly" (Alley 1992, 147).

Nevertheless, in *The Bone People* Hulme explores entanglements among rural places, Māori histories, imperialism, and the capitalist economy. These entanglements are evident in a scene in which Joe, Kerewin, and Simon travel to Moerangi for a holiday. Kerewin complains that the pine trees along the roadsides have replaced kahikatea. Pine trees were introduced to New Zealand in the nineteenth century and are heavily used in plantation forestry. Kerewin suggests that they look sickly: "This land isn't suitable for immigrants from Monterey or bloody wherever" (157). She feels anger on seeing the pine trees, "snarling to herself" and telling Joe, "I hate pines" (157). Kerewin's feelings about the trees are shaped by her interpretation of whether or not they are natives or foreigners, and more broadly by her anxiety about the unequal relationships between Indigenous and settler peoples in the aftermath of colonialism. The pine trees and the kahikatea stand in for uneven social dynamics among people. Kerewin's interpretation of the legitimacy of the trees' presence in par-

ticular geographic locales reflects her perception of proper human sociogeographic arrangements. The trees share social imaginaries with people.
Kerewin's assertion that the land is not suitable for immigrants draws
us in the direction of the troubled relationships between human migration and some histories of environmentalism.[22] Hulme quickly complicates overly simplistic perspectives on the relationship between environmental politics and migration, however. While Kerewin is scathing of the
pine trees, Joe is more accepting, suggesting that pine trees have their purpose. The kōwhai tree, living in coastal areas where its seeds fall into rivers
and the sea to be carried to other beaches, is also an emblem of Indigenous
peoples in this novel. It is a "sea-tree emblem for a sea-people, only the
people haven't woken up to the fact they *are* a sea-people yet" (126). If
the scene about the pine trees as aliens to some extent naturalizes what
stays in place, Hulme here complicates this perspective by also natural-
izing movement and dispersal. Moreover, she does not describe a world in
which people travel as opposed to the land. As the *kaumātua* or elder Tiaki
Mira observes, "The land changes. The land continues. The sea changes.
The sea remains" (336).

Kerewin's angry response to the pine trees also reflects her sense of
the injustice of a world in which the lives of nonhuman beings are heavily oriented toward short-term profit. It is much easier for pine trees to
endure in New Zealand than it is for kahikatea. Pine trees are cultivated
within hegemonic forms of economic life, while kahikatea are marginalized to fragmentary areas. Kahikatea forests were initially cleared for dairy
farming and timber materials such as butter boxes, but they are not prof-
itable within agricultural capitalism because their life cycle far exceeds
that of a capitalist. Taking several hundred years to mature, they are "not
fast enough for the moneyminded," as Kerewin puts it in *The Bone People*
(157). Although these forests once thrived in lowland, swampy areas of
New Zealand, they are now among the archipelago's most diminished ecosystems. Alternative ways of apprehending kahikatea, as part of a network
of people, nonhuman beings, food, memory, medicine, and cultural life,
are not allowed the same power as capitalist agriculture to shape life and
landscapes in New Zealand.[23] In the 1970s, environmental activism forced
the inclusion of kahikatea forest in a national park, and in 2010 the Nature
Heritage Fund, a government fund that finances environmental protection on private lands, purchased further kahikatea forest (Department of

Conservation n.d.a.). Today, then, kahikatea are marginalized to support flows of money, technology, and goods in the capitalist economy, but such flows also support their survival, raising the question of what hope would mean in a world in which the possibilities of protection and destruction seep together in such complicated ways.

The entanglement between struggles to create spaces for kahikatea and the economic system that Hulme sees as undermining these trees provides one way to understand the difference between *The Bone People*'s form and that of the classical utopias. *The Bone People* is not formally directed at the imagining of a different world in the manner of utopian literatures, partly because Hulme does not think her way beyond the entanglements between ecology and the capitalist economy. Hulme similarly understands Kerewin's subsistence practices only in terms of limited difference from the environmental losses unfolding in plantation forestry and other forms of industrial agriculture. Kerewin can practice a subsistence relationship with the land partly because she won a huge amount of money in a lottery. Susan Y. Najita suggests that the story about the lottery may anticipate the settlement between Ngāi Tahu and the Crown regarding breaches of the Treaty of Waitangi (2006, 113). The settlement provided Ngāi Tahu with economic compensation, among other measures. If the story of Kerewin winning a lottery anticipates this settlement, it reflects the material gains made by Ngāi Tahu and other Māori in long-term struggles for justice. The lottery allows Kerewin to own private property, a privileged position that she seeks to enforce. She has "discouraged anyone from coming on her land" (Hulme 1986, 15). On finding that Simon has entered her tower home uninvited she tells him, "People's houses are private and sacrosanct" (20). Her investment in private property has violent consequences: when Simon kicks in her guitar and steals her knife, Kerewin is so enraged that she allows Joe to beat him. Joe almost kills Simon and is sent to prison. Eventually Simon is moved from hospital to welfare homes. Kerewin's subsistence practices may break with the logics of plantation capitalism, embodying nonmarket-oriented relations with nonhuman coastal inhabitants, as well as with the people with whom she shares the food, but they rely on other angles of participation in the capitalist economy, including on land ownership, which presumably freed Kerewin from the need to sell her labor to pay rent.

So far we have seen complex entanglements among Kerewin's subsistence practices, rural ecosystems, and the economy that is diminishing these ecosystems. A similar pattern of complicity emerges around Joe, who draws on the private property system to protect a piece of land and its inhabitants. When Joe is released from prison, he retreats into the bush, or the forest. Unable to find a way from a bluff to the beach, he jumps and breaks his arm. Many things are broken around and by Joe, are unable or barely able to survive the way in which he lives, from cups and plates that are destroyed in fits of rage to his recurrent battering of the child Simon. His wife Hana and baby Timote have died. Joe's potential to endure, as well as that of the people and objects that are close to him, is particularly precarious.

In imaginatively addressing these conditions of existence, Hulme tells a story in which Joe becomes involved in practicing Māori cultural approaches to the land. Tiaki Mira finds Joe at the bottom of the cliff and moves him to the resting place of a canoe, a stone, a little god, and a mauri. *Tiaki,* to guard and to shelter, forms a basis for the concept of *kaitiakitanga,* guardianship and protection. A *kaitiaki* is "a person, group or being that acts as a carer, guardian, protector and conserver" (Royal 2009a, n.p.; see also Young 2004, 52). Tiaki Mira protects the mauri and other beings that long ago voyaged across the ocean to this place (363). Extensive environmental degradation has subsequently driven the mauri, the life force of the land, to become "despaired of us" (370). When Tiaki Mira dies, Joe inherits and becomes a guardian of the land. A solicitor tells Joe that he will receive the title to the land: "You will then own 796 acres of pakihi and private sea beaches. The land itself is nearly worthless unless you care to develop it. If you spent a million dollars and half a century, for instance, you might make a farm out of it. But that is all its potential, overt value" (376). He adds that Tiaki Mira told him "there was something of extraordinary value on the property that needed watching" (376–77). The solicitor initially evokes the future in a manner that intensely disregards the world that already exists, or more specifically the land and its inhabitants, but backtracks to suggest that something already present on the land matters and must be watched, connecting the future more carefully to the present. Joe subsequently protects the land by placing a *rāhui,* a restriction on the use of the area, that he marks by erecting carved posts (383). He perseveres with Tiaki Mira's efforts to protect the land from potential developers and gains a sense of momentum in his life.

At earlier moments in *The Bone People,* Hulme frames Joe as a bystander who watches environmental change unfold with alarm, helplessness, or indifference. He gains access and agency in relation to the land partly through inheritance. Tiaki Mira's grandmother had land rights that she protected within the *Pākehā* (European) framework of private property: "She made sure, pakeha fashion, that it would never pass out of her hands except to someone she was confident would look after what it bore" (370). If Hulme is critical of the social relationships involved in private property in other parts of *The Bone People*, here she suggests that they allow characters to maneuver toward a project that supports the varied beings that rely on the land.

As we see in these stories of Kerewin and Joe, and in contrast to *Erewhon*, *The Bone People* does not involve an imaginary of a promising world that is entirely different from that in which characters ordinarily live. Rather, Hulme imagines that people, as well as entities such as forests, actualize more limited, murky forms of difference in relation to hegemonic socioeconomic forces, as when characters draw on the private property system to support relationships with the land that are distinct from market-oriented agriculture. Acquiring private property and capital makes characters' existence less precarious and supports their efforts to live in alternative environmental ways, but Hulme is disturbed by such forms of life, for example, in suggesting that people may relate violently to others in enforcing private property. Moreover, her characters attempt to secure viable forms of environmental life in an economic system that damages such life. This does not mean that such forms of life are inevitable or easy to establish and maintain in relation to such conditions; they require agency in relation to land, time away from paid labor, and a means to support the people involved. If Butler in *Erewhon* observes the emotionally deranging impact of the chasm that opens up between his narrator and a privileged position within hegemonic social and economic arrangements, Hulme addresses characters whose material conditions of life lead into impossibilities. Without access to land and without a way to remove themselves from relentless industrial labor, characters' ability to care for the land and each other is battered if not nearly impossible.

Among its modes of engagement, *The Bone People* offers readers hope by imagining a present world that—in characters' varied efforts to regenerate the relations of human and nonhuman agents—suggests a future that is somewhat open and promising, in which people might find means to redirect the trajectories of environmental degradation and lingering colonial social relations. *The Bone People* evokes a future in which

Joe and Kerewin's tentative activities continue to grow, developing into more creative and critical forms of life. By the end of *The Bone People*, for example, Kerewin's, Joe's, and Simon's hospitality to each other has grown into a substantial communal life extending among local people and involving infrastructures such as Kerewin's new house, a communal space that "holds them all" (442). Such infrastructures are important because they go some way to imaginatively addressing those people—most people—who will never inherit or win resources such as land and money, and they also loosen Kerewin's and other characters' reliance on capital accumulation and private property. The latter forms of life are still present at the end of *The Bone People*, but they are not the only existing realities. Joe suggests that before the land and its life could entirely recover the "whole order of the world would have to change, all of humanity," but changed global dynamics are an elusive, fleeting dream in this novel (371). Hulme does not suggest that her characters could somehow overturn the entire global economic system, but rather marks their continued, critical engagement in it.

Endurance

In insisting on porosity between what already exists and what could one day emerge, Hulme underlines not only complicity but her concern for endurance. The concept of endurance directs attention and effort toward the unbroken, continuing existence of an entity or state within certain, murky, somewhat flexible parameters.[24] Only some forms of change mean the end of endurance. Rapid and even destructive change may allow a being, force, or process to endure. Its survival is broken not by change but by destruction so extensive that it no longer exists within the somewhat opaque parameters that defined its survival, such as being alive, or having a relatively distinctive form.

In *The Bone People*, characters' attention to endurance leads them to qualify, rather than eliminate, their struggles to change the world. Hulme suggests that not everything should be improved, made otherwise, or replaced by something better, in so far as we can direct our effort. Joe says of Simon, for example, "I resented his difference, and therefore, I tried to make him as tame and malleable as possible. . . . And I loved and hated him for the way he remained himself, and still loved me despite it all" (1986, 381). He makes a similar point about Kerewin, who does not fit within hegemonic models of sociality: "I was trying to make her fit my idea of what a friend, a partner was. . . . now I can see other possibilities, other ways, and there is still a hope" (381). Joe stops trying to destroy Simon's and Kerewin's relatively autonomous, distinctive ways of being in the world, but he does seek to change certain conditions of their existence, including by restoring relationships with family and attempting tó break his own pattern of drunken violence. Concern for endurance involves stepping back from efforts to change something and its encompassing world, but this move is not absolute. Politics of change become an uncertain, unwieldy site rather than are an inevitably compelling mode of engagement, but they remain important.

There is a further relationship between change and endurance in *The Bone People*: endurance does not only encompass actual people, ecosystems, or ways of life but also the potentials that they carry with them. Elizabeth Povinelli explores linkages between endurance and potential in the context of social projects that do not have a firm hold on emergence and survival but rather that precariously waver between actual and potential existence. Drawing on Giorgio Agamben, she argues that potential (a concept that I understand to designate capacity or resources for coming into being) is partly embodied and exists: "For Agamben potentiality has a dual nature: while the actual can only be, the potential can be or not be" (2011a, 9). If a person dies, for example, certain potentials are lost with them, because those potentials are inseparable from a singular, embodied, irreplaceable, and fragile life. The endurance, or destruction, of a person—and of anything else in the world—alters the present configuration of life and so inseparably who or what can shape future environmental politics.

As I have suggested, the characters of *The Bone People* undertake environmental practices that are different from industrial agriculture. But Hulme also describes dreams that are never fully realized in the space of the novel. Kerewin dreams of an ecology that remains largely unrealized throughout *The Bone People*. In her dream, a wrecked building sits on a bare and deserted land, but trees slowly emerge and "straggle" up the bare slope. The building is remade and joined by other buildings in a "bewildering colonisation" as daylight appears and people gather (1986, 428). Kerewin and local people do eventually work together to rebuild a communal space, the Māori hall, at Moerangi, but at the end of *The Bone People* the forest has not returned and nor have the people clearly begun to thrive. Instead of imagining future life forms that one day might repair damaged and regenerate irreparable ecosystems along these lines, Hulme suggests that the life of the present world embodies and bears this potential, from the survival of the mauri to characters' knowledge of how to care for it. In the last reference to the mauri in *The Bone People*, it "waits, and spins its magic in deep silence" (441). When Joe suggests that it would be impossible for the mauri to ever awaken, given extensive environmental damage, Tiaki Mira tells him, "Everything changes, even that which supposes itself to be unalterable. All we can do is look after the precious matters which are our heritage, and wait, and hope" (371). The future ecology in which the mauri re-awakens is inseparable from characters' current ability to take care of "the precious matters which are our heritage." Hulme cannot imagine the future apart from the question of how human and nonhuman beings are living (and dying) now. Because Hulme connects this future to existing life and its potentials, we return to her attention to how specific individuals and communities might become better positioned in relation to existing economic forms of life. Such attention is crucial without recourse to any future such beings might support. But it does have implications for how Hulme can engage the future, because she cannot entirely separate survival in the existing world from her fragmentary gestures toward an ecology that might one day emerge. Rather than telling a story in which everything in the existing world is made otherwise, then, Hulme imagines that some beings, projects, and ways of life might endure.

Indigenous Environmental Politics

Hulme also associates a promising future with Māori cultural approaches to the environment, perhaps appearing to lead us into the mire of early European views about Indigenous peoples as natural savages and later environmentalist stories about their "well-nigh Utopian dignity" in ecology (Jameson 2005, 18). Some environmental activists, literary writers, and filmmakers, among others, have represented Indigenous peoples as near-utopian figures who live well in nature, in contrast with modern peoples and their aggression against the more-than-human world. Such environmentally profound Indigenous figures appear in popular cultural materials such as James Cameron's film *Avatar* (2009), in which a population described as "Indigenous," the Na'vi, can connect their nerve-endings directly into the flora and fauna of the moon Pandora. Numerous scholars have suggested that such stories do not necessarily well reflect the complexities of Indigenous people's environmental histories and have primarily been created by Europeans. They argue that such accounts situate Indigenous peoples behind Europeans in a trajectory from nature toward civilization, failing to recognize that Indigenous peoples move in time and may want to live in cities or economically profit from their lands.[25]

Stories about the environmental virtues of Indigenous peoples migrate across and are mobilized in specific contexts, with disparate outcomes. Activists sometimes tactically seize on these stories to advance democratic concerns to make space for the perspectives of people who live in sites targeted for destruction or protection, or to address specific institutions involved in environmental struggles within accepted and recognizable imaginative frameworks (Raffles 2002, 150–79; Tsing 2005, 249–50). Their concerns for peoples' agencies in environmental life matter. Indigenous peoples have not always been upheld as a nobly vanishing population who are well entwined with nature. Although some European writers situated certain communities from the Pacific as living peacefully with nature, others framed the ocean as the home of pagan savages who degraded and wasted their habitats.[26] In numerous settler colonies in this ocean, and elsewhere, large numbers of European writers maligned Indigenous people's environmental life, in the context of resource extraction–oriented economy, wars for land and political control, missionaries' aspirations of converting heathens, and in science, schools, and legal systems, among other sites.

Such histories are evident in an archive from December 21, 1835, when Charles Darwin sails into the Bay of Islands, New Zealand, fresh from a visit to Tahiti. He recorded his experiences in *The Voyage of the Beagle* (2010 [1839]). Disembarking at "Pahia" (Paihia), Darwin quickly observes the "hovels of the natives," emphasizing their "diminutive and paltry" size, and remarking on their incongruence with the whitewashed, tidy cottages of the English, with their pleasing gardens of English flowers (172). Both the Māori and their houses are "filthily dirty and offensive" (173). After traveling across "so many miles of an uninhabited useless country" to a missionary settlement at Waimate, Darwin notes his pleasure at suddenly coming upon an English farmhouse and seeing that missionaries have taught Māori to plough fields and build houses with windows (175). These developments please Darwin not simply because they recall England and the creative capacities of Englishmen, but also because they spark "the high hopes thus inspired for the future progress of this fine island" (175). On December 30, Darwin leaves the archipelago on a less lofty note: "I believe we were all glad to leave New Zealand. It is not a pleasant place" (177).

Swept into the imaginative net woven by Darwin, Māori and the non-human beings of the archipelago are good only to be transformed from their small, dirty, and degraded status into a promising future modeled on English ecosystems, people, and culture. Cracks are already running through this story, as Darwin notes that Māori may have deliberately used fire to replace forest with fern, a food source, in the areas that he claims are uninhabited and useless, and that plant and animal species introduced from England are creating unanticipated environmental consequences (2010, 175–76). Nevertheless, Darwin was neither the first nor the last influential European intellectual to denigrate Indigenous people's environmental life. In Hawai'i, missionaries and literary critics maligned Hawaiian approaches to nonhuman animals as pagan, threatening, and incomprehensible (Wilson 2000, 191–213). In 1843, Reverend Sheldon Dibble writes in a history of Hawai'i: "The Sandwich Islands present some of the sublimest scenery on earth, but to an ignorant native—the great mass of the people in entire heathenism—it has no meaning" (qtd. in Wilson 2000, 193).

The power dynamics that shape environmental life are always on the move and being unsettled, but the legacies of these histories run deep. In a recent opinion piece in the newspaper *Taranaki Daily News*, Peter Moehu uses poignant humor to point out the asymmetries in the protection of places important to Pākehā as compared to Māori. He describes how the Taranaki regional and district councils allow multinational corporations to explore for oil anywhere that they would like to. As such, he suggests that a Māori-owned company will explore for oil in local cemeteries and a church, places that are historically important to European New Zealanders: "'Pakeha have been quite protective of sites they consider culturally important and have avoided drilling in those areas. This has left an opportunity for us to exploit." He continues that "the same cannot be said for culturally sensitive Maori sites, many of which have been poked, prodded and exploded in the name of oil exploration or progress" (2010, n.p.).

As theorists engage enduringly colonial power disparities in varied sites in the Pacific, they emphasize the inseparability of environment, social recognition, and political participation. Environmental struggles are not simply about determining which social group's environmental approach is most compelling, although this may be a concern; they are also about how environmental life reflects Indigenous peoples' authority and self-determination in relation to their lands, waters, and other resources. For example, Jonathan Goldberg-Hiller and Noenoe K. Silva suggest that struggles over the relationships among humans, pigs, and sharks in Hawai'i are inseparable from concerns for Indigenous political control; they are struggles for Hawaiians to "own and reconstruct these and yet to be imagined worlds again" (2011, 444). Such commitments do not preclude exchange and entanglement among peoples but insist on direct engagements with power and justice within environmental life, past and present.

In *The Bone People,* Hulme explores a colonial history that shaped an environmental life involving persistent inequalities and tensions. Tiaki Mira, we learn, grew up in a time when it was believed "that the Maori could not survive, so the faster they became Europeans the better for everyone, nei?" (359). Some of *The Bone People*'s sentences are structured to juxtapose the jarringly different imaginative relationships with ecology that people may inhabit in a present shaped by such histories. Kerewin sits alone watching the sea while on holiday at Moerangi with Simon and Joe: "The colour has faded out of the sky. It is grey, becoming darker as the world turns herself round a little more. The clouds are long and black and ragged, like the wings of stormbattered dragons. Or of hokioi . . . huge birds" (250). The dragon may refer to literary genres of fantasy, which Hulme taps into occasionally in *The Bone People. Hōkioi* is a giant bird in Māori traditions and is sometimes described as a name for a bird that had a three-meter wingspan and that was extinct by the time Europeans came to New Zealand and renamed it Haast's eagle. European histories of thought are present here in Hulme's invocation of the Earth's rotation on its axis. But this is also a "she" and probably refers to Papatūānuku, the Earth and Earth Mother. In transitioning uneasily from dragons to hōkioi, Hulme underlines troubled relations between ways of apprehending the ecology of this part of the world and indeed the Earth.

In *The Bone People,* Hulme insists on the creative ways in which people draw on Māori approaches in their relations with human and nonhuman beings, including the relational frameworks that bind people, land, and ocean and that are described by Kerewin, and infrastructures like the Māori hall. Hulme does not homogenize or simplify these approaches, however. For example, when Tiaki Mira dies, Joe inherits the land and becomes its guardian. After placing an embargo on the area, he leaves to reconnect with Kerewin and Simon, rather than attempt to live as did Tiaki Mira. Joe joins Kerewin and Simon in a family so new that "maybe there aren't words for us yet," says Simon (395). In *The Bone People,* Hulme imagines modes of sociality that to a certain degree baffle imaginative organization, that are shaped by various cultural and sociogeographic influences, and in which Māori politics, histories, and culture are vital. She apprehends, and to some extent imaginatively addresses, the colonial inequalities that still shape people's agencies in environmental politics.

Endurance and Beyond

Travel writer Chris Johnston suggests that *The Bone People* reflects the mysteries of a place named Ōkārito: the novel is "an elusive book. And Okarito is an elusive place" (2004, n.p.). Hulme lives in this small, coastal settlement, which is also home to a protected wetland and to a kiwi species known as *rowi*, of which just 375 individuals remain as of 2011. A Department of Conservation brochure about the bird records, "In a small area of forest near Ōkārito, rowi are fighting for survival" (2011 n.p.).

Much contemporary New Zealand environmental writing apprehends survival as a threatened, appreciated reality, the continued possibility of which underlies any hope that such writing might offer. Terms such as *survival* and *endurance* deeply reveal the contemporary imaginative and material force of colonial histories involving deliberate, almost entire, environmental disappearance and replacement. Perhaps the concept of endurance promises the physically impossible in response to such histories: unchanging forests, mountains, rivers, and peoples. The West Coast, bordered by the Southern Alps, a high mountain range that runs down the South Island, has been narrated in such terms, as wild, inaccessible, and timeless.[27]

If we turn to historical archives about Ōkārito, we find the traces of a different story about endurance. Ōkārito has been occupied on and off by Māori for more than 800 years. Europeans were exploring the area by the mid-nineteenth century. When the land surveyor Thomas Brunner passed through the area ("Okaritu") in 1846, he noted in his journal that "we found some natives" and described eels taken from the mud flats being served "to dogs as well as Christians" (1848 [1846], 9). Brunner may have seen *kurī*, sometimes known as the Māori dog, the Polynesian dog, or the South Sea dog. Kurī voyaged with people to the archipelago in around the thirteenth century but became extinct shortly after Europeans arrived (Keane 2009, n.p.). Māori used kurī in hunting birds such as kiwi, made cloaks of their fur and skin, and kept them as pets (Museum of New Zealand n.d.). Historian Alexander Hare McLintock writes in 1966, "The Frenchman Crozet, who was at the Bay of Islands in June 1772, noted that:

'The dogs are a sort of domesticated fox, quite black or white, very low on the legs, straight ears, thick tail, long body, full jaws, but more pointed than those of the fox, and uttering the same cry; they do not bark like our dogs'. According to Hutton, the dog was dull, lazy, and sullen in disposition" (McLintock 2009 [1966], n.p.). McLintock also observes the affection between the dog and Māori women, its use for food, weapons, ornaments, and cloaks, as well as its presence in Māori histories (n.p.; see also, Keane 2009).

The people at Ōkārito may have been caring for kurī, or they could have been caring for dogs that had recently arrived on the island with Europeans. Both possibilities remind that Māori had long been altering, and changing with, the ecology of this area, that their endurance did not involve stasis. Struggles directed at endurance orient us toward the possibility that certain life forms, projects, and memories might remain in existence over time, even though they are always changing and in turn are altering the world and its futures. But this work also politicizes endurance; who and what endures becomes a site of conflict. To appreciate certain aspects of what already exists in this world—even to want some dimensions of this world to be more or less the same tomorrow—is a precarious politics, when there is so much here that is diminutive and destructive.

But in my estimation, struggles for endurance matter in this world often characterized by incredible disregard and destruction. This does not mean that endurance is enough, however. The care of some life forms may also be a condition of their or others' destruction, for example. Struggles for endurance provide no certain answer regarding where people might seek to direct their agencies in these processes, but they do address all manner of loss. We could extend such recognition from the losses a politics of endurance might halt to the mourning or otherwise addressing of the losses that it may call into being. In addition, we might attend to the endurances that hardly seem bearable, are a long-walked path on the abyss of disappearance, including that embodied by Joe and those close to him at certain moments in *The Bone People*. Many additional modes of engagement also animate present well-being and evoke hope in *The Bone People*. The most striking of these engagements is sociality, actively cultivated ties among human and nonhuman beings variously defined as love, friendship, and family. Joe describes his hope as interwoven with his friend, and, for that matter, her survival: "The hope is still a hope while Kerewin lives" (381).

CHAPTER 2

In Search of Rain

Water, Hope, and the Everyday

When, if ever, does exclusive ownership of water begin? When the water crosses your property line, whether in a stream or under-ground? Is it yours if it falls from a passing cloud? Would that make the fluffy white cloud directly over-head your cloud?

Piliāmoʻo and Vivien Lee, "A Portfolio of Photographs by Piliāmoʻo.
Hoʻi ka Wai: The Waiāhole Stream Restoration."

WATER EXERTS A FORCE on people's experiences of loss, upheaval, and hope in Hawaiʻi writer Gary Pak's short story "Language of the Geckos" (2005a). One day the *moʻo* (geckos, water spirits, ancestors) who inhabit Gabriel Hoʻokano's house sense a rainstorm moving off the ocean. They become "boisterous" and there is contention among them (24). The rain falls for five days and five nights, flooding the land around the house and cutting the family off from a nearby town. "Strange things," "vintage" objects, and old newspapers with dates of no discernible significance begin to surface in the waters (26–27). "Dis funny kine weather making everybody funny kine, everybody jumpy," says Gabriel (27). Set by Pak against a historical backdrop of water diversion for the colonial-capitalist agricultural economy, particularly for sugar plantations, "Language of the Geckos" is a story of water falling back to the sites where it was displaced, and of the changed, communal forms of life that the Hoʻokano family build in the emergent waterscape. Pak, a writer born in Honolulu in 1952 of Korean heritage, a professor of English at the University of Hawaiʻi, and an activist who has been involved in social movements on Oʻahu, calls his short stories "my visions of what I feel should be" (2005b, xvi).

Water—moving on oceanic, atmospheric, surface, and subterranean pathways, falling into rivers and inhabiting pipelines, houses, and life forms—is almost everywhere tangled in environmental struggles in the

Pacific. But in this markedly amphibious area of the world, the first utopian writers primarily map human well-being onto the spatial templates of
islands, although their utopians do at times venture into the ocean or the
atmosphere. Thomas More's utopians even go so far as to carve their island
off from the mainland, creating an oceanic barrier between themselves
and the world beyond. Fredric Jameson argues that an enclave within a
broader social space recurs within the utopian literary form and marks
the radical difference of the utopia (2005, 15). It is not surprising, then,
that some utopian writers negotiate the presence of water in their imagined worlds with a measure of unease. In English writer Samuel Butler's
Erewhon (1970 [1872]), our narrator navigates a river gorge in search for
empty land. He seemingly cannot resist commenting repeatedly on the
river, figuring it as an unpredictable, threatening, and sentient being that
is capable of "ungovernable fury," "boisterous and terrible," "wide and
wasteful," "awful," and "muddy and horribly angry" (1970, 49, 49, 50, 55).
The river may ultimately enable the destruction of the utopian community
of Erewhon, since the narrator plans to take a gunboat up the river into
Erewhon and then to transport the utopians to plantations in Queensland
(256). Reinforcing but also seeping through utopia's margins, water is crucial to but not collapsible with utopian ways of life and aspirations.

   In the previous chapter, I explored how writers connect the endurance
of people, nonhumans, projects, and commitments with futures that are
promising and open, as these writers respond to the lingering power of
colonial period practices that positioned most existing life as a site to be
overcome by better futures. As they engage the present world, writers' explorations of hope become tangled with water, an element that shapes life
but that can be difficult to live with, in its often stormy return to the land
and dangerous relationships with economy. Postcolonial scholars have
often associated anti-colonial struggles over land with promising futures,
because land embodies the potentials of sustenance, independence, and
dignity.[1] But in Hawai'i, as elsewhere on the Earth, conditions of water
upheaval, diminishment, and injustice have also shadowed life for many
years, are a force in physical precariousness, economic impoverishment,
and political conflict. In late nineteenth- and early twentieth-century
Hawai'i, plantation owners oversaw the diversion of water from rivers for
sugar cultivation and other uses, undermining Native Hawaiian agricultural and fishing practices that are interwoven with the water.[2] Urbaniza-

tion and other processes damaged or destroyed many other aquatic eco-systems, including springs, pools, fishponds, bays, and reefs.

In this chapter, I explore the force that water exerts on literary writers' efforts to illuminate hope. A number of scholars describe hope as an awareness of the promise and openness of the future that takes form in people's connections with other beings, forces, and processes. Julianne A. Hazlewood argues that Afro-Ecuadorian, Chachi, and Awá peoples in the Ecuadorian Pacific create "geographies of hope," involving territories, ecological-cultural practices, agricultural diversity, and networks among different communities, even as they are increasingly surrounded by immense seas of oil palm plantations that are driven by demand for the biofuels used in climate change mitigation politics in the Global North (2012, 139). Their territories and networks are deeply interwoven into the possibilities of hope as a concept, such that in Hazlewood's essay the term *hope* refers directly to territories, social linkages, and agro-ecological activities rather than to an isolated emotion: "The communities of La Ceiba, La Chiquita, and Guadualito have cultivated hope and transformed it into inter-island and intra-island collaborative geographies of hope to re-assert the rights of themselves and Nature" (143).

Taking up this thread of hope that is inseparable from people's relations with nonhuman beings, forces, and processes, in this chapter I argue that water not only enlivens but sometimes also undermines and complicates literary writers' efforts to evoke promising, open futures, in its expansive trajectories around, above, and into the planet, its changeable forms, its capacity to destroy and sustain life, and its often hurtful entanglements with economy. In Pak's short stories, living people, ancestors, geckos, land topologies, and water, among other agents, draw a rainstorm to sites where water long ago vanished. Water's return allows a Native Hawaiian family to reestablish relative economic autonomy and sociocultural difference. Water also constructs transnational connections and shapes the family's interaction with these connections; in the context of renewed economic and social agency associated with water, one character can stop participating in U.S. military activities in the broader Pacific. Cathy Song's poetry, in contrast, takes us to the plantations where migrant women's intimate contact with water in activities such as cooking and bathing reflects and reinforces gendered, racialized labor arrangements. In tracing water's movements through and around bodies, Song apprehends hardships but also sees persistent activities through which people in small, quiet ways force some measure of openness into the imaginaries and practices of environmental life. Although Pak's and Song's works are different in many ways, both writers associate hope with water, a highly animated force that people and more broadly institutions are partly responsible for shaping but cannot entirely control. As such, their writings emphasize not only the hope but also the uncertainties and precariousness that take form in people's relationships with this enigmatic shape-shifter.

Return of Rain

When the moʻo of Pak's short story "Language of the Geckos" predict a rainstorm, they become skittish and combative, entering a "troubled state." Even the usually calm gecko Kopa is observed "skittering back and forth across the dusty screen faster than usual, as if anticipating a big storm" (2005a, 24). When the rain comes, it pacifies the household. As the rain continues to fall, however, Gabriel again becomes agitated, associating the unending rain and clouds with his sense of being not-so-subtly manipulated by his "wayward" dead brother Jacob, who has manifested as the gecko Kopa (23). Gabriel looks at the "always cloudy sky and the rain" and addresses Jacob: "'And den! You going float my house away or what?!'" (25–26). The atmosphere of promise and disruption escalates when with "ominous regularity" strange, vintage objects surface in the waters surrounding the house (27). These objects are "concocting a strange sense of time past and time lost" (28).

A major agent in this condition of disorientation is the distinctive waterscape of "Language of the Geckos." Water is temporally and formally unstable, and provokes temperamental responses. It may be tempting to leave it at this. After all, water is one of the more ungraspable substances, seeming to repel or overwhelm imaginative categories. Even an analyst of water as persistent as Gaston Bachelard finds that he cannot undertake a psychoanalysis of water, a rational and comprehensive survey of all the data of water images, because people's relationships with water are not as durable and solid as their relationships with earth, crystals, metals, and stones (1983, 6–19). He is forced to remain "emotional and personal" in his analysis of water (8).[3]

Yet, the rainstorm and lake of "Language of the Geckos" (2005a) do draw us in the direction of enduring environmental conflicts and injustices. In the story's first lines, we learn that the moʻo have long inhabited the property where Gabriel Hoʻokano lives with his wife Mary and his cousin Harriet. The moʻo remind us of the locality at a prior time, raising the question of what existed here before urban development. Later in the story, Pak briefly locates this property: the flood cuts the Hoʻokano family off from "Kānewai town" (27). Pak therefore leads us in search of this place that he names Kānewai. According to a number of contemporary archives, Kānewai is a locality in Mānoa Valley, now a densely populated area of Honolulu. Dennis Kawaharada writes that Native Hawaiians knew moʻo to inhabit the valley's cliffs, mountains, waterfalls, springs, streams, and pools. In "Language of the Geckos," the moʻo share Gabriel's genealogy and live on his house. Kawaharada describes moʻo as "water spirits, usually female, in the form of large lizards" and as ʻaumākua (ancestral spirits) and guardians of fishponds (Kawaharada 1999, 19; 20). Hawaiians grew *kalo* (taro) in Mānoa Valley by building ʻauwai or irrigation ditches that tapped streams and directed water onto agricultural terraces. These ditches eventually would return the water to its source stream (Culliney 2006, 213).

Fragmentary but tenacious archives characterize Kānewai as a pool. Writing in 1935, John Williams describes an underground pool named Kānewai and of importance to Native Hawaiians (Sterling and Summers 1978, 281). Dennis Kawaharada recounts a story by Emma M. Nakuina about twin rain spirits who run away from their stepmother to Mānoa Valley. The brother goes to a "pond" called "Kanawai" and digs a tunnel from there to fill a pool for his sister, but the pond dries up after foreigners arrive and damage the spring (Kawaharada 1999, 21–23). Geologists have added to these mappings of the site, describing how Pleistocene reef limestone was deposited there when the sea level was much higher than it is now, and lava flows and sediments settled over the limestone. The resulting karst topography features trapped underground water, sinks, subterranean streams, caves, and spring-fed ponds. William R. Halliday writes that "the name of Kanewai Field perpetuates the memory of a long-filled karstic pond; the easternmost of several perched water table ponds between Diamond Head and Punchbowl Crater" (1998, 143). Like many subterranean ecosystems, the unique karst ecosystems of this area have been heavily destroyed or damaged: filled and drained for construction; besieged by raw sewage and other materials.[4]

To the east, another ancient water ecosystem—a coastal, royal fishpond built by Hawaiians and known as Kānewai—still survives. Hawaiians

created hundreds of fishponds in marsh and estuarine ecosystems, cultivating mullet, milkfish, and other species: "By the time of European contact, Hawaiians arguably led the world in the art and science of fish husbandry, with potential harvests across the archipelago estimated at nearly
1,000 tons annually" (Culliney 2006, 101). They used sluice gates and
ʻauwai to modulate these waterworks' connections with streams, springs,
and the ocean (214). Most Hawaiian fishponds have been destroyed or diminished through filling, dredging, and other forms of construction, the
introduction of new species, pollution, and disrepair amid upheavals of
colonialism. Chris Cramer, of the Maunalua Fishpond Heritage Center,
writes of Kānewai and another nearby fishpond, "Despite their location
along busy Kalanianaole Highway, few can guess that behind the blue government property signs and shady coconut trees lie the only intact shore-
line ponds in Honolulu" (Cramer 2011, n.p.). Kānewai is a rock-walled
fishpond that receives fresh water from Kānewai Spring and tidal salt
water from Paikō Lagoon. It had a wooden double-gate system to modulate the tides and for trapping fish (Maunalua Fishpond Heritage Center
n.d.). The community organization Maunalua Fishpond Heritage Center
is working to learn about, protect, and revitalize the fishponds and to re-
energize people's relationships with these waterworks. One of the great
difficulties that they face lies in gaining access and permission to work
with the fishponds. Kānewai is currently both state and privately owned.[5]

In "Language of the Geckos," then, the lake appears at the site of a
long-vanished pool or a surviving but threatened Hawaiian fishpond; both
waterworks hold spiritual and material significance for Hawaiians. Pak
also draws us to further waterways destroyed or threatened by twentieth-
century development on Oʻahu. Through the name Kānewai, he reworks
Waikāne, and so gestures to the Waikāne and Waiāhole valleys, where rain
falls on Koʻolau Range and flows in streams to Kāneʻohe Bay. Kawaharada
describes these places as shaped by plentiful rain and notes that the names
of nearby ahupuaʻa (land divisions) reflect the prevalence of water, including "Waiakāne ('Water of Kāne'), Waiāhole ('Water [of the] āhole fish'),
Waiheʻe ('Slippery water,' or 'Water [of the] octopus')" (Kawaharada 1999,
33).[6] Between 1913 and 1916, the Waiāhole Water Company oversaw the
creation of a vast ditch system to move the water to a sugar plantation
owned by Oʻahu Sugar Company. The Waiāhole Ditch cut stream flow,
exhausted springs, and altered the ecosystems of the bay, heavily affect-

ing local fishing and farming communities (Berry 2006, 43–44). As the sugar industry collapsed in Hawai'i in the late twentieth century, local peoples' long term struggles to persist at Waiāhole-Waikāne-Kāne'ohe ignited around relationships between water, ecology, sociality, and economy. Landowning, governmental, and development organizations sought prolonged water diversion through the Waiāhole Ditch for residential and commercial projects, tourism, golf courses, and corporate agriculture. Community and Native Hawaiian organizations asserted that the water be allowed to run down the streams so as to support ecosystems as well as activities such as fishing and farming (44). They achieved the restoration of some water to the streams.

In "Language of the Geckos," water begins to rush back to threatened or destroyed places associated with the name Kānewai. In order to understand the disappearance—and later reappearance—of water in these areas, we need to engage the histories of water in Hawai'i. When the rain eventually stops, the Ho'okano family expects that life could return to normal: they imagine driving and shopping in Kānewai (Pak 2005a, 27). Yet, the lake does not recede. As time goes by, the family requires less and less food. Although this emergent ecology is only imprinted briefly and faintly in "Language of the Geckos," Pak's attention to consumption and driving suggests that the rainstorm makes imaginable a way of life that breaks with the capitalist mode of production. He links particular relationships between people and water, or "hydrosocial relations," with economy (Linton 2006, n.p.). Water was crucial to the establishment of sugar plantations in Hawai'i. By the late nineteenth century, this "thirsty" crop was economically dominant in the archipelago (Berry 2006, 42; Wilcox 1996, 1). Sugar companies took water far away from its parent streams, most controversially from the wet windward side of the mountains through tunnels to the dry leeward sides. By 1923, almost every stream in Hawai'i was being diverted for sugar. Of the emergent environmental conditions, John Culliney writes, "Dewatered and/or biotically decimated, many of Hawai'i's freshwater ecosystems were in ruins by about the 1920s. In the modern era, most of the rest, including the anchialine pools untouched by earlier developments, have been damaged or destroyed by a variety of new impacts" (2006, 219). Colonial-capitalist processes of water reorganization destroyed or deeply threatened the ecosystems vital to Hawaiian fishing and agricultural practices. In *Stolen Waters,* a documentary film about the

Waiāhole Ditch, independent video production company Nā Maka o ka
ʻĀina traces the health problems and hunger faced by Native Hawaiians
when the water was appropriated (1996).

To return to "Language of the Geckos," then, Pak conceives of the revitalization or return of water at Kānewai and Waiāhole-Waikāne-Kāneʻohe.
The waterscapes of "Language of the Geckos" reflect patterns of heavy
rainfall and quickly rising floods on windward Oʻahu, but they also point
toward submerged histories of water appropriation and upheaval in varied
sites and forms, as water returns to places from which it was made to disappear or where it was diminished. Water links people to the past through
its cyclical movements and physical return to places where it once existed,
but also because past water-related injustices reverberate in the present
world.[7] The rainstorm is a complicated archaeological site for Pak.

An Alternative Forecast

In water's cyclical traversals around the Earth, as well as in the traces that
precede rather than that only follow those traversals—such as changes
in atmospheric pressure that may allow beings to anticipate rain—water
is a reminder of the present world's relationships not only with the past
but inseparably with the future. In "Language of the Geckos," Pak suggests
that water's reminders of the past energize contemporary Hawaiian and
local community struggles to reinhabit ordinary relationships with wetlands, rivers, and the ocean and to live with hope of a more viable environmental life. Through a reference to the old Hawaiian-language newspapers
that appear in the lake and disorient the Hoʻokano family, Pak associates
water's return with contemporary and historical Hawaiian political struggles. Noenoe K. Silva writes that nineteenth- and early twentieth-century
Hawaiian-language newspapers and other archives reveal Hawaiian nationalist struggles that have been absent from most historical writing and
that show that Hawaiians were resistant in the face of imperialism rather
than passive and helpless. These archives have politically energized contemporary Hawaiians, who are reconnecting the past with the present
and the future (2004, 3–4).[8] When an archive surfaces in "Language of
the Geckos," Gabriel regrets not taking up his brother Jacob's fight to sustain Hawaiian life ways and acknowledges the potential of Jacob's struggles
to bring change. The newspapers remind him that he could be "making
all dis rain instead of suffering from it" (27). This point is more sharply

focused in *Children of a Fireland: A Novel* (2004), where Pak again takes up the Hoʻokano family's story and we learn that outsiders bought most of the Hawaiian land in the Waiola Valley and leased it to sweet potato farmers (57). Jacob resisted these processes of land dispossession and the destruction of his family's agricultural way of life, but Gabriel felt helpless and went to fight in the Pacific War (Pak 2004, 58, 186). Jacob blamed Gabriel for not supporting the family cause, "an accusation that angered and haunted Gabriel painfully" (2004, 58). To return to "Language of the Geckos," then, the newspapers lead Gabriel to acknowledge the capacities of Jacob's struggles (literally, to make rain, or we might say, to make water return), which he previously felt were hopeless.

As the water returns to Kānewai in "Language of the Geckos," it energizes further people and so Jacob's struggle spreads. Gabriel and his family revitalize loving relationships with each other and with the geckos and cows in "isolation" on the emergent island (Pak 2005a, 29). They begin learning "the requisite language," presumably the Hawaiian language (28). Pak connects Hawaiian cultural and economic autonomy with the reappearance of water, presumably because the water is crucial to people's ability to shape their relationships with nonhuman aquatic beings such as plants or fish. He evokes varied peoples' struggles to reestablish ordinary working relationships with damaged, threatened, or appropriated water in Hawaiʻi, including with fishponds, anchialine ecosystems, streams, springs, and bays. In the essay "Reservoir of Hope," D. Māhealani Dudoit describes peoples' direct practice of marginalized everyday relationships with water amid their political struggles to retain water in streams. She emerges through forest in Waiāhole Valley into the "uncommon sight" of recently planted *loʻi kalo* or taro terraces: "'We're fighting for the water,' Calvin Hoe tells me as together we clear the irrigation ditch of weeds. 'But at the same time we're fishing, planting taro. We're teaching the children. Well . . . we're teaching ourselves'" (1997, 161, 163).

In describing such emergent, amphibious forms of life as isolated, Pak may appear to ignore their entanglement in the wide-ranging spaces of water and economy. The terminology of isolation in "Language of the Geckos" resonates with the discourses of the local literature movement, a coalition of writers in which Pak is involved and which formed in the late 1970s, seeking to ground literature in local scenery, histories, ethnicities, language, and subnational community.[9] Rob Wilson emphasizes the important work of the movement but also notes that it has sometimes produced a problematic discourse of authentically local aspects of literature, such as language, style, and cultural attitude (2000, viii). He traces enduring U.S. stories about Hawai'i as remote and isolated islands in a vast ocean, following these stories as they migrate through the twentieth century in tourism, literature, and other forums. In these accounts of the femininity and remoteness of the "'South Pacific' scenery" (no matter, as he notes, that Hawai'i is in the North Pacific), "lost aboriginal treasure," and leisure, Wilson identifies a complicit stirring together of notions of Hawai'i as "pleasure periphery" and as site of commercialization and national expansion (x, xv, 86).

In "Language of the Geckos," Pak associates the rainstorm with the possibility that characters could disentangle their economic lives from the capitalist economy, linking water's return to characters' break with shopping and driving, but he does not ignore the island's connections to a broader world. The key is to turn our attention back from the land to the water. Strikingly, Pak uses the space of the hydrologic cycle to complicate the concepts of dislocation and isolation: the rain moves "in from the ocean" as "rainy clouds" and creates "a growing lake" (2005a, 25, 25, 26). Pak invokes the expansive pathways through which the sea exhales water into the atmosphere and water moves to the mountains, eventually falling as rain and cutting its way into and through the land. In tracing the spaces illuminated by water, Pak moves from sea through atmosphere to land.

He searches in these aerial and aquatic spaces for human histories and accountabilities rather than only for nonhuman forces. In the lake that forms when a rainstorm moves off the sea, the characters begin to find newspapers and vintage objects that remind them of historical events that occurred *in the sea*. In particular, the water carries traces of past U.S. military incursions in Asia and the Pacific. When a newspaper floating in the water triggers Gabriel's memory of joining the U.S. armed forces, Harriet is reminded of the death of her husband on U.S.S. *Indianapolis*, a ship involved in the Pacific War, based at Pearl Harbor on and off, and that carried the atomic bomb "Little Boy" to Tinian before the bomb was dropped on Hiroshima (26). U.S.S. *Indianapolis* was torpedoed while on a secret mission to Leyte in 1945, and its loss was overlooked. Around 300 people were drawn down into the ocean with the ship, and approximately 900 were thrown into the waters to drift for days, with few still alive when rescue finally arrived. In "Language of the Geckos," Pak imagines that the water, moving among sea, sky, and land, physically bears with it traces of these horrific histories. He challenges the common framing of Hawai'i as the most geographically isolated archipelago on the planet, describing instead the islands' entanglement in trans-Pacific histories involving the incomprehensible destruction of nonhuman and human life.[10] In *Children of a Fireland: A Novel,* Pak suggests that Gabriel participated in these U.S. military activities in the wider Pacific as a response to his experiences of colonialism at home in Hawai'i, specifically the dispossession of his family from their land and their agricultural way of life and their subsequent conflict and fragmentation (2004, 58, 186). When the water returns in "Language of the Geckos," characters begin to heal familial grievances and practice communal forms of life, creating alternatives to economic precariousness and hopelessness. The water supports different possibilities for life within the space of the island, then, but it also allows characters to find meaning and support outside of participation in the U.S. military networks around the Pacific, changing their relations with a broader world. Pak's characters do not eliminate all ties with life over the horizons, however. They remain flexible and expansive, able to remember past connections to U.S. militarism and maintaining certain colonial influences. For example, the cows, a recently introduced species, are crucial figures in the family, suggesting that Pak conceives this island partly in terms of new ways of conceiving sociality (2005a, 29).

Directing our attention toward the spaces beyond the island borders, the water suggests that the borders of the emergent community are more porous than they may at first appear to be. The short story form, as Pak reworks it, reflects the wandering environmental dynamics of water. "Language of the Geckos" is broken up by one middle section around which two other sections are juxtaposed. The story's form echoes the shape of the lake that it narrates. "Language of the Geckos" is short and fragmentary but references characters, events, and places in other literary works by Pak. We can struggle to follow what leaks from this story into other texts and contexts.

In particular, in "Language of the Geckos," Pak transforms the concerns of an earlier story, "The Valley of the Dead Air" from *The Watcher of Waipuna and Other Stories* (1992).[11] In "The Valley of the Dead Air," Pak takes a different angle on the revitalization of aquatic ecosystems, focusing on those people who live on land and use water that was stolen from the Ho'okano family. In the story, people from an ethnically complicated local community attribute a bad smell permeating Waiola Valley to Jacob

Hoʻokano, who is Gabriel's dead brother in "Language of the Geckos." As
Susan Y. Najita notes, the valley's inhabitants have tormented Jacob, undermining his people's survival through rumors that deny the existence of his
heirs, and living on land appropriated from his family (2006, 143, 151). Pak
also implicates their capitalist agriculture in environmental damage. The
valley residents suspect that a wind carried the smell "from the mangroves
and mud flats of the coastal area" and soon the valley's "earth began to
emit a terrible odor of rotten fish" (1992, 9, 10). These images of dead fish
and a stinking coast evoke diminished waterways. Pak links these environmental conditions to the community's support for water's incorporation
in the colonial-capitalist agricultural economy. Jacob's family was dispossessed of their land when they could not pay a land or water tax (11). The
valley residents are now using the land, and presumably also some of the
taxable water, for market-oriented agriculture: "How we going sell our
produce to dah markets?" worries one local resident when the rotten smell
emerges (12). Pak reminds readers that water is required to grow plants,
noting that when rain comes it "was as if the storm had nurtured the smell
like water nourishes plants" (14). He situates accusatory fish remains in
plowed earth: "While plowing one corner of his sweet potato field, Tats
Sugimura uncovered a hole full of fish scales and fish bones" (10). Pak
ties market-focused farming to stress on aquatic ecosystems. The valley
residents unwittingly occupy the position of the corporations and government agencies that have sought sustained water diversion from areas such
as the Waikāne and Waiāhole valleys for new kinds of capitalist agriculture
since sugar production's collapse in the 1990s (Berry 2006, 44). Windward
farmers, fishers, and community groups, in turn, argue that leaving water
in the streams will enable different possibilities, particularly Hawaiian
methods of taro cultivation, which support the health of stream, bay, and
estuary life (Dudoit 1997, 161–63).

The bad smell vanishes when the people from the valley admit their
entanglement in a colonial context and begin to support rather than undermine Jacob and aquatic ecosystems. They are honest about their mis-
treatment of Jacob and acknowledge that their life is complicit with the
appropriation of Hoʻokano land (Pak 1992, 16–18, 11). They also share their
produce with Jacob and each other, reorienting their agriculture toward a
local, nonmonetary, communal economy (18). Soon, the environments of
the valley revive: the community wakes to "the smell of salt, and the warm
winds that carried it over the valley swept up to the highest ridges of the

mountains, and there the warm air married with the cold dampness and thick clouds formed, and soon, with the shift in the trades, rain began to fall over the silent, peaceful valley" (19).

In "The Valley of the Dead Air," then, water returns in relation to a socio-culturally diverse community's emergent affirmation of Hawaiian struggles and a new dynamic between economy, land, and water. In "Language of the Geckos," in contrast, Pak explores the difference of what the rain might mean for Hawaiian characters, suggesting that water could in varied ways support Hawaiian independence. Placed alongside each other, "Language and the Geckos" and "The Valley of the Dead Air" represent the connected and yet different meanings of water-oriented struggles for the Indigenous Hoʻokano family and for the local people of Waiola Valley. Given the joy experienced by characters at the end of both stories, Pak evokes not only the deep tensions and fears that follow these different peoples as they cut their way toward the future—such as the status of the stolen Hawaiian land on which the residents continue to live in "The Valley of the Dead Air"— but also hope for water's capacity to support multiple layers of sociality and difference.

Alongside water's durable relationships with specific land formations such as mountains and watersheds, Pak also pays careful attention to the implications of water's temporal uncertainties. He is deeply preoccupied with water's shape-shifting capacities, at one point in "Language of the Geckos" referencing a multiplicity of water forms over the space of a page, including "rain," the "ocean," "wet air," a "lake," and "cloudy sky" (2005a, 25). This aquatic instability triggers unrest in the family: observing the skittish behavior of the moʻo in these conditions, Gabriel "found no rest when the moʻo were in such a troubled state" (25). Through attention to water's shifting forms and disruptive temporalities, Pak inserts a feeling for provisionality into the story, a sense that this world will continue to change.

In conclusion, we might understand "Language of the Geckos" as a kind of water and weather forecast, connected by memory and by the enduring patterns of rain to past forms of water as well as to present realities. A storm off the ocean brings water back to areas where it disappeared or was diminished, calling up histories of capitalist-colonial appropriation and degradation of water as well as local community and Native Hawaiian organizations that are struggling to care for an alternative life with water. For Pak, the word *communal* might better accord with the present world if water were allowed to run down the rivers: water allows people to grow food and so is crucial to relative economic autonomy; it also underlies people's agency in their relationships with nonhuman beings, including the possibility of caring for riverine and estuary life. Rather than only imagine this emergent ecology through the framework of an island, in following the water, Pak traces expansive passages through sea, atmosphere, and land and is drawn into an effort to navigate precariousness and agency partly through those spaces where wars, migrations, and economy have taken form. Water is a reminder of transnational connections and of how people are participating in those connections. The promising, open future evoked in "Language of the Geckos" is partly activated and shaped by water, including by the ways in which it orients people to the past and the future and to transnational spaces, as well as through the material realities it supports, such as cultivation.

Water, Intimacy, Economy

For Pak, water is never entirely separable from human activities and responsibilities, but it is not entirely collapsible with these either. In evoking hope that relies partly on water, Pak reminds us that we live in a world that will not always move in a way that we can entirely control, want, or survive. Indeed, Gabriel's initial response to the rain involves deep resentment and dismay. Insofar as people do have agency in environmental life, Pak insists on exploring modes of communication and participation rather than on efforts at domination. At the end of "Language of the Geckos," people, cows, and geckos alike begin to learn the "language of isolation" (2005a, 29).

But Pak emphasizes that the imaginary ecology of "Language of the Geckos" is far from ideal for all its inhabitants, and so that we should remain thoughtful about the story rather than view it as authoritative. His references to Mary, Gabriel's "common-law wife," and Harriet, Gabriel's first cousin, are particularly troubling (24). At Mary's insistence, and despite Gabriel's lack of enthusiasm for the idea, Harriet has begun to eat meals and stay overnight at the Hoʻokano house. When the newspapers drifting in the lake inspire Gabriel to talk of "history," Harriet experiences "a bitter memory" of the telegram she received on her husband's death on U.S.S. *Indianapolis* (26). On remembering this loss, she expresses desire to visit the cows, and states: "I'm going" (26). Yet, as Mary points out,

Harriet cannot leave because of the flood; she can only tenuously inhabit a world where she is trapped. In noting the legal status of Gabriel and Mary's relationship, Pak subtly suggests that the uncertain legitimacy of Harriet's presence in this place can be understood in the context of specific social regimes that organize peoples' relationships with land through private property and the nuclear family. In early nineteenth-century Hawaiʻi, missionaries sought to exile sexuality into an enduring marriage run by a husband and where divorce was almost impossible; the ownership and inheritance of property could be administered through this family (Merry 2000, 227–30). Sally Engle Merry observes that in a sea of imperialism, the king (mōʻī) and chiefs (aliʻi) sought to make the independent Kingdom of Hawaiʻi recognizable on European terms, taking up frameworks like private land ownership from the Anglo-American legal system (36). In the mid-nineteenth century, they adopted laws that reconfigured people's relationships with land, reinforcing the property-owning nuclear family and positioning women as subordinate to their husbands with few legal rights (96–97). The nuclear family, and the legal world that attended it, was very different from diverse Hawaiian practices of marriage and sexuality, including extended kin groups; it constituted "an enormous shift from the open kindred system of the ʻohana [extended family] with strong brother/sister linkages and relatively easy entrance into and exit from marriage" (Merry 2000, 97, see also 221–257). In "Language of the Geckos," Pak links Harriet's uncertain status in the Hoʻokano family home—her reliance on the goodwill of her cousin Gabriel—to historically contingent social institutions that position the home as belonging to Gabriel and Mary.

At the end of "Language of the Geckos," Gabriel, Mary, Harriet, the cows, and the geckos form a loving social life. Gabriel and Kopa revitalize their relationship, and Gabriel shares "this new experience with Mary and Harriet" (28–29). Pak associates agency with Jacob, Kopa, Gabriel, and the water. Through the figure of Harriet—through her claim on memory, not on history; through her precarious presence in a home that legally belongs to others; through her marginality to, and even her entrapment in, others' struggles for an alternative environmental life—Pak briefly illuminates a material world, involving laws and economic resources, that addresses people in different ways and that may impact on their commitments and their hope, as well as that hope—if any at all—that others associate with them. Harriet occupies a troubled position in relation to established, powerful social arrangements such as property ownership, but also in relation to emergent, marginal social arrangements that are gaining a grip on survival.

In order to explore writing about shadowy figures who may be difficult to see in the art of water-related social movements, I will turn now to Cathy Song's writing about migrant peoples' interactions with water on plantations in Hawai'i. Song was born in 1955 in Honolulu and has Korean and Chinese ancestry. Her first collection, *Picture Bride* (1983), which received the Yale Series of Younger Poets Award, can be read as an extensive, changing map of the experiences lit up when we are attentive to water. While Pak focuses on places where water was made to disappear, Song moves us to the plantations where the water arrived and to people who live and work with the water. She directly or implicitly references water throughout *Picture Bride,* including in all eight poems in the first section and in many of the poems that follow.

Most of the poems in *Picture Bride* focus on women who migrated to Hawai'i from Korea and China as well as their descendants. In the first poem in the collection, Song describes a twenty-three-year-old woman in the process of leaving Korea for Waialua Sugar Mill camp, O'ahu, to marry a man she has never met. In a sentence that stretches over seventeen lines of the poem, Song gestures toward the woman's potential oceanic journey. The boat has not yet left Korea and the woman remains there throughout the sentence. Her husband-to-be, in turn, waits alone outside a sugar mill in Hawai'i. Song then shifts abruptly to the woman's arrival in Hawai'i, leaving out the ocean journey that she anticipates in the previous line. Peoples' migrations from Korea to Hawai'i intensified after 1900, when federal laws banning Chinese immigration were extended to the archipelago and plantation managers sought to redress the labor shortage by pursuing workers from varied parts of the world (Takaki 1983, 25). They facilitated the movement of Korean women to Hawai'i in an attempt to orchestrate families and to settle the workers (121–23; Kwon 1999, 27). Some of these women are known as picture brides, in reference to photographs that were exchanged across the Pacific in the arrangement of their marriages. The missing water in the first poem of *Picture Bride* reflects historical silences about people's trans-Pacific movements, but it also evokes imaginative histories of the ocean as a world beyond that of human life.[12]

In *Picture Bride,* people live in damp and confined conditions in agricultural settlements on O'ahu. Rain drizzles outside houses, mud oozes past windows, mildew creeps along sinks, and mold grows on bodies.

Song particularly associates water with women and with their domestic labor, with cooking, care giving, and bathing, as well as with experiences of containment and depression. These women contribute labor to the material conditions of life that Pak's characters seek to alter in "Language of the Geckos." They are not directly involved in social movements, and their exhausting investment in the world—in interacting with water, in particular—does not return the striking environmental changes that we see in "Language of the Geckos." In tracing the relations between people and water, however, Song sees creative forms of connection that characters practice with each other and with the material world, and that reveal future openness and promise. She figures water as an element ideally capable of kinship, as able to wrap around and pass between peoples' bodies and to connect imaginatively and materially divided places and bodies. In tracking these aquatic dynamics, Song also finds ways in which people complicate given forms of relation, particularly those associated with family, gender, and nationalism, in small ways altering their present world and the ways in which it is shaping the future.

Song particularly focuses on fresh water, tracking it in a tangle of pipes, pools, baths, and bodies, and associating it with migrant women's domestic labor. In "Leaving," a poem set in the pineapple growing district of Wahiawā, she describes centipedes in the pipes, mildew around the sink, and mold on children's fingers (15). She often juxtaposes damp interior places and dry exterior places. This structural dynamic is visible in the second poem in the collection, "The Youngest Daughter," in which the narrator bathes her mother. Song evokes the narrator's experience of an enduring life inside the house.

The sky has been dark
for many years.
My skin has become as damp
and pale as rice paper
and feels the way
mother's used to before the drying sun
parched it out there in the fields. (5)

Song compares the narrator's moist, wan skin with the dry skin of her mother, who has worked outside. Although not without complications, this narrative of the confinement of women in damp indoor spaces forms a pattern that stretches throughout *Picture Bride*. A later poem, "A Dream of Small Children," describes a woman enclosed in a house, "as if in a fish bowl" (55). In "A Pale Arrangement of Hands," the narrator's mother lives at Wahiawā, where the rain falls around the house like a "fence" (75). With a "light, sad sound," her "damp dress" drops to the bathroom floor, her intimacy with water reflecting the closeness and claustrophobia of the habitat (77).

In these spaces, women use water in bathing, caregiving, and cooking, contributing to economy and social life. Women who lived on sugar plantations in Hawai'i worked in the fields as well as in homes, where they did laundry, cleaning, sewing, ironing, and food preparation: "Everywhere on the plantation—in the fields, mills, boarding house, camps—women contributed directly and indirectly to the process of production" (Takaki 1983, 80). Historical accounts of the plantations have sometimes elided the domestic labor that is particularly, although not exclusively, associated with women, perhaps reflecting the hegemonic imaginative fault line between labor and the domestic sphere, the latter conceived as a private space distinct from the capitalist economy.[13] Song's characters' labor is also marginal because they draw on water to create not only material products but affects, communication, and more broadly social relationships. For example, in "The White Porch" Song describes bathing as a gendered activity that is productive of social life: a woman's washed hair is "like a measure of wealth" (24). In enabling others to recognize her family's affluence, this woman undertakes biopolitical labor, or work that creates "not only material goods but also relationships and ultimately social life itself" (Hardt and Negri 2004, 109). Kathi Weeks observes that biopolitical labor may be unrecognizable within conceptual frameworks that associate labor only with "waged production of material goods" (2007, 235). In *Picture Bride*, Song explores women's occluded, and presumably unpaid or little paid, work of creating social relationships, but she also reveals the agency of water in such work, in its interactions with bodies, infrastructures like pipes, taps, and baths, and imaginaries such as cleanliness. If in *All I Asking for Is My Body* (1988 [1975]), Hawai'i writer Milton Murayama famously describes a plantation camp where even the spatial organization of "shit" in the sewage system reflects hierarchies among different ethnic groups, in *Picture Bride* Song draws attention to socioeconomic arrangements that are illuminated by people's intimacies with water (Murayama 1988, 96).

Song does not homogenize the lives of men or women, but she does trace relationships between women and water in disparate places and times and repeatedly evokes the unacknowledged labor that women contribute to these relationships. Drifting in *Picture Bride* from Hawaiʻi plantations to sites in China, Japan, Korea, the Pacific Ocean, Mexico, Switzerland, and the continental United States, she registers varied economic arrangements that materially and imaginatively associate water and women. The agency to shape these arrangements is usually attributed entirely to others: the waged laborers who cut sugar cane, the artists who paint women and water. For example, in several poems Song engages the art of Kitagawa Utamaro and the women it situates in amphibious habitats. A Japanese *ukiyo-e* (pictures of the floating world) artist of the Edo period, Utamaro is well known for *bijinga*, portraits of beautiful, idealized women. Some of the women in his artworks wear clothes and hair accessories that mark them as sex workers, their labor oriented toward shaping other people's experiences of pleasure, desire, entertainment, or beauty (Usui 1995, 3). Song emphasizes the artist's creativity but also that of the women: Utamaro's "presence" can be traced in the prints, and yet so can the ways in which the women "arranged themselves" before him (37). In "Girl Powdering Her Neck: from a ukiyo-e print by Utamaro," a woman "practices pleasure" by making up her face with the powder that "some other hand will trace" (39). Her skin evokes snow and her face appears in the mirror as if in "a winter pond" (40). In "Ikebana," a woman wears silk to create "the effect / of koi moving through water," while in "Beauty and Sadness: for Kitagawa Utamaro," several women appear to be bathing "in a mountain pool with irises / growing in the silken sunlit water," and another woman is "captured" in emerging from a bath (41, 37, 38). These women work to make apprehensible their physical likeness to water and its life, contributing to their own commodification and to social imaginaries of themselves and of water along lines such as purity, femininity, or gracefulness.[14]

In tracking water, then, Song is drawn into apparently private spaces and moments. In exploring people's relationships with water in such sites, she finds unseen contributions to economy and social life, as well as hardships and inequalities. Song's critical reflections on people's connections with water also extend to the ocean. She often animates the term *ocean* in thinking about people's experiences of being different from others, or of their exile by others to such positions of difference. In "Lost Sister," Song situates the ocean as a spatial force in migrant peoples' experiences of national fault lines and related precariousness. She tracks a woman who left China and "swarmed with others / to inundate another shore," sharply differentiating human communities in evoking different shores, and implicitly, the waters that lie between (52). Song underscores the depth of the fracture that these people have crossed, at least physically, by describing them as "locusts," a language similar to that of biosecurity stories in which the threat of nonhuman invasions is invoked in terms also used to describe peoples' movements and belonging (52).[15] Ideas of radical social differences heavily shaped plantation workers' lives, as sugar planters deliberately arranged and fostered ethnic and national divisions among workers in order to fracture political organization and weaken threats such as strikes (Takaki 1983, 24). Nineteenth- and early twentieth-century institutional archives of Hawai'i, such as court records, reveal a relentless ordering of people through rigid categories of identity (Merry 2000, 139). These divisions manifested in peoples' lives in terms of the types of jobs that were possible, the wages received, the spatial dynamics of living conditions, and in the experience and social interpretation of violence (Merry 2000, 140–43; Takaki 1983, 76–77, 92–93). For example, plantation camp blueprints from 1920 illustrate that "differences in identity were reflected in the design of houses" (Merry 2000, 143). These institutionalized arrangements of social life made it difficult to recognize the malleability of identities in the archipelago, and they elided the multiplicity of identities within ethnic, gendered, national, or other categories (139). In *Picture Bride*, Song associates peoples' relationships with the ocean with experiences of migration and of national and ethnic difference.

These associations between the ocean and migration are later absorbed into Song's descriptions of peoples' experiences of difference along other lines, specifically in gendered terms. In "From the White Place: for Georgia O'Keeffe," Song links the ocean to American painter Georgia O'Keeffe's experience of being positioned by art critics as radically other as a woman. O'Keeffe's husband Alfred Stieglitz situates O'Keeffe through "endless negatives," a reference to his photography as well as to his sense of her profound female distance: "He wanted to show her / the space between a man and a woman, / the oceans and plains in between . . ." (73). Stieglitz was an influential photographer and gallery owner who promoted O'Keeffe's art in early twentieth-century New York, first exhibiting her drawings at his 291 Gallery in 1916. Vivien Green Fryd observes that Stieglitz framed O'Keeffe's work in terms of "female anatomy and eroticism" and initiated an enduring critical tradition that heavily interpreted her works in gendered and sexualized terms (2003, 117). In 1921, Paul Rosenfeld writes of O'Keeffe's work: "Her art is gloriously female. Her great painful and ecstatic climaxes make us at last know something the man has always wanted to know. . . . The organs that differentiate the sex speak. Women, one would judge, always feel, when they feel strongly, through the womb" (qtd. in Fryd 2003, 126). O'Keeffe confronted gender-based understandings of her art and of her right to produce it, suggesting that "the things they write sound so strange and far removed from what I feel of myself," and asking whether "man has ever been written down the way he has written woman down" (qtd. in Fryd 2003, 126). Song associates the ocean with O'Keeffe's experience of being identified as wildly different as a woman: the waters do not simply mark a border but also a massive distance. Song's use of the ocean to portray O'Keeffe's experience deeply suggests how the ocean evokes associations with social difference, which are most directly traceable to migration in *Picture Bride*.

In this collection, then, Song explores hardships, disappointments, and modes of care that take form in people's relationships with fresh water and the ocean, as well as how these relationships may reveal dynamics of class, gender, nationality, and race. She draws us into the houses and working spaces where many people spend a large measure of their lives and where they work in intimate contact with water.[16] If the creativity of people in these sites is sometimes absent in histories of the plantations and of other sites, the water is likewise often imperceptible as a force in economy and social life. In places where people receive water steadily through massive infrastructures such as reservoirs, treatment plants, and pipelines, water is particularly easy to forget.[17]

A Different Hydrological Map

Like Pak, Song anticipates a different future for her characters in relation to a storm. When the rain stops in the third poem in the collection, "Easter: Wahiawa, 1959," the women and children can go outside:

we were all together
under a thin film
that separated the rain showers
from that part of the earth

like a hammock
held loosely by clothespins. (1983, 7)

The narrator's grandfather brings out a movie camera:

I looked from him to the sky,
a membrane of egg whites
straining under the weight
of the storm that threatened
to break. (7)

Evoking the film that holds water inside clouds, as well as that captures people in an image, Song links the cloud's containment of water to that of the family in the film. She extends this connection by suggesting that rain's threat to the order of the cloud also threatens that of the film. Water's activities have the potential to upset established representational patterns as well as environmental forms. The impending storm is a reminder of what has not yet come, of an imminent, different future.

But as rain falls in *Picture Bride,* it reinforces rather than changes the conditions faced by Song's characters. In "Leaving," Song reflects on the town Wahiawā, linking a woman's depression and enclosure with rain that falls like a "gray curtain" (14). In a later poem, the narrator recalls Wahiawā, where "rain fell like a fence around our house" (75). If in Pak's "Language of the Geckos," the water encircles the Hoʻokano house and enables a different socioeconomic life, in *Picture Bride* the rain further walls off characters within already isolated and claustrophobic spaces. Unlike Pak, Song does not associate her characters with collective struggles that force alterations in water conditions. Their absence from such struggles might be understood partly in the context of social restrictions and responsibilities, as well as economic impoverishment. They cannot easily be framed as resistant to existing water conditions, since their labor supports the running of the plantations. They have ties to social groups that were historically situated in precarious relation with land and water in Hawaiʻi through exclusionary laws related to naturalization and land ownership. Song does not frame them as overcoming their status as settlers in relation to Hawaiian peoples through the formation of nationalist or other claims on land and water. They would not stand out on any dominant map of the history of water struggles.

But Song does evoke small, creative ways in which both people and water interact with, complicate, and exceed given institutions and imaginaries. She traces water as it shape-shifts, moves around, and passes through entities such as people and nations. The water is involved in, a reminder of, and a way of visualizing the connections that people may build with each other and with other beings. These connections sometimes cross the sharply focused and enforced social borders that have heavily affected the lives of migrant workers in Hawai'i. In paying attention to the movements of water in the poem "Seed," Song makes imaginable the intimacy of the narrator and her lover, for example.

> Our meetings are conspiracies.
> I bring the water,
> you prepare the hunger.
> I portion out the spirits,
> the ritual of breaking bread.
> You part the water,
> come flying back to me
> on boneless wings,
> quiet fish. (25)

If in *Picture Bride* Song suggests that people's experiences are heavily marked by their categorization along lines that include gender, class, and nationality, and that these categories are entangled with imaginaries and infrastructures of water, in "Seed" she makes water part of a different politics of sociality. The first images trace the separation of the narrator and her companion. Their unborn daughters remain as potential embodied by their distinct bodies. Because water is able to wrap around their bodies, and is visibly reshaped by their interaction, it is through this element that Song recognizes their overlap, what they create together. "Seed" describes a fragmentary, apparently private, moment of a sociality, in which people complicate the overly rigid gendered categorizations associated with hardship and suppressed potential in some of the poems in *Picture Bride*.

Song repeatedly draws on water in imagining the connections that people forge with each other and with other entities. In "Blue Lantern," she describes two children in neighboring houses who listen as a man mourns his dead wife. The man's "grief washed over" them "like a tide" (13). The water runs between and reshapes around people's forms, representing the force of the man's sorrow on the children, illuminating the way in which people overlap each other, unsettling one another's seemingly evident boundaries. In "Hotel Genève," Song extends her exploration from people to varied processes connected by water, describing how the rain and the city "merged into one plane of vision" and how, in bathing, the narrator is "filled with the steam" (71). Rather than see life in terms of fixed, discrete entities, Song recognizes relatively differentiated but porous forms that are always on the move through their interactions. She shows that people are connected to each other and to broader ecosystems by tracing water's movements in and out of bodies.

In tracing the shape-shifting pathways of water, Song draws readers toward what seeps across the borders set up among people and other entities, and sometimes toward the ways in which people encroach on the categories into which they are placed. The poetry evokes small practices in which characters move through their lives in ways not entirely set up in advance and managed by social templates. These practices provide care, pleasure, freedom, or connection in everyday experiences, and in doing so they may support the material conditions of life on the plantations and beyond. But illuminated against the bleak waterscapes of class, nationalisms, and gender inequalities, they also reveal moments of openness in which people express their social capacities to work out their relationships in creative ways.

Song focuses on practices that may appear to be very socially narrow and temporally ephemeral: the intimacy of two lovers; two children who establish a profound connection with another's grief; a young woman who establishes a measure of autonomy from family rules and spaces. Such activities do not transform water-related thought and infrastructures in the decisive ways imagined by Pak in the context of coordinated social movements. Song's poetry is about "very quiet" people, in her terms (82). As many critics have noted, it focuses on people's daily, mundane practices (for example, Huot 2002, 352–53; Wallace 1993, 8). Song does not clearly calibrate these practices with a broad ideology such as nationalism. A number of scholars have associated socioeconomic and environmental creativity with people's everyday practices. Sociologist Asef Bayat argues that the ordinary activities through which people seek to navigate and better their lives may not only reinforce but quietly alter social life—its rules, relations, norms, distributions of resources and power—even when such practices are not framed as a political project. Bayat explores the force of

the persistent activities by which the poor, squatters, internal and international migrants, street children, the unemployed, housewives, and youths,
among others, in the Middle East and beyond—immense social groups at
this time of neoliberal globalization characterized by the weakening of
public sectors and by informal practices of survival—seek a "better life-
chance" (2010, 15, 19–20). Migrating to cities, illegally setting up shelters,
tapping into water and electricity supplies, pursuing education, and running businesses on sidewalks, they directly alter socioeconomic life rather
than ask governments or other institutions for such alterations (19). They
are not usually mobilized by clear organizational arrangements or collective ideologies, but their fragmented and yet often convergent practices
have a cumulative force on spaces, norms, and distributions of power and
goods in cities, communities, and states (14–20).[18]

To be attentive to writers who associate hope with people's everyday
practices requires engaging literary forms that cannot be accounted for
through a focus on imaginaries of a new world or even of a dramatically
changed world. Such attention matters because it allows us to see a different site of creativity, hardship, and potential. In contrast to Song's
poems, Pak's short stories, with which I began this chapter, much more
clearly imagine substantial, socially driven environmental change. Yet Pak
also evokes the ways in which people combine these struggles with everyday practices involving water, including in fishing and cultivating taro.
He engages contexts where these everyday forms of life were disrupted
and sometimes eliminated by such forces as the encroachment of private
property around aquatic ecosystems, the removal of water from rivers
and springs, and the growth of expensive coastal housing. People's direct
practices of an alternative, ordinary life involving water are supported by
their organized, tenacious clashes with those institutions and people who
would evict them from the land or take away the water.

Persistent Uncertainty

Although Song's and Pak's works converge in emphasizing the everyday
as a source of hope, they lie across fissures from each other in many ways.
They attach hope to people and to their differing positions in the world
as well as to diverse forms and activities of water. *Picture Bride* brings an
important perspective to a discussion of hope in focusing on everyday
creativity but also as a reminder of people who may be invisible in *both*

hegemonic and more marginal accounts of what in this world allows hope. Although Song provides a critical lens on the aquatic conditions that Pak's characters struggle to transform, her characters also economically survive through labor that sustains these conditions and so her poetry raises the question of how such people might be positioned in relation to Pak's imagined, promising world. The differences in Pak's and Song's writings remind us of the work not only of grasping toward alternative forms of life involving water but of continually opening up questions about present water conditions, those people and other beings who coexist with water, and their futures.

Continued curiosity regarding how people might live well with water is not simply a matter of choice. Both Pak and Song connect hope to people's intimacies with changeable forces that cannot entirely be controlled, from nonhuman beings to other peoples. They associate promising futures with exposure to, rather than entrenchment against, water, in its connections with and differences from people. Both writers consequently link hope to people's capacities to navigate surprising, fast-changing environmental conditions. The rainstorm that takes form in Pak's story "Language of the Geckos" accords with and supports a family's struggle to allow an alternative way of life, although it also alarms and threatens some characters, at least initially. In contrast, in Song's poem, "Easter: Wahiawa, 1959," a rainstorm entirely fails to converge with a character's hope that it will interrupt and force an opening in the possibilities of her everyday life. For Pak and Song, water involves vibrant forces that are never entirely collapsible with people's struggles to live well. But water can never be completely separated from human life, either, as is evident in these writers' insistence on tracking the creative and destructive relationships among water, the capitalist economy, social movements, and people's everyday practices. They associate hope with people's precarious but vital efforts to shape water through economy and social life but also with people's capacities to navigate the sometimes surprising, threatening trajectories of lives that they do not alone compose.

CHAPTER 3

Hope in the Poetry
of a Fractured Ocean

Allow me
to mend the broken ends
of shared days . . .

Hone Tuwhare, "Friend"

IN THE POEM "Kākā Point," from *Shape-Shifter* (1997), New Zealand
Māori (Ngāpuhi) writer Hone Tuwhare anticipates that *tītī* or sooty
shearwater will return from the ocean to the narrator's coastal home. In
their yearly migrations, tītī construct expansive connections through ocean
and skies from the southern to the northern reaches of the Pacific and
back. Tuwhare's narrator senses the world from which the seabirds will
emerge. It involves spaces and ways of life that are largely unknown and invisible and yet that shape the narrator's life, because the birds provide sustenance as well as a sense of home. At the end of "Kākā Point," Tuwhare
calls for the birds to survive and flourish: "Eat well—and mate well—so
that your woolly, roly- / poly progeny will thrive in their thousands for
us" (79). He anticipates and imagines, rather than describes, the return
of the birds. The poem never resolves this temporality of waiting, and as
such it is perhaps tinged with uncertainty regarding the dependability of
the birds and more broadly of the world in which they exist, a futuristic
openness onto which both hope and unease might be read. In 1998, indeed, the *Command* oil spill affected sooty shearwater migrating off the
California coast and consequently the populations who flew south and
landed on islands in New Zealand, leading to a transnational restoration
project. Migrating tītī are caught as the bycatch of commercial fishing operations and may be affected by climatic fluctuations.[1] Tuwhare offers no
sense in "Kākā Point" that his narrator could control or even profoundly
shape what happens in the world through which the birds travel, although
he does emphasize that the narrator participates in that world in eating

birds and fish, among other activities. The poem evokes the spatially diffuse beings and forces that can affect a life.

A view toward an oceanic horizon recurs in contemporary media that
engages the Pacific Ocean. In documentary films about sea level rise in
the Pacific, shots from islands out to sea evoke peoples' relationship with
climatic processes that are undermining their life but that they did not create.[2] In New Zealand European settler culture, the horizon has sometimes
marked distance and loss.[3] But in Tuwhare's poem "Kākā Point," and in
the climate change documentary films, the horizon evokes enigmatic intimacies; it is an attempt to represent the faraway and yet disconcertingly
close spaces that shape lives and futures. Life in and beyond the Pacific
is intensely connected, as evidenced by rising sea levels, oil companies
prospecting in deep waters, and the flight paths of missiles as well as of
birds. But in trying to follow these connections, we may struggle to move
through an ocean also marked by differences, and sometimes by uncross-
able fractures, between beings and their interests.

In the previous chapter, I explored literary writings that associate
hope—an awareness of the openness and promise of the future—with
water and so that draw us not only into national or local contexts but
through water's expansive trajectories in the ocean and atmosphere before
it falls as rain in Hawai'i. Now I focus more directly on literary writings
that situate peoples' present-world struggles to regenerate the connections
between human and nonhuman beings across long distances, including
through national borders, as allowing a relationship with a future that is
promising and open. A number of ecocritics have recently sought to turn
attention toward cultural production that evokes wide-ranging connections, complicating the heavy focus on local or national contexts in some
strands of environmental thought.[4] In some imaginative histories, the
Pacific Ocean allows hope precisely in offering a retreat from such connections, as a space of lonely islands where people have long stagnated in
their insularity from what lies beyond the beach.[5] In environmental struggles in the Pacific, however, activists have almost ceaselessly undertaken
their battles in relation to transnational entanglements, engaging empires,
corporations, and military networks. Their tactics include participation in
"unwanted entanglements," to draw from anthropologist Eben Kirksey's
discussion of activists' struggles for *merdeka* (loosely, freedom) in West
Papua (2012, 1). Faced with conditions of immense power disparity, West
Papuans manipulated violent connections with foreign governments, cor-

porations, and Indonesian politicians in order to work toward freedom: "Contingent alliances, sometimes even with the enemy, can open up possibilities in seemingly impossible situations" (15). Kirksey describes hope as animated by the tactical work of such alliances, in combination with expansive dreams of a life that is free from them.[6]

Literary writers from the Pacific, too, have long been aware of the ways in which life is entangled across the ocean. Some writers respond to peoples' precarious positions in an ocean with so much varied life by imagining the control of all that life, at least insofar as it affects a particular people. In *Utopia*, for example, Thomas More associates a promising world with utopian peoples' ability to powerfully manage their relationships with other peoples so as to secure utopian interests in a precariously connected and differentiated world. Their management strategies include aggressive elimination and subdual of others in combination with an emphasis on utopian security and insularity (1999 [1516]).

Alive to histories in which institutions have sought to speak for and control vast swathes of life through the waters and beyond, contemporary New Zealand poets Cilla McQueen, Hone Tuwhare, and Ian Wedde imagine that differences in environmental life—including in ways of imagining—are important for this world and its futures. The first poem that I discuss here, Ian Wedde's "Letter to Peter McLeavey: After Basho" from *Three Regrets and a Hymn to Beauty* (2005b), addresses colonial art and contemporary corporate and conservation accounts of environmental presents and futures that are encompassing, or that do not admit to any differences in perspective (Wedde 2005b). Wedde insists on the disparate futures that human as well as nonhuman beings might experience as promising. Rather than only associate hope with differences, however, the writers engaged in this chapter also suggest that the conversations and other exchanges made vital by such differences are a site of possibility. They explore how the transnational pathways of resource extraction and production, from milk, to timber, to aluminum, may unravel human and nonhuman lives. But they also imagine the present world as a site of struggles to alter transnational pathways. In the poem "Kākā Point," from *Shape-Shifter* (1997), Tuwhare imagines a "multi-lingual" ocean that can interact with its diverse life forms on their own terms and can support conversations among them (78). Conversations among peoples of the ocean do not necessarily facilitate environmental well-being, of course; they are also vital to processes of destruction and usually exclude the vast majority of people and other beings. In the last section of this chapter, I engage a poem that addresses such exclusionary dynamics. In "Tiwai Sequence," from the collection *Markings* (2000b), McQueen addresses the impacts of transnational aluminum production and consumption. She incorporates lines from the publicity material of an aluminum company into her poem, forcibly including the company in a dialogue regarding the environmental damage in which it is involved.

Hope in a Fractured Ocean

In suggesting that connections across transnational spaces—specifically those embodied by sooty shearwater migrations—offer hope but also provoke anxiety, as well as in observing the narrator's limited agencies in relation to such spaces, Tuwhare's poem "Kākā Point," with which I opened this chapter, is quite a different imaginative project than the early utopias that are set in the ocean. They famously associate promising modes of being with islands.[7] In *Utopia,* More tells us that on arriving in the land that would later become known as utopia, King Utopus "caused fifteen miles space of uplandish ground, where the sea had no passage, to be cut and digged up. And so brought the sea round about the land" (1999, 50). For More, an island offers a possibility of drawing back from and warding away the world, to some extent. The sea has long been a space into which to push people away from limited social worlds, in a combined and often lethal effort to encompass a life and its possibilities as well as to abandon that life.[8]

More's island may be luminous, grabbing hold of attention, but *Utopia* also reflects his imaginative struggle with coexistence on a planet involving many unruly forces scattered across space. He does not suggest that the island is entirely insular. Indeed, it is quite permeable, but the utopians can deal with relationships beyond the island in limited ways and largely on their own terms. They practice overflow colonialism, for example. When their population grows too large, they expand into other lands, by violence if they meet resistance (1999, 63). More's utopians therefore have limited but significant agency in relation to what falls outside the utopia, at least in terms of how it affects their lives.[9]

More's sense of the utopian status of these peoples' substantial and aggressive agency in relation to others draws us in the direction of the more recent colonial and military networks that have stretched around and deep into the ocean, seeking to grasp, shape, and direct much, if not all, of its life. Empires have been conceived partly through oceanic rather than island-based spatial frameworks, including the American Pacific, the British Empire, the Japanese South Seas *(nanyō)*, and the French Pacific.[10] A recent press release describes the U.S. Navy's Pacific fleet—a network of ships, aircrafts, sailors, and civilians positioned around the ocean—as having "command and control of more than 45 percent of the earth's surface" (Navy.mil. 2006).

Many contemporary literary and theoretical writers from the Pacific critically engage histories in which institutions have sought to control the present reality and plan the future of multitudes of other beings. New Zealand European writer Ian Wedde observes the dreaminess of artifacts and archives of early European exploration in the Pacific, arguing that they see a promising ocean in a lost past or a redeemed future but studiously avoid imagining futures in relation to the socially fractured realities of the present, including the conflicts surrounding imperialism (2005a). He suggests that the rainbow in Māori artist Emare (Emily) Karaka's collage work *Ka Awatea* (1991) is a symbol of hope within the Ringatū faith, but in contrast to European exploration archives, "this hope rises in a present that's pictured as fragmented and complex" (2005a, 93). *Ka Awatea* suggests that hope emerges in a fractured world—a world of conflicts over compelling modes of life and futures—and as such, hope is also myriad, a term for many experiences.

Wedde's poems take up this thread of a fractured present world and of the differing claims on hope that this world might allow for. Born in 1946, Wedde has published numerous poetry collections, novels, and works of cultural criticism. He has been influential within humanities institutions in New Zealand and beyond, including in working at Te Papa Tongarewa— the Museum of New Zealand, at Auckland University, and as poet laureate.[11] In "Letter to Peter McLeavey: After Basho," a forty-section poem, Wedde explores the environmental imaginaries of colonial art and governmental and corporate advertising (2005b). He rebukes those archives that do not acknowledge any differences in the ways in which human and nonhuman beings apprehend environmental life. He suggests that differences—cultural or otherwise—matter in environmental politics, because they offer pathways to address the uneven impacts of colonial injustices such as the destruction of forests. They can also disrupt business as usual by sparking tensions around the meanings of existing environmental life and its potentials. Although Wedde makes often sharp claims on the present realities and imagined futures that allow for hope, his poetry is also marked by uncertainty and by attention to its own limitations, and so makes space for the perspectives that others might bring. As he reflects, "Most of my poems are concerned with how we live, how we should live, & are political in these senses. At the same time I think I seldom tell; I enquire. So people reading my poems are questing *with* me not being told *by* me (though I have my convictions & am certainly vain enough to lay them on the poem & 'the reader' from time to time)" (Wedde 1973, 185).

In "Letter to Peter McLeavey: After Basho," our narrator, a poet, sets out from Wellington or nearby, searching for an understanding of beauty, among other phenomena. In the poem, Wedde recontextualizes phrases that he finds circulating in governmental and corporate discourses, interrupting their ordinary logic to illuminate the politically charged ways in which they apprehend promising modes of being. Pausing at Ōhingaiti, a rural area settled for the building of a railway viaduct as well as for farming, Wedde incorporates a phrase or a sentiment taken from the website of the multinational dairy company Fonterra: "On Fonterra's 'Milk' website / there's only one health, / it's green and '100% pure'" (41).

Fonterra's interpretation of health and environment, as they already exist, and implicitly as they should exist, is designed to speak for and apply to all human and nonhuman life, without limits. The slogan "100% pure," which is used on the website of the Crown entity Tourism New Zealand, elides the environmental changes that people and nonhumans shape over time.[12] It may also direct attention toward certain places that look like they could be pure while making it difficult to think about environmental politics through less obvious sites such as cities and economy. The term *green* has long been associated with environmental loss in some archives from New Zealand, and today a well-known, if politically embattled, discourse situates the archipelago as "clean and green."[13] Insistence that health is green elides the diversity of the life that we could call green as well as different colors that are important in Māori culture and in alternative environmental politics. In "Letter to Peter McLeavey: After Basho," Wedde insists on the significance of red and crimson, among other colors (49). Fonterra's positioning of green and pure as terms that can speak without limits for health and environment works to marginalize beings that do not easily fit within these imaginative categories.

The concepts of greenness and purity are not simply tools that focus certain visibilities and invisibilities in the present world. They are vague, aspirational terms that call up an ecology that *should be,* and that histori-cally have been drawn on to evoke encompassing, global futures.[14] Making claims about how others do and should live, including across national bor-ders, has been crucial to environmental politics. Such work might involve confronting a company that is carrying away a rainforest on roads and ships, or revealing the demands for biofuels used in climate change mitiga-tion efforts in Northern industrialized economies and how they interlock with the establishment of monocultural plantations in the Global South. But when environmentalists represent the realities and futures of others, they can undertake marginalization and imposition, especially if such rep-resentations are aggressively circulated and implemented in conditions of power disparity and constructed in ways that elide their limitations and the potential for different approaches.[15]

In "Letter to Peter McLeavey: After Basho," Wedde makes the limitless agendas of companies such as Fonterra brush up against commitments, spatial practices, and lives that they would ignore. He apprehends fractures in the ways in which people and other life forms might interpret present as well as promising forms of environmental life. At Ōhingaiti, our narrator directly takes a phrase from advertising materials for the Peach Teats brand of manufactured teats, which are used for rearing calves: "Peach Teats—calves love 'em" (41). On New Zealand dairy farms, calves are removed from their mothers and raised separately to enable greater efficiency and productivity in the milking process. Wedde returns to these calves two pages further into the poem: "I just know 'Peach Teats' calves / think their mothers are beautiful: / more beautiful than 'Peach Teats'" (43). The lines ask us to think about the elisions at work in the notion that calves love Peach Teats, specifically the processes by which calves are separated from their mothers for the production of milk. They also critically engage the link that the Fonterra and Peach Teats companies make between milk pro-duction and well-being. The dairy industry is a force in extensive environ-mental degradation in New Zealand, including in the pollution of water-ways and in high methane emissions.[16] In suggesting that a calf would prefer its mother to Peach Teats, Wedde suggests that we cannot simply conflate the well-being of the calves and a corporation, and more broadly that we cannot simply reconcile preferred modes of being across beings. Although he makes a claim on the experiences of another being, he draws attention to the narrator's role in making the claim and so its limitations.

Wedde also evokes differences in how people might imagine promising futures. From Ōhingaiti, our narrator travels further inland to the area of the central volcanoes, Ruapehu, Ngāuruhoe, and Tongariro. In section "8 Te Porere," he references an earthwork redoubt at Te Pōrere and repeats a phrase that is associated with it: "Ziklag is the name for this Pa" (43). Te Kooti Arikirangi Te Tūruki, a nineteenth-century Māori leader, is supposed to have said these words when he saw the *pā*, or fortification, in 1869 (Binney 1997, 185). Several years earlier, the government imprisoned Te Kooti without trial on Wharekauri in the Chatham Islands. While imprisoned, Te Kooti founded the Ringatū faith, which held that the Māori prisoners would be saved by God as the Israelites had been in the Old Testament: "Te Kooti's was a faith that offered hope to the oppressed" (Waitangi Tribunal 2004, 170). Te Kooti escaped from Wharekauri back to the North Island along with a community of 298 prisoners known as the *whakarau*. The group initially attempted to peacefully retreat into the North Island, where Te Kooti wanted to develop the religious community. But there came a turning point as they were provoked by the Crown's aggressive pursuits and forcible acquisitions of land to which Te Kooti had rights at Tūranga. In 1868, Te Kooti and the whakarau attacked Tūranga, executing 29–34 settlers and 20–40 Māori who had been involved in land transactions (Waitangi Tribunal 2004, 204–5). In subsequent conflicts with the Crown, they sustained many casualties, including between 86 and 134 individuals who were shot without trial on capture by Crown forces (244). Te Kooti evaded capture, eventually withdrawing into the Rohe Pōtae or the King Country and continuing to develop the Ringatū Church, which is still active today.

At Te Pōrere, the place to which Wedde comes in "Letter to Peter McLeavey: After Basho," Te Kooti and the whakarau fought government forces, were defeated, and fled. Historian Judith Binney argues that in naming the pā "Ziklag," Te Kooti anticipated his people's future in terms of both failure and hope, referring to the defeat of the Israelites by the Amalekite peoples at the town of Ziklag as well as to King David's subsequent pursuit and defeat of the Amalekites: "If he did utter this remark at Te Porere, he was predicting a fearful doom for the besieged *before* battle, but also offering a later resolution" (Binney 1997, 186). Observing the creek and the birds that now exist in this place, in "Letter to Peter McLeavey: After Basho" Wedde also ponders what the whakarau might have aspired to amid the cold, wind, snow, and sleet of September–October 1869.

I wonder if the whakarau freezing in their flooded trenches
looked up at Ketetahi's steam
and imagined immersing themselves
in the healing pools at Tokaanu (Wedde 2005b, 44).

Wedde does not speculate on these peoples' relationships with the future with any certainty, but the lines evoke imaginings of material well-
being, security, and recovery. In referencing Ziklag, Te Kooti's name for
the *pā* (fortification), Wedde also suggests that practicing and developing
the Ringatū faith and retaining land and autonomy were likely important
imaginings for this group. He engages fractured social dynamics, referencing the emergence of a specific social group and faith as well as the conflicts of imperialism. If early in the poem Wedde observes the corporation Fonterra's claim that there is only one health, which is green and pure,
through the story of Te Kooti and the whakarau he ponders the social differences and power dynamics that shape peoples' relationships with the
present world and the future.

In "Letter to Peter McLeavey: After Basho," Wedde suggests that colonial New Zealand art may elide such fractures, tracing continuities between this art and contemporary corporate and governmental discourses.
He observes that in 1841 English painter Conrad Martens painted the
settlement of Kororāreka, also known as Russell, in a way that elides conflict between Māori and Europeans. In Martens's painting of the town
and the bay that lies beyond, Wedde sees "a posed group of Maori" and
suggests that they "imagine the town burning" (52). The line refers to the
tensions smoldering between Māori and settlers at that time, as well as to
the invisibility of this conflict within the painting. A few short years after
Martens painted Kororāreka, Ngāpuhi leader Hōne Heke would repeatedly cut down the town's flagstaff in protest of European settlement and
of the Crown's efforts to undermine Māori sovereignty. In 1845 he would
attack and sack the town, and war would break out between Ngāpuhi and
the Crown (Taonui 2009a).

Wedde describes ideological continuities between these colonial paintings of New Zealand and contemporary governmental infrastructures
related to environmental protection. He suggests that conservation infrastructures position people in an all-seeing perspective and so elide differences and limitations in ways of seeing. In section "12" of "Letter to Peter

McLeavey: After Basho," he comes across a viewing platform, a structure
that is a common in conservation and tourism in New Zealand.

From the viewing platform
I can see the forest:
there are no trees in the way.

From the scenic lookout
I view from above
what's best understood from below.

Spectacular while spread out,
expansive although deep,
only its remoteness can touch me. (47)

The forest can be seen because the trees that once inhabited the site of the
lookout are gone. The viewing platform figures the relationship between
people and forest as one of separation, positioning people not to see their
situation in but their distance from the forest. It allows not so much a
reconciliation of people and nature as a reconfiguration of perspective
through which the forest emerges as an entirely separate object. This way
of seeing the forest is made possible by deforestation as well as by the construction of the viewing platform. More broadly, Wedde perhaps observes
that the forest becomes an object of acute awareness at a time when it is
mostly gone. At this point in the poem, the narrator has traveled through
Cambridge and Ngāruawāhia in Waikato, a region once covered in waterways, wetlands, and forest but where European settlers comprehensively
eliminated existing ecosystems for agriculture and timber, as they did in
other low-lying plains expanses of New Zealand.[17] The forest, Wedde observes, has been transformed into churches: "They're everywhere / the
forest isn't" (47). The viewing platform supports the idea of a view without limitations, uncertainty, or complicity.

Wedde suggests that we might rather understand the forest from
within, a vantage point that brings us up against limitations in perspective
and that also recognizes the forest's involvement in human life. A forest
is creative in ways that seep well beyond what we might recognize as its
spatial borders, providing food, wood, watershed protection, and habitat,
and shaping soil and climate. It is a relatively distinct entity with murky

borders. If we do not see the forest's connections with human life, we cannot engage many of the injustices entangled with its loss. In particular, Wedde emphasizes the long histories of human presence in the forest and some of the wrongdoings that have characterized this presence. In section "13," which directly follows the section on the viewing platform, Wedde writes of Te Mahuta Ngahere, "the father of the forest" (48). The lines refer to Tāne Mahuta, thought to be New Zealand's largest surviving kauri tree, and Te Matua Ngahere, considered to be the archipelago's second-largest living kauri tree (Department of Conservation n.d.b.). Probably more than 2,000 years old, Te Matua Ngahere lives near Tāne Mahuta in Waipoua forest, where the local people are Te Roroa (Department of Conservation n.d.b.). The names evoke the trees' genealogical links with other beings, and so are a reminder of interconnection rather than of distance.[18] Māori have lived in this area for around 1,000 years, using the kauri forest for food such as birds and pigs, as well as for gum, wood, and medicinal plants (Waitangi Tribunal 1992, 5.2.6). The Crown put Te Roroa under pressure to survey and sell most of their lands quickly and cheaply, particularly from the 1870s onward. Te Roroa faced many injustices in relation to the Crown's inadequate provision of reserves, and the land surveying and sales, including the low prices paid. They lost most of their lands and other resources, experienced state failures to support their welfare and development, saw the desecration or destruction of their *taonga* (treasures), and faced difficulties in working with Crown institutions regarding management of the forest: "By the 1920s, they were coming to resemble 'the sea-birds which perch upon a rock' because they have no other resting place" (Waitangi Tribunal 1992, 5.1). The settlement between Te Roroa and the Crown included cultural and economic redress. Almost all of the northern kauri forest is gone, however. It was felled to make way for farmland and for timber. In the following section of "Letter to Peter McLeavey: After Basho," titled "14 *Hokianga,*" Wedde observes that the children of Te Mahuta Ngahere "became the church at Pakanae / painted by Eric Lee Johnson" (48). If we do not recognize peoples' relationships with the forest, as well as the differences that characterize such relationships, it is impossible to take responsibility for histories of environmental injustice.

Attunement to differences in perspective also allows space for alternative politics in relation to nonhuman beings. Many nonhumans will fall away from encompassing narratives about what exists in this world and about what hope might mean, whether these narratives involve greenness, purity, or health. Such narratives may allow certain beings to more easily be wiped out of this world with little, if any, regard. Moving into the far north of New Zealand, Wedde arrives at Muriwai beach. Here he writes of Colin McCahon, a New Zealand European painter who lived from 1919 to 1987. Suggesting that McCahon finds nothing special about the beach or sea at Muriwai, Wedde narrates the sea in plain, descriptive words such as "matt dry sand, slick wet sand, foamy backsuck" (54). McCahon, suggests Wedde, cries because "beauty this plain / doesn't stand a chance" (54). While working at Muriwai during the early 1970s, McCahon observed the interactions between a gannet colony and the coastal land forms, creating a series of paintings known as *Necessary Protection*. The series explores the concept and aesthetics of protection that could help support both human and nonhuman life in this place, drawing inspiration from the ways in which nonhuman beings take shelter within the forms of the coastal ecosystems and expressing fear regarding their potential degradation, particularly given the power of the scenic to determine what ecosystems are protected in New Zealand.[19] McCahon explains these concerns in a fragment about the land and the shrub known as *manuka*, written in 1977: "Up north the manuka hangs fiercely to the land form. It is a protective skin, it protects the land it needs and the land gives it life and a season of red and pink and white flowering. Take the manuka and the land is lost. This situation is the one I refer to in all the paintings and drawings that belong to the family I call *Necessary Protection*" (1977, n.p.). Necessary protection does not designate a one-sided exchange but rather reciprocity, as the manuka protects the land and so the land can in turn sustain the manuka. The concept rejects insularity, in suggesting that we cannot live without others. It also resists efforts to dominate others, in insisting on the importance of agencies different from our own.

In "Letter to Peter McLeavey: After Basho," Wedde takes up McCahon's concerns about life forms that do not fit within dominant stories about what protective relations should be cultivated. During the road trip he picks up phrases from tourism and other forms of consumer economy, particularly those that implicitly value certain landscapes and interpretations of aesthetics, including "Untouched World," "spectacular beauty," and "Scenic Tours" (63, 64). Beauty, for Wedde, is "something / else" (65). A search for a never fully graspable elsewhere that we might call beauty takes Wedde to a beach at Mitimiti that is covered in "plankton scum": "it's what the mullet eat, / it's what Ralph Hotere dips his brush in: / calligraphy of black salt" (50). The inconspicuous mullet and the plankton scum, if a source of inspiration for artists (and in New Zealand artist Ralph Hotere's case, perhaps literally, since Hotere incorporated materials like shells or sand in his works), do not fit within the dominant interpretations of the beautiful, special, and worth saving or paying for. These ecosystems do not meet hegemonic criteria for protection and yet in profound ways they protect life, including that of the mullet and the artist. Throughout "Letter to Peter McLeavey: After Basho," Wedde renovates the aesthetics of beauty, paying attention to what might be seen as plain or ugly. At Mitimiti, he observes the way in which the black water of a lagoon becomes silver at dusk and reflects the stars at night. "Frugal and cunning," this is a form of beauty that "makes do" (51). Wedde associates beauty with a more diverse range of sites and processes than may be evoked by terms such as scenic, untouched, and spectacular. But perhaps more importantly, he suggests that apprehensions of beauty should be continually open to experimentation.

In my reading, then, in "Letter to Peter McLeavey: After Basho" Wedde associates hope with contexts fractured along lines that include species and social group. He asks readers to recognize differing perspectives on the present realities and imaginary futures that might allow for hope, a relationship with the future that includes openness and promise. Peoples' efforts to maintain their distinctive perspectives on environmental life—both as it exists and should exist—have sometimes been aggressively undermined by powerful, militarized forces, as Wedde suggests in engaging the resource-related wars of nineteenth century New Zealand. Recognizing differing perspectives on both the present world and promising futures is important to projects of addressing the uneven—indeed, wildly disparate—impacts of processes such as capitalist forest extraction, in which some make their fortunes and others find themselves adrift in charred and hacked landscapes. Such recognition makes space for the unsettling passions, dreams, and tensions that characterize this environmental life, allowing the disruption of business as usual with struggles regarding the environments that could and should be.

Conversations at Sea

Although Wedde's poetry apprehends relatively distinctive forms of environmental life, it also emphasizes the relations and mobilities that cross and shape such forms of life, such as the movements of trees in the context of capitalist resource extraction and the way that such movements also mobilize individuals or groups in opposition. Pacific peoples have long participated in expansive relationships across and into the ocean. In this ocean, however, we come up against long-standing cultural histories that situate people as living in remote and lost island worlds rather than as shapers and theorists of an ocean that binds as much as it isolates. Across numerous European literary, political, and film archives, and in much academic scholarship through to the 1970s, the Pacific Ocean is figured as the home of primitive peoples who live on contained islands, from modernist artists' yearnings for the life of the savage to salvage anthropology in the threatened heritage sites of unexplored cultures.[20] Despite, and beyond, these stories, the ocean is important within past and contemporary ways of living in the Pacific. Epeli Hauʻofa observes that the myths and legends of Pacific peoples traverse land, the ocean, the underworld, and the atmosphere at cosmological scales, and reflect not just imagination but material histories such as exploration, migration, kinship, and trading (2008a, 31). Paul D'Arcy suggests that these oceanic life ways have been disrupted by colonial institutions that defined islands as isolated spaces, as well as by material reconfigurations since, such as the processes by which Pacific nations rent the rights to fish within their EEZs to large, foreign corporations, with as little as five percent of the reported market value of catches coming back to Pacific Islanders (2006, 168). Although the sea's linkages with people have been battered, it is nevertheless still tracked through by environmental, kinship, economic, and political connections. In the last two centuries, people have continued to negotiate relationships across borders, as is evident in archives such as treaties, petitions, press releases, and art works. Rather than take Oceania as a space of islands in a distant sea, Hauʻofa argues that we apprehend a "sea of islands," a perspective that emphasizes "the totality of . . . relationships" in and beyond the water (2008a, 31).

A luminous imaginary of relations and differences among oceanic life forms takes form in the poetry of Hone Tuwhare, a Ngāpuhi writer who was born in 1922 and died in 2008, and who is one of New Zealand's most recognized and important poets.[21] Tuwhare published many volumes of poetry and served as poet laureate. The 700 printed copies of his first collection, *No Ordinary Sun* (1964), sold out in New Zealand in ten days, and the collection was reprinted thirteen times, in three editions, up to 2001 (Hunt 2011, 16). Tuwhare was posted to Hiroshima with occupation forces shortly after the atomic bombing and is well known for his poetry about nuclear concerns. *Shape-Shifter* (1997), which I discuss here, pulls together poems and prose works by Tuwhare and color paintings by New Zealand artist Shirley Grace. Most of poems in *Shape-Shifter* take the form of dialogues in which Tuwhare speaks with the land, water, wind, trees, birds, and significant people, engaging topics such as Māori culture and politics, language, colonialism, sex, and love. And, as Robert Sullivan notes, many of the poems are preoccupied with the sea: the collection tastes "salty" (1998, 6).

At the end of "Kākā Point," the poem with which I began this chapter, Tuwhare imagines the return of *tītī* (muttonbirds, sooty shearwater) to the coastal waters near the narrator's home. Tuwhare lived at Kākā Point on the South Island's East Coast. Just down the road, the Department of Conservation's (DOC's) proposal to create a marine reserve at Nugget Point has been contested for many years.[22] When I passed through Kākā Point in the southern winter of 2006, the words "No reserve" were painted across the sides of buildings and on signs. Yearly, sooty shearwater undertake startling migrations, flying north from breeding sites on New Zealand islands and other southern locations to sub-Arctic waters and back. Rakiura Māori undertake a seasonal harvest of sooty shearwater chicks, a food source, from islands around Rakiura or Stewart Island in southern New Zealand. A hint of anxiety that the seabirds will not survive washes back across "Kākā Point" in the last line, where Tuwhare calls for them to flourish and to provide continued sustenance.

Tuwhare situates the potential that sooty shearwater will return to Kākā Point and will thrive not simply within a local, coastal place but on a planet involving multitudes of beings.

> Way out and beyond, I sense a whole World in movement
>   and flex. On the same latitude, Chile nudges, just
>   over the horizon.
> And because the Sea is multi-lingual, I share
>   its collective heart-beat, with all poets, in all
>   lands, joined together by oceans of applause—and
>   a fine mutuality of taste, for fish (and chips, please). (78)

In describing the sea's linguistic capacities as well as its heartbeat, these lines broadly observe that the sea is an agent that expresses itself in and responds to the world. Te Ahukaramū Charles Royal describes vital and textured relationships between Māori and the sea. He notes that certain Māori traditions situate life as emerging from the sea and tell stories of the underwater world, including of the deep sea. Such traditions show respect for the complicated forces that the sea exerts on life: "Water was considered to be an energy possessing myriad characteristics, shapes and natures. It upheld life, yet was also able to bring terrible destruction. This energy with all its forms, moods and expressions is called Tangaroa. The common translation, 'god of the sea', does not adequately convey its meaning" (2009b, n.p.).

As well as situating the sea as a relatively coherent being through the image of its "collective heart-beat" in "Kākā Point," Tuwhare evokes the kaleidoscope of life forms that shape this being, including people. Many of the poems in *Shape-Shifter* engage these life forms, expressing concern that some might be overlooked in the oceanic fabrics of which they are part. Most of the ocean's life forms are "scaled to be overlooked," as U.S. poet John Updike puts it in "Transparent Stratagems," a poem about the ways in which deep sea animals are adapted for camouflage and visibility (2001, 88). In "Big Whale Itch," Tuwhare explores the difficulties of recognition at sea. He addresses entities so small that they are virtually indistinguishable from seawater, as well as forces that stretch vertically and horizontally through large swathes of the planet. The currents, wind, and moon "incite the waves" to war with the land, shaking the narrator's crib or small, coastal house (16). As all this unfolds, "the great Earth-ball continues on its / course, oblivious to local and minor insurrections" (16). The land finally coaxes the sea to be quiet by giving it "three billion grains of sand," and the waves retreat (16). Tuwhare ends "Big Whale Itch" with a much smaller life. The narrator examines the sea, hoping to see a ship running into the wind's "shoulder; a lurching sea-animal perhaps—just briefly / imploring the sky to scratch its nose, back, arse" (16). The sea-animal appears in the middle of the line and is separated out by the semicolon and the dash, so that it formally lurches out of the sentence. The lines direct attention toward large-scaled entities, such as the sea, as well as toward what exists within and sometimes crosses their borders, or the small lives that Tuwhare pulls, and that indeed may leap, from the ocean. Through these abrupt scalar shifts, the poetry is crafted to attune readers to immense forces such as the sea as well as to the small beings that are caught up in them.

Although Tuwhare's poetry evokes a multiplicity of marine life forms, it does not suggest that they are entirely discrete. In many poems in *Shape-Shifter*, he observes disparate beings clash or otherwise engage each other. The poem "The Sun Is a Truant" describes the interactions of rocks and the receding tide. The waters abandon the rocks but will return to engulf them in a "frenzy and furore of embracings—seeded with high / emotional overtones I find . . . excessive" (83). Through the imagery of intimacy, here "seeded," Tuwhare asserts the creative exuberance of the relationship between the rocks and the water.

The volatile dynamics of difference and connection that mark environmental life can be anxiety provoking in suggesting that many beings affect one's life and yet are different from that life and cannot be controlled. *Shape-Shifter* is a reflection on the present realities and potential futures of such connections; it suggests that people could be present with other marine life forms in ways that extend beyond recognition and attachment to conversations. Imaginative projects related to the apprehension and aesthetic renovation of marine life forms have not always supported these life forms to thrive or even to survive. Since the advent of industrial fishing in the nineteenth century, fishing corporations have sought new ways to sense and catch more of the elusive beings that swim or drift in the waters or that shelter on underwater mountains, plains, and abysses. In addition to utilizing technologies such as sonar, global positioning systems, new net materials, spotter planes, and hydraulic winches, some companies have worked toward new imaginative possibilities for sea creatures. For example, in the late 1970s, commercial fishers learned of the presence and lucrative possibilities of a fish known as the slimehead in deep waters such as the Chatham Rise in New Zealand (Fahrenthold 2009). The fishing industry reimagined the fish through the more appealing name orange roughy, and an industrial fishery was established. Between 1979 and 1997, orange roughy at the Chatham Rise infamously fell to an estimated 20 percent of their pre-fishing populations, while other species caught as by-catch also declined (Clark et al. 2000).

Rather than seeking only to enable aesthetic attachment to marine life forms, in *Shape-Shifter* Tuwhare imagines conversations between human and nonhuman beings about promising forms of oceanic life. To return to the poem "Kākā Point" and its concept of a "multi-lingual" sea, here Tuwhare evokes the different modes of expression and capacities for communication that characterize oceanic life (78). Tuwhare's sea can listen to and speak with other beings in ways that reflect their own modes of engagement. Moreover, it can support them to communicate in ways that involve their differing languages and knowledge. The Pacific Ocean has been a site for efforts in such communication in varied intraoceanic social movements, such as Moana Nui, a coalition for dialogue and action involving activists, academics, and others, and in governmental institutions such as the intergovernmental environmental organization SPREP or the Secretariat of the Pacific Regional Environmental Programme, which fosters trans-Pacific cooperation in areas such as climate change and pollution. Tuwhare's image of a multilingual sea evokes not only vibrant, if tenuous, realities of dialogue, but also a sea that *could be,* a sea that might be better shaped by communication that reflects the varied terms of its communities. Rob Wilson calls such a form of communication "heterological," describing the profound injustice of a world in which the U.S. judicial system would likely not recognize an eighteenth-century shark hula poem as an archive that establishes a chief's claim on the Big Island of Hawai'i (2000, 210). Even when Hawaiian environmental politics are engaged within that system, they "can only be validated, not by the communal force of native animism, but by truth claims of Western material archaeology and cultural anthropology" (210–11). Wilson advocates that people listen for alternative narratives of the land and sea at least partly on the terms of the communities who produce such narratives, rather than "presume to judge and adjudicate their wisdom in some all-mastering Hegelian kind of way" (2000, 210).

While Wilson focuses primarily on human forms of communication, Tuwhare's imaginary of a multilingual ocean encompasses many oceanic beings, human and nonhuman. Tuwhare's sea can listen and express itself to varied forces.[23] In an interview, he suggests that speaking with beings such as houses, rain, or the weather is a "very Maori thing":

> When you go to a marae, you address the house. You do your homework, of course, and you find out what the name of the house is—and you address it as a person. Well of course, it *is* a person; it's named *after* a person, you see. Just like mountains too, you know; or trees; and we name rivers. But whatever I talk to, whoever I talk to, I hope I'm talking *with,* not talking *down.* (qtd. in Manhire 1988, 275–76)

Tuwhare's narrators often speak directly to the ocean, addressing it as Tangaroa. As Frank Stewart notes, Tuwhare's poetry involves conversations with the sea, trees, the sun, and others, rather than simply speaks to or about them: "On friendly terms, Tuwhare addresses them all, along with a world of sacred objects that listen to and return this talk" (1993, 3). In listening to and speaking with the ocean, Tuwhare treats it respectfully, acknowledges its relatively distinct agency, and gauges, within limits, its changeable moods and activities. He also emphasizes his intimate, ancestral relation with the ocean. To see an ocean as a conversational entity is to see how it is dense with interacting beings, many capable of knowing their world and of expression and response. But the poetry does not provide a neutral angle on what the ocean might say to people or to others. The sea's expressions always take form through its exchanges with the poet. For example, in "Big Whale Itch," Tuwhare tells us that the "voices of the Sea" chant "ingenuous lies" into his ear, but that the ocean also "secretes a million / anonymous hulks of ghostly truths . . ." (16). He emphasizes the uncertainties that mark this communication, attributing them at least partly to the sea's wily, volatile, playful character.

In *Shape-Shifter*, then, Tuwhare imagines a present ocean already tracked through with connections, including exchanges in which nonhuman beings communicate with each other and into which Tuwhare also enters. Most of the poems apprehend the dynamics between such beings with humor and pleasure. But they are often also tinged with grief, and sometimes with rage, as they traverse the environmental practices of institutions such as logging companies. Tuwhare affirms conversations as an angle of engagement in such an ocean, if such conversations grapple with the difficulties of recognition, with distinct forms of expression, and with limitations in understanding. His imaginary of a multilingual ocean evokes not only a present world but also calls for a future shaped by peoples' limited capacities for openness to the beings who live in different ways in the ocean and to what such beings might bring to conversations about environmental life.

Like the other poets engaged in this chapter—McQueen and Wedde—Tuwhare is unique for having contributed to art works by New Zealand Māori artist Ralph Hotere; such art works not only thematically reflect on but formally embody conversations with multiple participants. Hotere's art takes names, forms, or fragments of text from poetry, while the poets in turn incorporate his art into writings. The works actualize exchanges among different materials, and evoke some of the difficulties and potentials of such exchanges. Jonathan Mane-Wheoki identifies two main sources for

Hotere's use of poetry in lithographs. On one hand, such a practice draws from the heritage of New Zealand European artist Colin McCahon, who wrote words into his paintings (Mane-Wheoki 1997, 234). On the other hand, the works engage the Māori custom in which *"taonga tuku iho* (treasures handed down from the ancestors) gain significance also from having words 'attached' to them *(he kupu kei runga)"* (235). Mane-Wheoki also notes that this practice has moved to some extent from spoken to written attachments of words since the introduction of reading and writing.

Hotere (Te Aupōuri) was born in 1931 and died in 2013, and is possibly New Zealand's most influential contemporary artist. His art, which is often described as intensely political, interacts with varied contexts of environmental injustice, including with war, nuclear weapons, and colonialism. Cilla McQueen tells a story in which he protested a proposal to place an aluminum smelter near the settlement of Aramoana in the South Island. He dumped black paint over the sign marking the planned smelter site, and then processed a Xerox photo of the blackened sign into a painting (McQueen 2000a, 43). Although Hotere's art often expresses disagreement with present-world injustices, it also formally embodies generosity and openness toward others. It offers perspectives on environmental life to others, but also positions what others might bring as important. Such art is an effort in being alive not only with but to others. As Wedde writes in an essay, "The collaborations in the art are like a love of conversation. What we love in this art is not so much what it is, as what it has already been" (1997, 11). The meanings of these art works are social, built in a space stretching between companions. Yet a conversation involves the differences of these companions. Without these it would not be required.

One such conversation takes form through Hotere's and Wedde's shared interests in pathways to sea, whether taken by birds, peoples, or pollutants. Wedde published a poem titled "Pathway to the Sea" as a booklet (1975) and Hotere provided its cover art as well as incorporated the motif of a pathway to the sea into other works. In Wedde's poem, the narrator digs a drain in her backyard to keep rainfall and sewage from reaching the ocean, because, she tells us, when you live in the "universe" there is no outside to which wastes could be exiled (12). The narrator interrupts the story about the drain to comment on corporate plans to build an aluminum smelter at Aramoana, or "pathway to the sea," a coastal salt marsh, sand spit, and settlement of a few hundred people near the entrance to Otago Harbour and the city of Dunedin in the South Island. The smelter would detrimentally shape the myriad, often hidden, pathways that air, water, and other entities take to the sea, as well as those pathways that the sea might take back into terrestrial life.

Wedde's narrator attempts to live differently in relation to ocean pathways, specifically by building a drain that will stop sewage and other materials migrating to the sea. But in the thick of this project, she comes up against the complicating activities of human and nonhuman beings. Other people help her with the drain, but she expresses deep resentment when some of them abandon the project along the way (6). She also encounters nonhuman beings that shape the project in disparate ways, such as the rain that washes the dirt back into the drain (7). Interactions with such beings are by no means easy or productive along the lines that the narrator would like. Just as it is shaped by these heterogeneous beings, the project also has unanticipated effects. A pear tree grows wild while the narrator is preoccupied with the drain and forgets to prune it back. The tree gobbles water and starch from leaves and roots, presumably affecting the "bonvivants the / earthworms" who "served" the tree (10). The narrator imagines rather than sees most of these interactions among nonhuman beings. Indeed it is likely that she does not, and could not, apprehend most of the beings that animate and are affected by the project. Although varied participants are important in the narrator's efforts to intervene in pathways to the sea, not all of them willingly take part or benefit.

"Pathway to the Sea" also formally illuminates these concerns for being with others who inhabit this world in a different way, in so far as the poem partakes in a loose conversation involving multiple participants. Hotere created the cover art for the poem, and also built further works about Aramoana. Along with artist Bill Culbert, in 1991 Hotere created an installation involving fluorescent light tubes, pāua shells, and rocks running 30 meters along the floor and titled *Pathway to the Sea / Aramoana*. Peter Vangioni suggests that the installation represents the flight paths of Otago Harbour birds, reflecting the words that are written on it: "TENEI TAKU MANU TE RERE ATU NEI—HE KARERE NO TE WHITINGA MAI O TE RA / PATAIA MAI NO HEA KOE? KO WAI KOE? This is my bird that flies to you a message from where the sun rises. It asks from where have you come? Who are you?" (2005, 18). The words ask the viewer to understand that they too share in the artwork, that they are an active part in its life, and likewise to be attentive to their involvement in the sea. But they also request that the viewer clarify the specific pathway that they have taken to the sea or to the art, to be accountable for their unique relationship to a collectivity. Concern to orient attention toward the inseparably collective and personal dimensions of activities such as the building of drains or the viewing of paintings runs through Wedde's "Pathway to the Sea" and Hotere's and Culbert's *Pathway to the Sea / Aramoana*. But the conversations in the works do not only involve convergences. They illuminate persistent differences in approach, as the relatively focused meanings created by the words in poetry are juxtaposed with the often austere colors, lines, and circles of Hotere's art. Gregory O'Brien notes that Hotere's works are intensely formal, that in them "language and meaning have been almost extinguished," whereas the words of the poetry provide somewhat more direct meanings (1997, 13). The different approaches in the paintings "place stresses on each other" and evoke tensions regarding the meanings that could be taken from the art (57).

Although Hotere, Tuwhare, and other artists make statements about existing environmental life and potential futures, including across long distances and sometimes at the scale of the universe, in Wedde's terms, they usually make such statements in a conversational manner. Their works are formally marked by the differences of multiple participants; such differences encourage viewers' engagement. Their works imagine, call for, and in a small way embody worlds involving interactions, and sometimes conversations, in which varied life forms are agents. Allowing for another being to express itself, and so stepping away from the early literary utopian dreams of aggressively controlling others in the ocean, which I discussed early in this chapter, requires some measure of openness to what exists in the present world and to the futures it may hold, because we cannot entirely anticipate what another being will bring to us.[24]

Unwanted Relations

Literary writers situate the different ways in which human and nonhuman beings live with the ocean, as well as the interactions, particularly the conversations, made necessary by such differences, as a reality that allows for hope. But they also engage the more desolate interactions that often dominate life in the ocean, such as economic networks and institutional forms like nations that heavily affect but in profound ways exclude most oceanic life, including from political participation. Pacific peoples have long sought agency in difficult, unequal relationships with other peoples and institutions, including in transnational relationships that reach well beyond the ocean. This is evident in the archive of a presentation to the Treaty on the Non-Proliferation of Nuclear Weapons (NPT) Review Conference Preparatory Committee in New York, where Palauan (Belauan) intellectual Richard Salvador works to alter the relationships between sites in the Pacific and an institution based in New York, and more broadly to gain agency in relation to the meanings of nuclear weapons as they are constructed in international forums (2002). He writes about what nuclear weapons have meant for his people and for Indigenous peoples throughout the Pacific. He also gestures toward the deep inequalities that mark such transnational dialogues, describing the difficulty of speaking about nuclear weapons in a format that does not reflect his or other Indigenous peoples' ways of knowing. He and his colleagues struggled to tell their story within the NPT forum requirements, to "confine an issue with broad implications on the environmental and human health contexts of Indigenous peoples' existence into the narrow limitations of the NPT" (1).

Cilla McQueen's poetry, the last work I engage in this chapter, imaginatively experiments in the transformation of often bleak, sedimented transnational environmental connections. Her collection, *Markings* (2000b), engages transnational aluminum production as a force in environmental degradation and in persistent colonial social injustices. Incorporating publicity materials from an aluminum smelter, McQueen's poetry evokes and in a small way embodies a world in which such corporations would be forced into the open and into critical dialogue about the environmental injustices in which they are involved. McQueen is a well-known European New Zealand poet who was born in Birmingham in 1949 but who came to New Zealand when she was four. She has published multiple collections of poetry and also served as poet laureate. Hotere and McQueen, who met in 1970, were married, and he engages her poems in artworks while she observes his art in poems and critical writing (O'Brien 1997, 103).[25]

McQueen's *Markings* is a collection about people who live intimately with the sea, primarily at vantage points on the South Island's southern East Coast. In a series of four short poems toward the middle of the collection, McQueen writes of a small group of people who catch and eat mutton birds and octopuses. In "A Wheke," our narrator addresses a person who holds an octopus, an "elusive wheke, with distant power" (36). If we read this fragmentary poem alongside the other poems in *Markings*, such as "Bluff Song (i)" and "The Autoclave," we might understand the fisherperson to be the narrator's husband and to have Māori heritage. In "A Wheke," the man pulls the skin from the octopus against the somewhat ominous backdrop of a red western sky (36). In the following poem, "A Crayfish," McQueen describes how crayfish can walk long distances on the seafloor but may be caught by the wheke (37). Situated alongside each other, the two poems suggest that there is no clear disjuncture between human and nonhuman practices of sustenance at sea. Two further short poems that follow, "Birds" and "Hearts," describe people catching and eating mutton birds, the tītī or sooty shearwater that we also encounter in Tuwhare's "Kākā Point." McQueen opens "Birds" with a communal scene in which people talk and laugh by the fire (38). The narrator speaks to a person who goes out into the stormy night to catch tītī. In "Hearts," McQueen describes several people who eat the hearts that power the tītī during its migrations across the Earth (39). In these poems, McQueen observes peoples' relationships with each other and with nonhuman sea creatures in the context of small-scale, subsistence fishing and harvesting. The poems mainly focus on people who share food, laughter, and conversation, realities drawn partly from respectful but at times violent relationships with nonhuman beings.

McQueen places these poems alongside longer works that engage the most visible operations of industrial economy on the land and sea. A number of poems situate infrastructures such as pylons, aluminum smelters, and large ships as jarring and disruptive in coastal landscapes. In a long poem titled "The Autoclave," our narrator looks across the bay from her home, weaving yarn and observing the rhythms of tide and wind. She notes that black swans bear a grassy weed that smothers the cockle beds. A container ship arrives, "tall as an office block and as foreign to the landscape" (16). McQueen juxtaposes this language of the ship's homogeneity and immensity with the multiple textures of the bay at low tide, described in the preceding stanza: "Pale yellow, white, pale green, / olive, taupe, blue-grey" (16). After her house burns down, the narrator moves south to Bluff, looking out across the water at the Tiwai Point Aluminium Smelter. McQueen describes the almost militaristic, automated animation of the smelter, evoking the ways in which its operations seem immovable and pre-decided by distant powers: "Pylons walk westward / two by two into the distance" (29).

In their juxtaposition, "The Autoclave" and the short poems, "A Wheke," "Birds," and "Hearts," may appear to leave us staring out across a fissure between industrial production and communal, subsistence, economically small-scale ways of life; the latter ways of life might then be said to embody compelling forms of present life and offer promising futures. But if these poems are read in relation to other poems in the collection, it becomes clear that McQueen implies that the people described in "A Wheke," "Birds," and "Hearts" are also entangled with colonialism and industrialization. In a number of poems in *Markings,* she suggests that the narrator's ancestors migrated as colonists to New Zealand and Australia from St Kilda archipelago, Scotland, while her husband's people are Māori. Industrial infrastructures also reflect social arrangements shaped by these colonial histories, specifically because they are set on Māori territories. In "The Autoclave," McQueen describes a freezing works as a "sarcophagus" over an ancient pā (29). A further poem, "Tiwai Sequence," observes the aluminum smelter at Tiwai Point, describing petroleum coke arriving at the smelter from California, liquid pitch from Korea, and alumina from Australia. To understand the use of the space, however, we need to engage its deeper histories, and see how industrial infrastructures were layered over sites important to Māori communities: "Once this was the site of a Maori toolmaking factory. / Now the aluminium smelter covers the area entirely" (43). The small social groups briefly articulated by McQueen in "A Wheke," "Birds," and "Hearts," and the aluminum smelter, have both taken form partly in relation to colonial history.

By drawing materials that are directly taken from the institutions of industrial production into poetry, McQueen further locates her critique in relation to, rather than beyond, such processes. In "Tiwai Sequence," our narrator takes a public tour of the Tiwai Point Aluminium Smelter, which lies to the south of Aramoana. McQueen notes that the smelter uses about the same amount of electricity as Auckland, the largest city in New Zealand. She also observes that it contributes to rising sea levels by expelling greenhouse gases, blows harmful materials out over the sea, and leaves abandoned stores of dross around the town of Bluff (41–43). The poem incorporates phrases that apparently are taken directly from the tour guide, such as "Any residue of harmful substances / merely blows out to sea" (41). Recontextualized in McQueen's poem, the phrase speaks of incredible disregard for the ocean and reliance on the wind. As in this example, "Tiwai Sequence" incorporates publicity materials that situate the aluminum smelter in a positive light, formally overlapping poetry and aluminum production. We might understand such an overlap in broader ways, including in terms of the infrastructures through which literature is distributed and on which it imaginatively draws. McQueen suggests that most people are in meaningful ways distanced from the smelter's ordinary operations, describing the narrator as taking an organized tour of it. But her poetry also evokes modes of participation in aluminum production that are perhaps difficult to see, as aluminum animates many aspects of everyday life. Aluminum is, of course, heavily used, including in vehicles, buildings, and cables. The complicities between industrial production and poetry do not simply lead in the direction of despair, however. In animating the smelter's publicity narratives in "Tiwai Sequence," McQueen makes these materials speak in a conversation regarding the smelter's environmental impact. If the publicity narratives were initially crafted to provide an authoritative account of the smelter, rather than to enter a dialogue, McQueen forcibly draws these materials into a conversation by situating them in "Tiwai Sequence" and thereby making them interact with concerns regarding climate change and colonial history. In emphasizing complicity and difference, "Tiwai Sequence" might spark not so much an effort to drive an aluminum smelter elsewhere on this planet as reflection on the impacts of aluminum production and consumption.

In parallel to the aesthetic of McQueen's poetry, which takes materials from an obvious site of industrial capitalism, many of Hotere's art works draw on demolition materials such as old corrugated iron and aluminum, fluorescent lights, window frames, stainless steel, and lacquer. These discarded materials are often imagined as the exhausted remainders of production and consumption, as too degraded, difficult, or dangerous to have further use value: an old, crumbling window frame; charred wood from a ship fire; rusting aluminum. Using tools such as sanding discs and blow torches, Hotere worked with these materials to create modes of being that were not anticipated or wanted in the dominant discourses and activities associated with industrial production. In particular, the art works bring people into contact with the materials that remain after the cycle of production and consumption, disrupting the processes that remove these materials from view and that imaginatively position them as inert waste. As Jane Bennett argues, seeing the persistent liveliness of waste materials, rather than forgetting them as "dead or thoroughly instrumentalized," enables recognition of nonhuman powers that affect human well-being, such as chemicals buried beneath houses, and that at this very moment may be affecting lives and futures (2010, ix).[26] In emphasizing that the materials embody ongoing processes, such as rusting and softening, Hotere's artworks orient viewers not only toward present realities and possible futures but also to the past. They challenge the idea of the new often associated with commodities, suggesting that such commodities have been assembled from elements that have been on the move over billions of years.[27] Iron, for example, is isolated from iron ore by smelting and is combined with other materials to make alloys like steel. Yet iron is not simply reducible to these processes. This element (Fe) composes most of Earth's core and is common in its crust. It was created when massive stars or supernovae burned and exploded, scattering elements such as iron through space (Sparrow 1999, 9–10). Iron not only precedes the human species but exceeds human efforts to control it. Because iron reacts to water and oxygen, it corrodes (or "rusts") through time. Hotere's art draws on the supposedly exhausted materials of industrial production and works them into modes of being that highlight their continued presence and liveliness, including in emphasizing and encouraging processes such as rusting. The artworks suggest that our relationships with these materials are a site of openness. Rather than simply positioned as exhausted commodities, aluminum and other materials might be drawn into critical environmental projects that draw attention to the costs and the afterlives of industrial production.

Hope and Politics of Disconnection

Hope might seem to be impossible in the face of the dauntingly complex connections that bind life forms, materials, and processes throughout the ocean, as well as through time, and that are often characterized by terms such as *climate change* or *capitalism*. In this chapter, I have explored literary writings that offer hope through stories of present oceans where myriad beings live in different ways but also interact and sometimes converse, including across long distances. These works suggest that such conversations do, and might further, extend between human and nonhuman beings and reflect differing modes of expression. At times they imaginatively force such conversations with uncooperative institutions, as is evident in McQueen's poetic engagement with the words of an aluminum company.

In concluding, it is vital to remember here that conversations do not always inspire hope. A different form of environmental imagining undertaken in Pacific literatures involves destroying certain connections rather than negotiating them through dialogue. In "Warawara, Pureora, Okarito," a poem first published in 1978 and reprinted in *Shape-Shifter*, Tuwhare calls for the obliteration of particular connections between native forests, government, and corporations. The poem takes its name from forests that became a site of conflict between environmental activists, the New Zealand government, and logging industries. All these forests were milled, and their remainders protected after long struggles.[28] In the poem, Tuwhare observes that government agencies have allowed private enterprise to fell and remove kauri, tōtara, and kahikatea (90). Through legislation, land purchases, and logging, these trees come to be linked to company bank accounts and to the luxury homes and paraphernalia of millionaires. Describing "yachts" and "mansion," the latter pointedly in the singular, as the products of logging, Tuwhare suggests that a few people are enriched while many people are in profound if not absolute ways absent from the relations among forests, government, and companies (90). Such people receive nothing directly from the sale of the trees.

In "Warawara, Pureora, Okarito," Tuwhare evokes a past in which people managed to break down specific connections between companies, government, and forests, and insists that such a mode of engagement remains important: "Bastards: / Stop your raping of the land. / Fuck off" (90).[29] He addresses these lines directly to "Private Enterprise," an abstract name that could encompass the workers who cut down trees and the institutions and individuals that direct the deforestation and sell, transport, or purchase the timber, evoking a network of lives, forces, and materials that no doubt would take us across the planet (90). Tuwhare instructs "Private Enterprise" as to how they should live, unceremoniously telling them to go away. He invites no conversation, as emphasized by the empathic full stops that follow the lines "Stop your raping of the land" and "Fuck off"— the only full stops in the poem (90). If Tuwhare usually offers hope in terms of strong connections among humans and nonhumans across long distances, particularly in terms of conversations, here he insists on a different angle of engagement, specifically on peoples' abilities to create ruptures between native forests and the networks that we call deforestation. At Pureora in 1978, indeed, activists physically occupied trees, blocking destructive relationships among the forest, bulldozers, government, and corporations, and eventually forcing the permanent protection of the remaining forest (Young 2004, 187).

Living well with the ocean is a continual experiment, as one mode of engagement—a conversation, an outright refusal—may be provocative or critical in one context and yet empty or oppressive in another. Likewise, rather than see the connections that people forge through the ocean only in terms of the violence and inequalities that they so often mean, we might also see the struggles for survival, justice, and repair that are entangled with them. Such ambiguities are evident in the varying attitudes of dejection and hope that mark the decades of artistic exchanges between Hotere, McQueen, Tuwhare, and Wedde. In the years between "Pathway to the Sea" (1975) and "Letter to Peter McLeavey: After Basho" (2005), for example, Wedde's tone grows bleaker. The latter poem, which remembers Hotere's interventions at Aramoana, also references Colin McCahon's *Beach Walk* series of paintings. This series depicts McCahon's walk on Muriwai beach in memory of the Pākehā poet James K. Baxter, whose spirit had traveled along Muriwai as part of the Māori spirit path taken to Cape Reinga (Simpson 1995, 180). Surveying the sand, sky, and waves in section "22 *Muriwai*," Wedde finds that McCahon could be crying:

> Beauty's
>
> nothing to write home about
> and if McCahon's weeping again
> it's because beauty this plain
> doesn't stand a chance, any more
> than his footprints do, the knobbly big toes
> pressed more urgently into black sand
> on the way back, but written off
> all the same
> by the same simple waves,
> the ones that keep coming. (54)

In the water, Wedde reads and simply places side-by-side precariousness and future desolation, as well as defiant survival. This quality of reversal appears commonly in these artists' works. It is a reminder of openness, that not all is given, hope held together with potential losses to come.

CHAPTER 4

In a Strange Ocean

Imagining Futures with Others

NEAR THE END of Australian writer Richard Flanagan's *Gould's Book of Fish: A Novel in Twelve Fish* (2001), William Buelow Gould, a convict who has been transported from England to a penal settlement on Tasmania, tells us that his paintings of fish, which a settlement administrator compels him to create, might be a way of "smuggling hope" (386). Gould suggests that people and fish are involved in this activity of moving hope among sites, beings, and times, although not all in equal and survivable ways. One might think, on the face of it, that hope is a *human* mode of engagement. Noting that hope and despair are concerns always "deeply tinctured by human suffering," Angus Fletcher observes that "as we reach into the present century our glut of despairing misery and hopeful outcry is . . . vast" (1999, 521).

But who is *we*? Literary writers have long associated hope with peoples' relationships with the nonhuman beings of the Pacific, although these relationships have not always involved concern for the desires and well-being of all involved. Most inhabitants of the ocean are not human. The first nonhuman beings emerged in the ocean around 3.3 billion years ago, with terrestrial life taking form just 400 million years before the present (Mitchell 2010, 25). Nonhuman beings are irreplaceably present in literary accounts of promising ocean futures, including as raw materials to be transformed into profit, food, or medicines. In an early literary archive set in the ocean, English writer Francis Bacon's *New Atlantis,* utopia is made possible partly by invasive research on nonhuman animals. European travelers sail from Peru into the South Sea in search for China and Japan but become lost in "the greatest wilderness of waters in the world" (1999, 152). They stumble across the island of Bensalem, on which utopians have established a scientific society named Salomon's House: "The end of our Foundation is the knowledge of Causes, and secret motions of things; and the enlarging of the bounds of Human Empire, to the effecting of all things possible" (1999 [1627], 177). The utopians' work at the parameters of the Human Empire includes prolonging life, imitating meteors and the heat of the sun, and making fruit sweeter. They enclose animals, including fish, experimenting in medicines, poisons, and surgeries. They also alter animals' growth trajectories, reproductive processes, and physiology, and combine varied beings to create new types.[1] While nonhuman beings are vital in this world, Bacon does not acknowledge their ways of knowing, a concern which would profoundly trouble the description of the island as a utopia. The utopians' research is directed toward improving human well-being, including in the areas of spiritual life, diet, life expectancy, and pain alleviation. The term *human* is deceptive here, however, because the human lives of *New Atlantis* are clearly stratified; the utopia's secretive scientific society does not extend to all the inhabitants of Bensalem.

As well as becoming fuel for the futures imagined by others, nonhuman beings live and die amid the exhausted spaces of efforts to produce such futures. In the poem "Da Last Squid," Native Hawaiian poet Joe Balaz observes marine animals who are positioned in some of the most diminished spaces of the economy. A man named Willy Boy catches the last squid from the effluent infused waters of an abandoned marine conservation area, which lies between an industrial park and a derelict desalinization plant (2003, 8–10). The Pacific Ocean is home to thousands of islands where nonhuman life forms evolved in relative isolation and where high numbers of endemic species took form. Many of these species have become endangered or extinct through human activities such as excessive hunting and fishing, habitat destruction, and the introduction of new animals and plants.[2]

Environmental writers today face an uncountable mosaic of nonhuman lives that have been diminished and destroyed around the ocean. They often seek to ruffle the assumptions that underlie stories such as *New Atlantis*, insisting that hope is a relationship with a promising, open future that relies on the connections between nonhuman and human beings. Through the recognition that nonhuman beings know the world and that people can grasp and respond to these ways of knowing, albeit within constraints, these connections, which may be a source of hope for some and mean destruction for others, can be reshaped to better support varied beings. Early in *Seeking the Sacred Raven: Politics and Extinction on a Hawaiian Island*, for example, U.S. journalist and veterinarian Mark

Jerome Walters asks, "What possible hope can we offer to the ʻalalā, to other species, or to ourselves?" (2006, 23). Traveling to Hawaiʻi, Walters traces the ecology of the disappearance of the *ʻalalā*, an endangered bird, from Hawaiian forests: the histories of ranching and logging; the transformation of people's relationships with land through private ownership; the introduction of new species such as cattle, goats, and sheep; the troubled institutional politics of endangered species in Hawaiʻi. His book spans the time before and after the ʻalalā became extinct outside of captivity. Hope, Walters suggests, could be part of the existence of the ʻalalā rather than simply of people, if only people could give hope to the ʻalalā, a possibility that is by no clear means still available.

In some European cultural histories, hope has come to be imaginatively located in the private, interior world of an individual.[3] In the previous chapter, I explored literary works that suggest rather that transnational environmental exchanges, including conversations about the impacts of wide-ranging processes such as aluminum production and consumption, are a site of possibility. Such conversations might allow pathways to address the contributions aluminum production makes to climate change, among other environmental processes. This chapter focuses more directly on literary stories that evoke hope through attunement to the relationships of human and nonhuman animals, specifically to the rapid loss of fish in industrial fishing and to people's efforts to interrupt this loss.

In *Gould's Book of Fish* (2001), Richard Flanagan explores hope in the context of the lives and deaths of Indigenous peoples, convicts, fish, and colonial administrators in a nineteenth century penal settlement in Tasmania. Flanagan, who was born in 1961 and lives in Tasmania, is a well-known European Australian writer. He has published five novels, winning a Commonwealth Writers Prize for *Gould's Book of Fish*. Tasmania lies to the south of mainland Australia, on the border of the Pacific Ocean and the Southern Ocean, or the Indian Ocean, depending on the archive.[4] It is home to hundreds of islands, seamounts, deep sea-floor fractures, kelp forests, rocky shores, and beds of sea grass. To the south, these ecosystems are marked by high levels of endemic species (Peat 2010, 150).

In *Gould's Book of Fish*, Flanagan suggests that penal settlement administrators' dreams of progress rely on but do not benefit all human and nonhuman beings in the colony. Heavy fishing and forestry, the appropriation of Indigenous peoples' life worlds, and the brutal control of the convict-laborers materially and symbolically constitute progress in administrators' terms. The convicts' claims to hope likewise draw on their relationships with nonhuman beings, because these relationships shape the possibilities that are evident to them, from death and torture to escape and survival. Flanagan suggests that hope is not simply an individual mode of engagement; it is nourished by assemblages of beings, human and nonhuman, and sentient and nonsentient, or by an "extended, virtual body," to draw from anthropologist Sylvain Perdigon (2008, n.p.). Writing of Abu Saeed, a Palestinian refugee who illegally operates a taxi in Lebanon, and who faces a future involving likely dispossession of the car and possible arrest, Perdigon argues that Abu Saeed's hope relies on actual and potential actions extended across other bodies (his wife and child) and objects (a car): "To pawn one's hope, as I believe Abu Saeed then did, to somebody else's presence, is also to constitute an extended, virtual body, that may include other persons and things, an abode of virtual actions, which bears witness to yet another dimension of the connection of hope and care" (n.p.).

As we have seen in *New Atlantis,* hope that relies on cultivation of an extended abode of action involving varied objects and lives, human and nonhuman, does not inevitably correlate with the well-being of all involved. In *Gould's Book of Fish,* Flanagan suggests that our narrator Gould's hope could never be entirely conflated with the experience of another human or nonhuman being, but that this hope might come to be better shaped by Gould's efforts to get to know, and respond to, others. Rather than tell a story of a promising island, Flanagan weaves in and out of stories told by different, although interconnected, narrators. Although these narrators interact with each other, their stories cannot be entirely reconciled into an absolute, singular account of the settlement, including of hope. In concluding, I briefly engage a more recent novel, *The Unknown Terrorist* (2006), in which Flanagan suggests that social dynamics related to national security are diminishing the possibility of constructing more just forms of life with the ocean and the world beyond.

A Genre of Progress

In the opening pages of *Gould's Book of Fish,* we encounter Sid Hammet, our narrator, who is living in present-day Hobart, Tasmania. He acquires and refurbishes old furniture, selling it to tourists as the authentic remnants of a romantic oceanic past. While sifting through a junk shop one day, he comes across the *Book of Fish.* This book, which contains writing as well as watercolor paintings of fish, and which appears to be the journal of William Buelow Gould, has a "mesmeric shimmer," smells of the salt carried in the winds of the Tasman Sea, and feels silky (2001, 1). Soon its cover begins to glow with "pulsing purple spots" and "speckled phosphorescence" (13). Turning the soggy pages of the *Book of Fish*, Hammet senses that he is "reading words written at the very bottom of the ocean" (24). He leaves the book briefly at a bar and returns to find it vanished. Feeling sorrow and unrequited love for the lost book, he decides to rewrite it. But on visiting the home of his colleague Mr Hung shortly after the loss of the *Book of Fish*, Hammet peers into an aquarium containing a seadragon. He feels that the seadragon is communicating something, before suddenly falling through the glass and sensing the seadragon passing back into him.

In what follows, we are drawn into the world of the person to whom the *Book of Fish* is attributed—William Buelow Gould—as well as into that of the fish that Gould painted and the people with whom he lived in Van Diemen's Land, now known as Tasmania. Gould is sentenced to transportation to Van Diemen's Land for forgery in 1825 and is then convicted of further crimes and sent to Sarah Island, part of Macquarie Harbour penal station. Tobias Achilles Lempriere, the surgeon of the settlement, requires Gould to paint fish that are caught around the island. In Gould, as well as in Lempriere and other characters, Flanagan draws loosely on actual historical figures, small traces of whose lives can be found in the archives of nineteenth-century Tasmania.[5]

Flanagan describes Sarah Island as a place where imperialism, war between Indigenous peoples and settlers, and the penal system are drawn together in a world marked by immense indifference to the hurt and destruction of others as well as by idiosyncratic practices of care and love. Shortly after Gould has been transported to Van Diemen's Land and has fled his work assignment, he travels along the coast, coming across a dead Indigenous woman who had been "staked out on the ground, abused in a most dreadful fashion & then left to die" (69–70). His companion, Roaring Tom, "began to wail & screech. He was a wild animal & it was a long time before I could have him halt his awful keening" (70). Humans have been present in Tasmania for more than 35,500 years (Cameron 2005, 4). British settlement on Tasmania began in the early 1800s. In the following decades, the people of this place waged a war of resistance against the settlers who were heavily encroaching on their territories and resources.

During this conflict, Indigenous peoples were harassed continually and their ordinary life was undermined, including by bounty hunters who pursued them around the island (Reynolds 2012, 57–58). Despite the violence that they faced, their resistance created disarray in the settlement, with the colonial government establishing martial law in 1828 and situating Indigenous peoples in conflict areas as "outside the law as enemies of the king" (60). The government eventually sought to displace them entirely from mainland Tasmania to offshore islands. Historian Henry Reynolds writes of Tasmania, "In just over 30 years the Aboriginal population fell by at least 90 per cent; the survivors were exiled to Flinders Island where deaths accelerated" (47).

Tasmania, and particularly Sarah Island, is also known for state brutality against convicts who were transported there during the nineteenth century. Sarah Island, which lies in Macquarie Harbour on the west coast of Tasmania, was a site of secondary punishment for those people transported to Van Diemen's Land and then convicted of further crimes. Approximately 72,000 convicts, many of them working-class people sentenced for petty crimes, were transported to Tasmania from 1803 to 1853 (Reynolds 2012, 138–40). Their transportation provided a vital labor force for the colony (Maxwell-Stewart 2010, 415–18; Reynolds 2012, 137–63). Ian Brand records that George Arthur (1784–1854), colonial governor of Van Diemen's Land, described Sarah Island as necessarily "a place of such strict discipline that they [the convicts] may absolutely dread the very idea of being sent there" (qtd. in Brand 1984, 50).

In *Gould's Book of Fish,* the Commandant of Sarah Island expresses mercury- and laudanum-fueled imaginings of Sarah Island as a grand nation defined by his rule, a place of immense wealth, beauty, and power, which attracts people from all around the world (100–102). He oversees engineering projects to construct this imagined nation. After reading accounts of railways in Europe, he is inspired to imagine the National Sarah Island Railway Station. The convicts build a railway track in a 200-yard line, and in a loop around that line, and the Commandant purchases a steam train after "selling the Gordon River & the Great Barrier Reef" and begins an "endless circling" on the train (166, 170). Gould is strapped to the front of the locomotive and told to paint his experience. The Commandant wants him to paint this new world as "Hope & Progress," but Gould's painting reveals only "desolation" as well as a stargazer fish (173).

Fish, desolation, hope, and progress are woven together into shifting and contested, but often deeply sedimented, relationships in the penal colony. Progress is a common way of describing lived realities, as well as a world to come, in many early European archives of settlement in Australia (Koshin 2011; Reynolds 2012, 39–40). Seeing progress involves connecting the past, present, and future in terms of a "unilinear path of social improvement and material prosperity" (Koshin 2011, 6). Progress, suggests Fredric Jameson, can be understood as the projection of a good future and the causal linkage of that future to certain matters of the present, specifically to the capitalist economy, through a teleological narrative (2005, 228). Claims regarding progress can work to elide or invalidate other ways of reading present realities and potential futures. The Commandant's description of the National Sarah Island Railway as progress makes it more difficult to see or care that this railway was enabled by theft of Indigenous people's land, the felling of the forest, and the control of the convict-laborers. Indigenous peoples, nonhuman beings, and convicts might not see the railroad as embodying social improvement and material prosperity. Jameson writes that the concept of progress is an effort to destroy what Habermas calls a sense of "time open to the future," meaning not so much that the future is uncertain but that it could be a "*disruption* . . . of the present*" rather than a continuation of what already exists or "a prolongation of our capitalist present" (2005, 228). Hope, in contrast, is not possible without an apprehension of future openness, and so of the potential for disruption of business-as-usual. Hope is a relationship with a future not locked into a single trajectory but that rather is a site of possibilities and of varying claims; this future is evoked by the unsettling struggles of the present world. In *Gould's Book of Fish*, however, the Commandant discursively attributes a single meaning to hope in a way that elides, and perhaps undermines, other potential ways of reading the present and relating to the future. Flanagan's capitalization of the terms *Hope* and *Progress* reflects the commandant's insistence that these modes of engagement can only be defined in one way: the railroad, or more broadly, the dominant, existing configuration of economy and social life means Hope and Progress.

Gould writes of the convicts, "We knew our part in it all was not to benefit from these dreams, but to give our lives over to transforming them into brick & mortar, into glass panes & iron lace" (Flanagan 2001, 103). Many of the people who were made to struggle to actualize these dreams were archived in convict reports. The existence of these mysterious reports is much rumored among the convicts, and Gould comes across them when he learns that he can push aside a stone in the ceiling of his cell and climb into a room above. Here he finds the settlement registry, the records of the island made by the Danish clerk Jorgen Jorgensen. These will be "the only enduring memory of our strange world" (281). The convicts are not permitted to write their own records or to have their pictures taken. They are "faceless people who have no portraits, who only exist beyond their bodies as a sentence of exile, a convict indent record, a list of floggings" (384). We might not expect the convict report to be a genre of writing connected to the imagining of a promising world. Perhaps such writing simply documents the past and present, fixing people within an authoritative and reflective story controlled by the state. Flanagan, however, primarily situates the reports as an imaginary of an alternative world and as a mode of engineering designed to elide the gap between that world and reality. As Gould reads the records, he begins to realize that they describe a penal colony that is absolutely unfamiliar because it is entirely without the immense suffering that he has experienced. The reports are designed to confirm Governor Arthur and the Colonial Office's imaginaries of the penal colony. The Commandant has ordered Jorgensen to create the records "in a way that would accord with expectation" and so Jorgensen has gone about reworking "all that barbarity & horror of our settlement as order & progress" (284, 285).[6] But Jorgensen has extended the project of fictionalizing the penal colony even further. Through the reports he has sketched an intricately detailed "alternative world" in which the colony is benign and good, and where an ordered system constitutes a rational society (284).

If we turn from *Gould's Book of Fish* to historical records that were made on William Buelow Gould, we catch a glimpse of the ways in which the convict reports were tangled in efforts to create a world rather than simply to reflect one. The *Index to Tasmanian Convicts* contains records of around 76,000 people, including files on William Buelow Gould. One of these files is divided into boxes in which notes on Gould are recorded in several ink colors and handwritings. The boxes are defined by categories such as Trade ("Artist"), Head ("Large"), Complexion ("Sallow"), Nose ("Aqueline"), and Marks ("Several Blue marks . . . on left wrist"). The largest space is provided for Offences and Sentences. Here the report describes Gould as spending time in solitary confinement after an incident that seems to include Gould accusing the assistant superintendent of "having a dislike of him" ("William Buelow Gould" n.d.). The file also records Gould's wife's petition for reduction of his sentence. The aesthetic of the file takes the form of preestablished boxes, into which Gould's life before, during, and after the penal settlement can be fitted. If Gould did make an accusation against the assistant superintendent, for example, this accusation is placed within the box that records Gould's Offences and Sentences, rather than, say, in a box for State Offences. The template of the record has substantial agency in relation to the story told and the lives it engages. Gould suggests of the registry: "The world no longer existed to become a book. A book now existed with the obscene ambition of becoming the world" (291).

An impassable gap lies between the world imagined in these reports and reality, and yet such files nevertheless exert a significant force on reality.[7] The registry enables colonial administrators in Hobart and London to see the penal settlement as progressing satisfactorily, and so the Commandant can proceed with his undocumented profit-making schemes, which include selling the wilderness of Sarah Island to a Japanese trader (169–70, 182). The reports also facilitate the ongoing control of the convicts. Because they are cumulative and can affect assessments of future conduct, they situate people within a history that is virtually impossible to escape. Gould is caught in "our past & the future decreed by the Convict System" (103). If progress is a story that is designed to lock the present world and future into a particular economic and social trajectory, the convict report is the necessary accompaniment of progress, containing those people who, in their pain, terror, and imprisonment, and in their threatening liveliness, seep away from and might contradict its story.

Colonial administrators and settlers extended their exertions of an imaginative and material order to the Indigenous peoples and the nonhuman beings of Tasmania. In the world of *Gould's Book of Fish*, natural historians are busily collecting and categorizing the nonhuman life of Tasmania, and indeed of the planet, and this research is interwoven with ideas about progress as well as with more personal projects of social mobility. Tobias Achilles Lempriere, the surgeon of the settlement, orders Gould to paint fish caught around the island. Lempriere aspires to social recognition though his classifications of fish, and he specifically seeks entry into an elitist scientific institution known as the Royal Society. During the eighteenth century, scientists were coming to situate nature as less wild and more "pliant and predictable," a trajectory that Hugh Raffles argues is represented by Linnaeus's *Systema Naturae* (Raffles 2002, 116). In *Systema*

Naturae, Linnaeus arranged animals and plants into categories that are still in use today, such as species, genera, and order. Scientists sought to arrange life forms globally into this order (Olsen 2010, 5). In *Gould's Book of Fish,* we are told that *Systema Naturae* inspires Lempriere to establish a scientifically defined separation between the natural and human worlds (120–21). Gould observes that Lempriere's projects of collection, classification, description, and circulation sound like an effort "to recreate the natural world as a penal colony" (129). He recognizes the ideals of order, knowing, and discipline that mark both natural history and the penal settlement, but also the material linkages between imperialism and science, including the transnational commercial possibilities revealed by the study of the nature of Tasmania.[8]

Nineteenth-century scientists also mapped people into racial and geographic categories. Australian Indigenous peoples were usually placed with nonhuman animals near the bottom of a supposedly scientific hierarchy of being.[9] In *Gould's Book of Fish,* Lempriere stretches his project of classification to Aboriginal peoples, placing their pickled heads into barrels and sending them to Britain. He states that these people, like dogs and fleas, are a distinct and inferior species and that we must know this common idea as science (232–33). Lempriere's natural history project involves the mapping of differences among beings and the organization of these differences into hierarchies structured through ideas such as civilization and progress. On hearing Indigenous peoples' heads shouting at him, he yells in reply, "How overjoyed they ought be at the prospect of working together on such a mighty project of Science & finally be of some use to Civilisation" (231). Lempriere's project does the work of justifying the violent realities of the penal colony: the appropriation of Indigenous peoples' life worlds, the control of the convict-laborers, the destruction of nonhuman beings such as trees for profit.

In *Gould's Book of Fish,* then, the Commandant and others make claims on a present world—specifically involving a railroad and more broadly the engineering of Sarah Island into a place of wealth and fame—that embodies and promises Progress and Hope. They attempt to lock progress and hope into an authoritative, singular narrative about what exists and should exist. Indigenous peoples, convicts, and nonhuman beings exceed the confines of this narrative, in the evident violence, loss, and hurt that they face. The convict reports as well as the archives of natural history are carefully orchestrated presentations of the necessity of this violence. Yet these reports, which are all that is left of many human and nonhuman lives of the penal station, need not be read in such a complicit way. Drawing particularly on the fish paintings that Gould was compelled to paint for science, Flanagan imaginatively constructs different stories, told by those who are not to benefit from the Commandant's imaginary island or from progress and hope but who are crucial as labor or raw materials.

Ecology of a Penal Colony

The convicts and the nonhuman beings of the penal colony are drawn together in often desolate ways, their relationships marked by pain, rage, and death. The penal system administrators use the island and its surrounding ocean to ensure that the convicts cannot easily escape with their lives. As a forest fire rages across the island at the end of the novel and Gould waits for execution, he observes, "For some convicts the accumulating dust in the air was one further oppressive element of a natural world that existed only as a gaoler" (363). Even when Gould does flee the prison complex, traversing among the island's waterfalls, rainforest, ravines, and limestone tiers, he cannot escape the reach of brutal forms of power. He comes on a tree, initially mistaking Indigenous people's ears, nailed to its trunk, for its bark (318). Such unpredictable and yet comprehensive reminders of conflict mean that the convicts feel continual fear and uncertainty regarding what might lie hidden in this ecology. For example, Gould observes a beautiful sky, but it "seemed brittle, as though it might at any moment break apart & reveal something awful behind all that glorious light" (70). Indeed, in the next scene, he comes upon a burning hut in which someone is crying. Flanagan here theorizes a continuation of the mode of state power that underlies transportation, the destruction of a person's relationship with a familiar, reliable material world.[10]

In engaging the ecology of the penal colony, Flanagan describes many forms of punishment that involve the manipulation of convicts' intimate relationships with water, an element that people internalize for survival and yet that is very threatening to their lives.[11] When we first meet our miserable narrator, Gould, he is incarcerated in a cell (a fish cell, in his words). The cell has been built on the coast, below the high-tide mark, so that prisoners must cling to its ceiling when the water rises or they will drown (43). By this point, Gould has already experienced several other forms of water-related torture. He angers a ship captain while traveling to Tasmania and is subsequently placed in a box and towed behind the ship, "dropped for a full minute into the Pacific Ocean inside that bubbling black wet box of slimy oak" (66). Flanagan also describes Gould's experience of a punishment called the Cockchafer. It is a waterwheel on which the convicts have to step and then climb for ten hours: "We had to become as water" (79).

All these punishments associate the convicts with water, an element long situated as external to civilization in some European imaginative histories. In their association with water, the convicts are symbolically exiled to a marginal realm, even while they are held on the island. Their exile is combined with imprisonment, enabling power to be exerted over their lives in a space of socially uncertain, ghostly status. Michel Foucault describes historical connections between water, liminality, and imprisonment in *Madness and Civilization: A History of Insanity in the Age of Reason*, tracing a "Ship of Fools" in "the imaginary landscape of the Renaissance," a strange "drunken boat" that glides through the rivers of the Rhineland and Flemish canals, conveying its disturbing peoples from town to town (1988, 7). He suggests that the practice of setting people perceived to be mad adrift on the waters symbolically establishes their liminality but also their containment: "Confined on the ship, from which there is no escape, the madman is delivered to the river with its thousand arms, the sea with its thousand roads, to that great uncertainty external to everything. He is a prisoner in the midst of what is the freest, the openest of routes: bound fast at the infinite crossroads" (11).

Yet, if the water is in certain ways associated with alterity in *Gould's Book of Fish*, the waterwheel and the fish cell also reveal state manipulation of the intimate relationships, and even the overlaps, between a person and water. They materialize particular relationships between Gould and water so as to gain agency over his psychological and physical state. The fish cage and the box towed behind a ship are technologies that subject people to hurtful intimacies with water, drawing on water's capacities to surround, enter, and possibly drown a human being. Since the purpose of water-related torture is not the immediate death of the person targeted, however, these waterlogged cages also rely on a person's fishlike ability to float on, swim beneath, and even to internalize water, and to survive, at least for a time. The waterwheel is a punishment that activates a person's ability to embody the formal malleability and continuous movement associated with water (in Gould's words, to "become as water"). But if these technologies are modeled on and animate a person's chameleonic capacity to in certain ways "become as" water and fish, they also rely on the differences of the entities involved, activating the excruciating pain and exhaustion that will be felt by a person who must fight to become like water on a waterwheel and the profound threat to the existence of a person who is enclosed in water.

Flanagan describes torture that literally puts the convicts into the place of fish or water. In elaborating state practices of forcibly altering people by manipulating their relationship with water, he asks readers to engage the form and sociopolitical context of connection and closeness between materials and beings rather than simply to affirm such connections. Neel Ahuja suggests that scholars in animal studies have sometimes idealized transpecies intimacies and have done so without adequate geopolitical tact, or in his words without attention to "the geographies by which humans are positioned differentially in relation to other species" (2011, 144). Writing about a CIA practice of torture involving the enclosure of a person with an insect and so of creating "a space of transpecies intimacy within the torture chamber," he argues for greater engagement with state, interstate, and extrastate use of animals in aggression against certain groups of people (129). In *Gould's Book of Fish*, Flanagan suggests that the convicts' experience of being forced into overlap with fish and into intimacy with water does not necessarily portend their well-being or survival, insisting that such transformative interactions between beings and materials be engaged in their specific contexts rather than affirmed in abstract terms.

In reading poetry by detainees, Ahuja argues that the transpecies intimacies that take form in spaces of incarceration cannot entirely be predicted or managed by the state (2011, 139–41). Likewise, in *Gould's Book of Fish*, the meaning of the forced metamorphosis of a person who is brought into intimate contact with water is not simply dominated by the penal settlement administrators. When a man, a machine breaker from Glasgow, is fatally hurt after falling on the waterwheel and becoming stuck in it, the wheel comes to a halt and the convicts talk with him as he dies. He "admitted that he wished he was a real Villian," and, Gould suggests, "We roared our approval" (80). The convicts for a moment transform the meaning of the waterwheel. Rather than an apparatus for the punishment of individual crimes, it becomes a critical, collective site through which to name state violence. A raucous energy emerges in the group in these conditions. In this scene, they cannot put this energy to any use beyond their words and other expressions and their effort to live, but it does reveal that they remain irreducibly different from the state in the claims they make on the world.

Smuggling Hope

What stories might have been told by the convicts, who were put in files and made to create paintings but who had little to no ability to shape these archives on their own terms? As the convicts are transported across the water toward the island, Gould sees stars reflecting in the ocean, "as though there were a thousand candles burning just beneath the surface of the still dark water, one light for each soul of every dead convict buried on the small isle of the dead to our right" (98). The many stories of metamorphosis among human, book, and fish in *Gould's Book of Fish* can be understood in the context of Flanagan's interest in telling the stories of the convicts who died on the island or who disappeared into the surrounding waters. In certain ways these people were transformed or physically absorbed into the sea, perhaps into fish too. Hammet observes that the *Book of Fish* seems to have been written at the bottom of the ocean (24). With the wariness of someone writing from the perspective of long-vanished beings, Flanagan fictionally recreates the stories of Gould and of the fish who were caught and painted at the Macquarie Harbour penal station.

In contrast to the very elaborate futures imaginable to the Commandant, for Gould future possibilities appear narrow and desolate, and so the future is a very difficult site for him to engage. On arrival at Sarah Island he is physically incarcerated in a "saltwater cell of an inescapable & putrid destiny" (208). He describes his entrapment in space as well as in a temporal trajectory where a frightening and painful end has already been determined, and he does not often engage the future because there is little there that could offer solace, meaning, or momentum. When he flees the penal station into the wilderness and is recaptured by the constable Musha Pug, he observes that no salvation or even comfort could be provided by the rebellious bushranger Matt Brady, science, the Commandant's dreams, God, the future, or the past: "There were only Musha Pug's boots, & after they had landed one more blow on my cheek & were skating over my mouth I kissed them. I kissed them because they were all that I had left to love" (359). Gould can find small measures of agency and comfort in interacting with his present condition.

There are times, however, when hope flares among the convicts, needing only a fragile basis to stir and spread, especially in relation to the chances of escape from the prison. As a fire roars across the island and threatens the settlement toward the end of *Gould's Book of Fish*, the convicts sense that escaped convict Matt Brady may be coming to free them. They begin "a wild dreaming of a new country to be" and focus "expectantly" on the mountains (366). These dreams have only a tenuous basis in rumors regarding Brady's plans for a revolution. Hope emerges among the convicts, then, but Flanagan does not suggest that it necessarily portends, or even in the lived moment constitutes, an experience of well-being. Gould's ability to feel that his hope is meaningful is heavily constrained by his condition of imprisonment, as well as by his archived convict history and its implications for his future.

Flanagan does not overstate the significance of hope in the contingent conditions faced by Gould, but both Gould's fish paintings and Flanagan's novel might be understood as technologies that are "smuggling" hope, in Gould's terms, by addressing the reader regarding potentials for intervening in their often destructive relations with other beings (386). The fish paintings, Gould tells us, are not intended for science or art, but rather are to make people laugh and think, to give them company and hope, and to remind them of those they love and who love them. Yet, people do not want his paintings to be so lively, he suggests. They prefer art that offers dead animals and imprisons people in a securely classified past. But "this business of smuggling hope might make them wonder, might be the axe that smashed the frozen sea within, might make the dead wake & swim free" (386–87). Gould's effort to smuggle hope does not simply mean that people's connections with others give hope, which after all could mean all manner of desolate realities, from torture by water to the destruction of a fish species for profit to the forced removal of Indigenous peoples from their homelands, all activities into which a minority might read a promising future. Rather, Gould describes hope as actively conveyed among different beings, places, and times.

Through the many stories about metamorphosis in *Gould's Book of Fish*, Flanagan defines the hope that Gould would smuggle. It is hope that is drawn from people's efforts and capacities to get to know something of the worlds of other beings, specifically of fish, and so that is shaped by the interests and expressions of those beings. Toward the end of the novel, Gould is about to be hung, is shot, falls into the ocean, and transforms into a weedy seadragon. He then lives in the sea until present day, when he is caught by Mr Hung and placed in an aquarium. We are then drawn back to the beginning of *Gould's Book of Fish*, where Sid Hammet finds the *Book of Fish*, peers into Mr Hung's aquarium, and is suddenly pulled into the body of the weedy seadragon/Gould, while the weedy seadragon/Gould moves back into Hammet's body. The weedy seadragon/Gould, having become Hammet, are then able to tell their stories. They rewrite the vanished book of fish.

One possible meaning of metamorphosis is the movement of all life toward sameness. This is an ideal, and a gathering reality, that Flanagan sees in the British imperial project of incorporating other life worlds. After spending time painting the fish and getting to know them, Gould begins to feel that he is unwillingly becoming a fish. He senses with alarm that the fish have begun to "enter me & I didn't even know that they were colonising me as surely as Lieutenant Bowen had colonised Van Diemen's Land" (214). The novel is set at a time when fish are very literally entering human bodies, and more broadly are being transformed into capital. Sealing, whaling, and fishing, among other industries, fueled the penal settlement economy (Nash 2003, 44). In many archives of Tasmania at this time, people observe rapid marine environmental change, including destruction of whale, elephant seal, and fur seal populations, and of the forests interlinked with coastal ecosystems.[12] In *Gould's Book of Fish*, the motif of metamorphosis evokes the attrition of nonhuman beings through their incorporation into the British Empire, and an emerging world in which only some species can flourish, at least for a time. As Gould finishes painting the leatherjacket, which he describes as a very gentle fish, he begins to wonder if "as each fish died, the world was reduced in the amount of love that you might know for such a creature" (200). He worries about "this destruction of fish, this attrition of love that we were blindly bringing about, & I imagined a world of the future as a barren sameness in which everyone had gorged so much fish that no more remained, & where Science knew absolutely every species & phylum & genus, but no-one knew love because it had disappeared along with the fish" (200–201).

Gould's reference to the disappearance of fish is expressed through the physical connection that he has forged with the contemporary character Sid Hammet, and so it simultaneously evokes historical and present world environmental change. In Tasmania, as elsewhere, the disappearance of oceanic species is not always well documented, especially in the cases of noncommercial animals and plants that cannot easily be seen from the coast and that are not tracked by specialist researchers (Edgar, Samson, and Barrett 2005, 1295–96). Edgar et al. write that just one species of mollusk is registered as threatened under the Tasmanian Threatened Species Protection Act, but that most of around 1,000 Tasmanian mollusk species have not been seen alive since the mid-1980s, for example (1295). The introduction of new species, overfishing, habitat destruction through practices such as trawling, climate change, and flow of silt and nutrients from land into coastal waters are among the processes that have affected Tasmania's marine ecosystems. The vast kelp beds off the East Coast of the archipelago have shrunk by around half since 1944, for example (Edgar et al. 1296).

In *Gould's Book of Fish*, metamorphosis evokes not only incorporation and destruction but also the potential for alternative relationships between people and fish. The story of Gould becoming a weedy seadragon does not imply that either being is destroyed through a movement from two into one, or from past into future. Their metamorphosis is a multidirectional process of becoming partly other, or of being altered through environmental life. Gould wants the chance to write of "his protest, his rage and hate and fear of this shitty world" (383). He must become a fish in order to survive the gallows, escape the settlement, and hold open the possibility of one day telling his story. Flanagan repeatedly links metamorphosis with survival in *Gould's Book of Fish*. In the scene in which Gould is punished with other convicts on the Cockchafer, or the waterwheel, Capois Death, a convict who was born in San Domingo and was previously a slave, describes how his ancestors could levitate, fly, and then dive into the sea and swim "as one with the fish until one was a fish," and Gould ponders how this might be possible (82). Becoming water, or perhaps a fish, would allow endurance and even freedom.

When Gould finally becomes a fish and swims away from the settlement, he retains his experiences of being a convict, but he also comes to inhabit the experiential world of another being, the weedy seadragon. Interest in nonhuman beings' ways of knowing marks varied contemporary scholarship in the humanities and social sciences. Such scholarship also emphasizes that nonhuman beings may gain a grasp on human experiential worlds and shape their activities accordingly. Eduardo Kohn argues that multifarious beings (or "selves") apprehend and represent their worlds, noting that representational systems are not only symbolic but involve icons such as "the cryptic coloration of a lizard's skin" and indices like "a windsock or a monkey's alarm call" (2007, 5). He writes about the Runa of the upper Amazon, who interact with the forest in hunting and other activities. In the forest, they engage an ecology of varied beings, and in order to do so well they must be able to inhabit the interpretative worlds of others, although this can never be done with certainty: "When one does so, attributes and dispositions become dislodged from the bodies that produce them and ontological boundaries become blurred" (7). The dogs who live with the Runa must also learn to navigate within social worlds shared with humans. Survival and living well require the ability to grasp something of the ways in which varied beings apprehend the world, even though these apprehensions, and indeed even those experiences that we claim as our own, cannot be understood in full (9).

In the context of people's relationships with marine life, it may be particularly difficult to imagine practices of ontological boundary blurring, or of swimming into the strange, albeit also familiar, oceans known to others. Some European cultural histories position marine animals as unfeeling and irrational, describing fish on mass as "cold," and targeting whales, squid, and sharks as insensible and unpredictable machines.[13] Many nonhuman beings cannot survive long once they are brought to the ocean surface, if they can survive this journey at all. They are impossible to keep in aquariums: "Researchers have only half-jokingly described research on mesopelagic organisms as 'forensic'" (Sweeney, Haddock, and Johnsen 2007, 808). Most people do not have the economic means to travel into these deep waters. Scientists, activists, and other people and institutions use media to draw people into the seas that might be known to nonhuman beings. These media open up a multiplicity of perspectives on how particular animals might see, feel, and hear the sea.[14] Sure enough, in *Gould's Book of Fish* Gould gets to know the fish as they die, having been pulled out of the ocean so that he can study and paint them. His art, he tells us, provides a "natural history of the dead" (63).

These encounters with dying fish have a transformative impact on Gould, nevertheless. He lives in a place where "in order to survive & prosper it was important to feel nothing for anyone or anything" (258). Yet when he spends a lot of time in the company of the fish, he begins to feel that he needs them (213). He must observe the fish carefully in order to paint them, and "all this painting & repainting began to affect me" (214). He eventually becomes a weedy seadragon, learning that fish feel and think:

"Our thoughts are our own & utterly incommunicable" (397). The term *thirst* cannot capture his unbearable need for water, for example (391). Yet, familiarity is also part of the strangeness of becoming a fish. In the stargazer fish Gould senses something "not alien but familiar. Yet I could not say what the nature of that familiarity was, nor why it at first disturbed me so" (161). He later tells us that there is something "irretrievably fishy about us all" (392). He already existed in continuity with, rather than only embodied difference from, the stargazer, so in shape-shifting into a fish, he did not become something entirely other than what he already was.[15]

The lives of Gould and the fish collide in transformative ways, then, but this collision does not inevitably support the well-being of either Gould or the fish. It means the death of the fish and the prolongation of Gould's life. When Gould is sentenced to death, the jailor Pobjoy seeks to profit by selling Gould's paintings and works to continually postpone the execution (258–59). Flanagan seeks to differentiate among a range of relationships between people and fish, while also suggesting that people's ability to maneuver in these relationships is profoundly constrained by economic and social contingencies. As Gould increasing becomes aware of the experiences of fish, he realizes that this relationship takes the particular form of "the inarticulable fear of many fish & my unrequited love for them" (382). He feels love for the fish as beings that are not the same as him, and realizes that he cannot entirely own this love: if we eliminate fish, he tells us, the future will be a "barren sameness," without love, wonder, or mystery (201). Even though Gould's love emerges from his interactions with the fish, and the fish are agents in this love, it cannot be conflated with the feelings of the fish. In connecting with other beings, Gould comes up against differences in experiences. His love begins to feel larger than his body, situated in complicated assemblages of beings, and yet also smaller, as only one way of making sense of those assemblages.[16] Flanagan most broadly associates love with the ocean, without which Gould's love of fish would be impossible. As Gould flies through the water as a weedy seadragon, he finds that "the sea was an infinite love" (396). Flanagan's point is not that all ocean creatures love each other, but that the ocean is a multitude of densely interwoven singular lives, and includes Gould, the fish, and the love which they form: the "ocean is impossibly complicated, interconnected, turbulent and nonlinear, and it touches every part of life," as journalist Alanna Mitchell writes (2010, 27).

The weedy seadragon is particularly significant as a being who is visibly

affected by the life forms and materials of the ocean. A watercolor painting of a weedy seadragon, labeled as a leafy seadragon, is among the few
remaining traces of the life of the real person known as William Buelow
Gould (Figure 1).[17] Gould's weedy seadragon painting and his other illustrations of marine creatures in *Sketchbook of Fishes* are now held at the
Allport Library and Museum of Fine Arts in Tasmania and are listed on
UNESCO's Memory of the World Register (Gould ca. 1832). The weedy
seadragon captivates early European explorers, who note its unusual
form, changing colors, and likeness to seaweed. In 1804, French naturalist
Count Étienne Lacépède encounters a weedy seadragon and describes it
as "decorated with small flames" (qtd. in Olsen 2010, 216). English naturalist George Perry notes "the strange and eccentric arrangement of shapes
in this singular animal" (Perry 1811, n.p.). English scientist George Shaw
describes a "most extraordinary species; far exceeding all the rest of the
genus in the singularity of its appearance, which is such as at first view
rather to suggest the idea of some production of fancy than of any real existence. . . . Its great particularity however consists in the large, leaf-shaped
appendages with which the back, tail, and abdomen, are furnished" (Shaw
1804, 456). Penny Olsen suggests that the weedy seadragon takes on and
inhabits aspects of other oceanic modes of being, specifically those of the
seaweed and the water, although not in a dominating or destructive way:
"Their small, almost completely transparent, fins undulate to move them
sedately through the water in a swaying motion, completing the illusion
of floating seaweed. Their colour assists in the subterfuge, changing according to location, diet and emotional state" (Olsen 2010, 219). An intimate relationship with the ocean sustains but also endangers the weedy
seadragon. The IUCN (International Union for Conservation of Nature)
lists the animal as "near threatened" in the context of habitat degradation
through the discharge of storm water and sewage and declines in kelp,
among other processes (IUCN 2006). Gould tells us that the seadragon
and other fish experience their relationship with him in terms of "inarticulable fear" rather than love (382).

Given the fear that is felt by the fish, Flanagan explores not simply how
Gould is transformed through interactions with these fish, but whether
this transformation could be shaped by the ways in which the fish express
their experiences and by Gould's capacities to engage those expressions
and make a difference in the lives of the fish. As Gould looks at the fish,
"still dying, the occasional mortal flap of the tail or desperate heave of the

Figure 1. William Buelow Gould's weedy seadragon painting from Sketchbook of Fishes (ca. 1832), which inspired Richard Flanagan's novel Gould's Book of Fish (2001). Courtesy of the Allport Library and Museum of Fine Arts, Tasmanian Archive and Heritage Office.

gills signalling their silent horror was not yet ended, the more I looked into the endless recesses of their eyes, the more something of them began to pass into me" (257). Gould recognizes pain and disagreement in the fish's batting tail. It is a moment when his interests and those of the fish clearly do not coincide, because the deaths of the fish enable him to paint and so to prolong his life. In a world not marked by this particular contingency, the survival of the fish could well coincide with the interests of Gould because the fish are an important source of his love. Gould cannot save the fish in the context in which he lives, however. His desire for survival, his love of fish, and the struggle of fish to live are countervailing forces that pull at him in ways that he cannot reconcile.

Unlike the fish he painted, Gould ultimately survives, transforming into a weedy seadragon and swimming away from the settlement. Several commentators, including Flanagan in *Gould's Book of Fish*, speculate that William Buelow Gould imbued the fish illustrations in *Sketchbook of Fishes* with the human characters of the penal station: the pot-bellied sea horse, the kelpy, the stargazer, among others, speak of both fish and of peoples of Sarah Island. In representing people as fish in the paintings, Gould could have sought to express experiences that he was forbidden to record. Flanagan takes further the idea that the paintings convey people who have metamorphosed into fish. In *Gould's Book of Fish*, metamorphosis designates people's capacities to get to know other beings and to be changed by this process.

To return briefly to *New Atlantis*, Bacon tells a story of a promising island. It is not difficult to imagine the existence of multiple imagined and perceived worlds on this island, not all of which feel promising. But Bacon gives no sense at all that the utopia's nonhuman animals, and indeed even that most of its people, actually experience this utopia. Concern for the capacities of fish for expression, the extent to which we can engage these expressions, and the political and social change that such engagement might shape, are completely absent from *New Atlantis*. Flanagan also tells stories of an island in *Gould's Book of Fish*, but he emphasizes differing experiences of this island. As the forest fire rages across the island, for example, the Commandant speculates on the possibility of capitalizing on the resulting charcoal, while the convicts begin dreaming of escape, everyone "remarking upon the fire only as a prolongation of our various worlds" (364). The Commandant's hope, no matter how firmly defined as the definitive experience of Hope, is not the same as that of the convicts.

These scenes evoke differences among people's experiences, but also the complicated ways in which such experiences are shaped through coexistence. The life forms described in *Gould's Book of Fish* are somewhat molten in relation to each other. Gould does not simply reject the Commandant's story about hope, for example. In his diminished conditions of life, he transforms this story into another story in which he could be someone other than a convict. The idea that the convicts will build the world dreamed by the Commandant, even though they will not benefit from that world, enables "some alternate idea of ourselves, some steam engine by which we could remake ourselves & our world" (103). This is not the only imaginary that allows Gould to hope, of course. Sometimes he builds a relationship with a promising future through efforts to escape, rather than through dreams of thriving in a material reality dominated by the Commandant's aspirations.

While not seeking to merge characters' different modes of being into one definitive account of hope, Flanagan suggests that hope emerges from connections among beings and that it is possible, within constraints, to alter these connections so that particular claims on hope come to better interact with the interests of others. More concretely, Gould's hope comes to be tempered by the experiences of the fish, even if it is never fully collapsible into those experiences. As I have suggested, Gould feels hope when the world seems to reveal the potential of his survival. But this hope becomes increasingly tinged with and complicated by his relationships with the fish. As he spends time with fish, he sees their hurt, fear, and loss, and worries about a loveless future without them. For Gould, hope comes to be animated by efforts to disrupt the excessive loss of fish from the ocean, rather than simply by his survival. He smears his protest across his cell walls using his excrement as ink, "in the hope he hopes not forlorn—that love will still at this last bid find him if he can but dig deep enough into his own decay" (384). Love, for Gould, is not possible without the fish, and so his hope relies on an intervention in their loss. Yet, his grasp on survival remains precariously locked into the deaths of the fish for his paintings. Transforming the relationships between humans and nonhumans requires engagement with the economic and social contingencies that do not entirely define but that heavily shape such relationships.

Because of the impossible dilemmas that he faces, Gould seeks to smuggle hope through time to a potential reader or viewer, in telling the reader of the destruction of fish and the consequent "attrition of love that we were blindly bringing about" (200). Through his paintings, he attempts to push hope across not space but time, to someone who might then get to know and love fish and who might struggle to halt their destruction. Indeed, many years later, Gould's words and paintings affect our contemporary narrator, Hammet. On reading the *Book of Fish*, Hammet grows curious regarding the experiences of fish, speculating on the "melancholy" of the weedy seadragon that is imprisoned in Mr Hung's aquarium: "As well as wonder, it shimmered sadness" (37). Flanagan does not naively assume that the viewers of Gould's paintings will inevitably experience more economic and social openness in their relationships with fish than did Gould. Such an assumption is evident in some media about environmental activists who brush up against fisher people in the Pacific.[18] Rather, Flanagan suggests that only in the present, in its relationships with the future and the past, can collective actions transform economic and social institutions.

Flanagan extends his interest in how Gould's hope might be shaped by nonhuman beings' concerns to the ways in which such hope could also engage the Indigenous peoples who live on Sarah Island. If the chances of escape allow convicts a relationship with a future that is partly promising and open, such hope cannot be conflated with the interests of the first peoples of Tasmania. On fleeing the penal station into the wilderness, Gould and Capois Death intersect two Indigenous men who kill Capois Death—a man of African heritage from San Domingo—after he provides an affirmative response to their question regarding whether he is "numminer," which he understands to mean "ghost" and Gould interprets as "white man allied to all the horrors inflicted by white men upon blackfellas" (319). Many of the most brutal scenes in Gould's Book of Fish describe Europeans' violence against Indigenous peoples and, as in the scene in which Capois Death dies, the ongoing, socially convoluted force of this violence. We are told that a sealer bashed Twopenny Sal's baby boy to death and took her as a slave. She is said to have killed their subsequent children.

As Gould spends time with Twopenny Sal, getting to know her and other Indigenous peoples who live on Sarah Island, he increasingly comes to see his relationships with them in terms of varying, albeit limited, potentials. After fleeing the prison and traveling across the wilderness, and near the point of starving, he runs into Twopenny Sal, with whom he has shared an intimate relationship, as well as Tracker Marks, who tracks bushrangers for the settlement police. Gould sees that British infantrymen have cut off Tracker Marks's nose and ears because he did not lead them to the bushranger Matt Brady. "Then," he records, "Tracker Marks did something that had I journeyed a thousand miles through a hundred wildernesses to find this one place, I would never have anticipated. He was extending his arm. He was reaching toward me. With the back of his fingers, on my cheek & lips, he was touching me" (324–25). Gould is almost never touched by another person with tenderness. His physical interactions with other people usually fill him with pain. The moment is a reminder of potential for, and tenuous realities of, engagement and care.

Gould is particularly changed through his relationship with Twopenny Sal. Ronald Bogue notes that Twopenny Sal offers Gould the significance of the circular scars on her calves (2010, 201). She describes one of these circles as "Sun" and as "'Palawa,' her word for her own people," and the other circle, which is "bisected but not broken by a single line," as "Moon" and as "Numminer," a word that Gould believes means ghosts and white men: "They believed England was where their spirits went after death to be reborn as English men & women, that the white men were their ancestors returned" (271). Later she tells Gould, "Gould numminer, but long time before you were Palawa" (340). Reminding us that we are offered Gould's interpretation of Twopenny Sal's knowledge, Bogue suggests that this knowledge situates people, animals, and the land in terms of relationality: "The violent opposition of 'them' and 'us', while not necessarily ignored or passively accepted in its practical, sociopolitical guise, is metaphysically overcome" (Bogue 2010, 204). Apprehending relationality among varied beings and the land does not necessarily mean ignoring differences but does complicate ideas of absolute divides (Bogue 2010, 204).

As Gould gets to know Twopenny Sal, he comes up against both connections and differences, not only feeling pleasure but increasingly becoming aware of his responsibilities in relation to her losses. When she comes to visit Gould in his cell for one last time, he sees that she is pregnant and asks who the father is. She replies, "Cobber," or friend (260). Gould realizes that he cannot expect or demand to be the father, because Twopenny Sal has had to survive the unimaginable upheaval of her people by gaining resources through intimate relationships with varied men of the settlement: "Do you think I was only gaoled? I wished to cry out as she turned to leave & rapped thrice on the door for Pobjoy to come & open—for I too was the gaoler" (260). Gould realizes that his love of Twopenny Sal cannot simply be conflated with her experience. Such a realization is significant if we think forward to that moment when a bush fire runs across the island and, sensing freedom, the convicts begin "a wild dreaming of a new country to be" (366). It is striking here that the convicts take on and inhabit the language of a new world that Flanagan associates with the Commandant and more broadly with imperialism. In his relationship with Twopenny Sal, Gould begins to realize that this world is not simply his to dream, that his interests and those of Twopenny Sal are not simply the same. The scene suggests that any European dreaming should, and can, engage the concerns of the Indigenous peoples of Tasmania.

Flanagan formally crafts Gould's Book of Fish to embody dynamics of difference and connection among the inhabitants of the island, not so much telling a story of a promising island as threading together the stories of distinct narrators. These stories overlap but also contradict each other. For example, the afterword, which takes the form of a colonial secretary's correspondence file on Gould, contradicts Gould's own account of his experiences in the preceding pages. Gould, we are told in the afterword, had multiple aliases, including Sid Hammet and the Commandant, the names of characters who are distinct from Gould in the main body of the novel. The afterword also suggests that in 1831 Gould drowned while trying to escape Sarah Island (404).[19] Through such contradictions, the novel illuminates the uncontainable complexities of the living and of history rather than imaginatively establish control over their stories or indeed over the experiences of the readers. As I have suggested, writing and art were woven into violent exertions of power in the penal colony. A number of talented painters, writers, and journalists were transported to Tasmania for crimes such as counterfeiting (Reynolds 2012, 140). They created archives for settlement administrators, including letters, paintings, reports, and books. These archives shaped their own and other convicts' present experiences and futures, as well as the historical records of their lives. Toward the end of *Gould's Book of Fish*, Gould flees the penal colony into the wilderness, traveling in a wild state of near-starvation and grief. He comes across a book, the content of which corresponds to his unfolding reality. He is "entrapped in a book, a character whose future as much as his past was already written, determined, foretold, as unalterable as it was intolerable. What choice did he have but to destroy that book?" (336). *Gould's Book of Fish* makes sharp claims on past and present struggles to regenerate in many ways irreparable relations between human and nonhuman beings. But, in its fissures and ambiguities, it is also crafted to provoke readers' thought rather than to dominate their comprehensions of the world and efforts to shape its futures.

Strange Oceans

Countless archives tell us that the ocean is strange. In the early European writings about the marine ecosystems of Australia, we might find the sea-dragon, flying through a kelp forest, a "strange and eccentric" animal who is "decorated with small flames" (Perry 1811, n.p.; qtd. in Olsen 2010, 216). A contemporary tourism advertisement describes "the most wonderful and magical destination on Earth," that is to say, Tasmania: "It's out there on the edge of the world" (Tourism Tasmania 2010a, 2010b). Some European cultural histories heavily emphasize the difference of the ocean and its islands as compared to the ordinary sites of human life. In *Gould's Book of Fish*, Flanagan describes strangeness not so much as characterizing the reality of another being's life, but rather as a dynamic process of interaction that alters not only how we see others but also how we can know ourselves. Gould swims into strange oceans by connecting with others and becoming aware of the possibilities for maneuverability in relation to the hurt and loss, as well as the well-being, that take form within these connections. In particular, Gould connects with fish and begins to fall in love with them. To love, in this context, is to enable another being who is not the same to reach out and touch you, so that you might realize that this love is neither entirely your own nor fully collapsible into the experience of that being. It is to experience hope, joy, and loss, among other facets of life, in connection with another. Through his relationships with fish, Gould begins to realize that the activities that allow him to feel hope, specifically the fish paintings that promise his survival, mean violent death for the fish. Gould begins to associate a promising future not only with his own survival but also with that of the fish. Although he has little room to maneuver in the world in which he lives, he attempts to smuggle hope by encouraging future viewers of his paintings and readers of his words to connect with fish as feeling and knowing beings. The paintings keep alive Gould's hope that a person might care about and act to intervene in the heavy loss of fish from the ocean and so, also, from their life. They are a technology through which Gould pushes this hope onto other people. The fish, in this way, might also come to be "given" some of the hope of survival that was once only available to Gould.

The ocean of *Gould's Book of Fish* may also be strange because it does not exist "on the edge of the world" but rather is deeply connected with terrestrial life. Flanagan explores specificity partly through the ocean, apprehending differences related to the medium—air or water—in which people and fish can most easily exist, as evidenced by the fish who die after being ripped out of the ocean, or by Gould's desperate struggle to survive the high tide by clinging to the ceiling of his coastal cell. But Flanagan's ocean is not simply different. Environmental and economic processes stretch through and beyond its waters, as is visible in the agonizing pathways of fish from the water into human bodies, aquariums, paintings, and more broadly the economy of the empire. Flanagan associates empire, capitalism, and urbanization, among other processes, with marine environmental change.

At this time when the ocean is such a complex and important force in climate change, fishing, and pollution, among other processes, literary studies is marked by heighted interest in "oceanic" or "sea" literatures.[20] In its amphibious approach to politics, ecology, and economy, *Gould's Book of Fish* is perhaps a reminder of the potential limitations of such a framework. It suggests that thematically selected literary archives that look the most like "the ocean"—for example, that primarily or entirely take place at sea or otherwise significantly accord narrative space to the sea—are not the only archives that speak in important ways about the ocean. *Gould's Book of Fish* imaginatively navigates ties between marine environmental change and economy, national security, war, deforestation, and cities. Its approach accords with critical methods in Pacific literary studies, where scholars rarely if ever isolate "maritime" literatures, fictional or otherwise, from other kinds of literatures.[21]

While *Gould's Book of Fish* might, perhaps, stand out in an ocean-focused framework, for example, it is much less certain that Flanagan's more recent novel *The Unknown Terrorist* (2006) would be recognizable within such a framework. Yet, the novel offers insights into linkages among the ocean, national security, and economy. *The Unknown Terrorist* sharpens the concerns regarding state violence that mark *Gould's Book of Fish*, tracing a number of terrified and dying human beings, some of whom are dumped into the waters. Set in Sydney at a time when the War on Terror reverberates in state practices, media discourses, and people's everyday interactions, *The Unknown Terrorist* elaborates several days in the life of Gina, also known as the Doll, a twenty-six-year-old woman who works as a pole dancer at a club named the Chairman's Lounge. The Doll spends an intimate night with a stranger, Tariq, and wakes to find that he is being described as a terrorist in the national media and that she is being featured with him in a surveillance photograph. She subsequently becomes a terrorism suspect, is hunted, and her life is rapidly destroyed. *The Unknown Terrorist* evokes the tangle of the state, media, and corporations through which cultural imaginaries of the threat of terror are shaped. But it also emphasizes ordinary people's participation in this world, the ways in which their loneliness, fears, and hurts seep into their social interactions and particularly into casual, everyday indifference to the suffering of others. Flanagan sees no deep reflection on the ways of life said to be threatened by terrorism, characterizing these life ways partly in terms of economic fissures between rich and poor, state terror, social indifference to people who are desperate and hurting, and unfolding environmental catastrophe: "Who would wish to change any of it?" (28).

At the end of *The Unknown Terrorist*, Flanagan describes the women, naked, waiting to dance for the clothed men who watch from below and for the clothed man who manages the Chairman's Lounge. These women, he suggests, "understand without knowing that not far away, on an ever rising sea, the scattered corpses of those that don't belong float for the shortest time like storm-tossed kelp leaves, before disappearing forever" (320). The women sense that others hold the economic, political, and social power to destroy their lives and that such destruction could unfold without attention or redress.[22] Some of the people who are dumped in the ocean are described in more detail in *The Unknown Terrorist*. On first seeing a broadcast of her photograph, the Doll unsuccessfully struggles to control her panic, seeking hope that might "hold her up as flotsam does a drowning man. But there were no words of hope, only a dimly perceived sense that something unknowable had changed, something terrible had taken place, and her life was no longer as it had been" (97). In a more literal instance of lives that disappear into the ocean, Flanagan engages the oceanic pathways of people smuggling, repeatedly referring to twelve men who have been brought from Shanghai into Sydney in a shipping container. Tariq was supposed to collect them but by this point he has been described in the media as a terrorist and killed. Trapped in the container in the harbor, the men are dying of thirst. At the end of the novel, we are told that a prawn trawler heads out into the sea, "loaded with twelve corpses that need to be dumped" (319).

The illegalities that some people face in their relationships with the ocean—that place for "Names without Graves, Graves without Names"—more often surface in discussions of human rights than of environment in the Pacific Rim.[23] Moreover, the characters of *The Unknown Terrorist* are not amenable to definition as environmentally concerned. The Doll's main aim is to save money so that she can buy an apartment and commodities. Shopping allows her to hold at bay the feeling that she does not belong in this world. Yet, *The Unknown Terrorist* is relevant to environmental thought on the ocean for exploring how social conditions related to national security are linked to the definition and defense of economic aspirations, with profound environmental implications. The television news program on which the Doll first sees herself and Tariq is quickly followed by an advertisement: "'It's so empowering to keep your skin supple,' the television said in a voice softly American" (96). Flanagan suggests that the media draws together messages regarding insecurity with imperatives to consume. He repeatedly links the economy, ocean, and climate, for example, in describing mansions and designer apartments alongside the "nearby globally warmed Pacific Ocean" (18). *The Unknown Terrorist* maps connections between events that might seem to be isolated in spaces such as cities and that are sometimes called human rights violations—such as the state and media persecution of the Doll—and environmental processes unfolding at sea and elsewhere.

The conclusion of *The Unknown Terrorist,* unlike that of *Gould's Book of Fish,* offers no story that might illuminate hope. Tariq ends up shot and rotting in the trunk of a car. The Doll has no chance of escape through metamorphosis. She is shot dead at the pole dancing club. Flanagan maps faint but unmistakable potentials at earlier moments in *The Unknown Terrorist,* seeing realities of care, joy, and playfulness among people who come to be categorized as each other's enemies within the media, the government, and often even within their own expressions. The Doll, who has troubled relationships with men and describes herself as usually indifferent to them, "had perhaps harboured the secret hope that in the future she would discover more about Tariq" (109). Facing critique for not having asked Tariq where he came from, the Doll feels that such questions had not seemed necessary: "For one night they found something beyond the answers of home and history" (109). It is not that Flanagan fails to see that home and history matter within people's lives: *The Unknown Terrorist* is an often furious and complicated examination of the variegated forces that home and history may exert on people's lives. Flanagan insists that these are not the frameworks that matter to people all the time. In their capacities for sociality, people are not always defined through these frameworks. But these capacities are destroyed with great indifference in *The Unknown Terrorist.*

In an interview on a current affairs program of the Australian Broadcasting Corporation, an entity owned by the Australian government, journalist Kerry O'Brien implicitly criticizes Flanagan for the relentlessly desolate tone of *The Unknown Terrorist:* "Did you really intend to write such a bleak book?" Flanagan responds that in Australia people are "more frightened" and "more frightening," and describes backsliding in terms of freedom as well as injustices in the distributions of wealth and power. O'Brien replies, "That's a pretty grim view," and Flanagan adds, "It is, but it is hard to have any other view at this point in time. But I think there are always sources for hope and I try and take my compass from the hope, but this book, there's been too much faked jubilation about our prosperity and I'm tired of hearing about how to invest our super and about rising property prices" (Australian Broadcasting Corporation 2006). Flanagan is put on the defensive regarding the bleak perspective of *The Unknown Terrorist,* a novel that after all is about naked women who dance above clothed men and who are denigrated by some of those same men for doing this work. It is also a novel about people whose lives are destroyed through their inaccurate identification as terrorists, and people who are left to die of thirst in a shipping container and then dumped at sea. Flanagan's refusal to evoke hope in the ways that he sees as usual in Australia, specifically through prosperity or national security, and indeed his refusal to evoke much hope of any form at all, and the journalist's implicit criticism of that refusal, raises the question of how we might understand the relationships among hope, loss, and responsibility. Is hope a mode of engagement that disrupts an effort to grapple with loss and responsibility, as seems to be implied in this interview? I take up this question in the following chapter, exploring how literary writers negotiate relationships between hope and loss in the context of nuclear weapons testing programs. These writers and Flanagan, if we return briefly to *Gould's Book of Fish,* make a claim that hope emerges in facing, rather than in mollifying or forgetting, loss and responsibility. Rather than a cover-up, in the words of Gould, hope "might be the axe that smashed the frozen sea within, might make the dead wake & swim free" (386–87).

· CHAPTER 5 ·

Utopia Haunted

Loss and Hope in the Nuclear Pacific

we can always ask, where and what kind of place is the place of despair and hope

Angus Fletcher, "The Place of Despair and Hope"

DURING THE 1980s, New Zealand Māori (Te Aupōuri) artist Ralph Hotere named a number of lithographs *Black Rainbow*. He gave one of these lithographs to Samoan writer Albert Wendt in 1986, and Wendt, in turn, titled a novel *Black Rainbow* (1995a [1992]).[1] When Wendt's narrator, Eric, first sees a *Black Rainbow* lithograph on the second page of this novel he says, "I didn't understand it but I liked it. Can you really have a black rainbow?" (10).

What kind of world is that of a black rainbow? Hotere produced the black rainbow lithographs to mark nuclear bombs detonated by France at Moruroa (Mururoa) Atoll during the 1980s. France, the United Kingdom, and the United States exploded hundreds of nuclear weapons in the Pacific between 1946 and 1996. The black rainbow motif recalls the Greenpeace ship *Rainbow Warrior,* which was bombed by French Secret Service agents in Auckland Harbour in 1985, shortly after it was used to evacuate Marshallese people from Rongelap Atoll, which had been radioactively contaminated by U.S. nuclear tests, and just days before it was due to voyage in protest to Moruroa Atoll. The black rainbow also draws us toward other oceanic peoples and places affected by nuclear weapons, recalling Japanese writer Masuji Ibuse's novel of Hiroshima, *Black Rain (Kuroi Ame)* (1969 [1966]). The blackened rainbow of Hotere's and Wendt's works marks the destruction of ecosystems and lives in a part of the world that has often been described for its vibrant colors. French artist Paul Gauguin famously associated the Pacific with intense color in his works, commenting in his journal of Tahiti, *Noa Noa*, "The landscape with its violent, pure

colors dazzled and blinded me" (2005 [1919], 26). In opening a collection
of literary works, *Nuanua: Pacific Writing in English since 1980*, Wendt notes
that *nuanua* translates as "rainbow" in many Pacific languages and that this
motif well evokes the cultural, linguistic, and environmental diversity of
the ocean (1995b, 1).

Many of Hotere's works draw on black: "Everything Hotere touches
turns to black . . . ," writes David Eggleton, "all the objects he makes, all the
shapes he renders, all the colours he finds, are freaked with jet" (2000, 62).
The writers and critics who engage Hotere's work associate black with loss
but also with potential, creativity, and ordinary life, much of which is spent
in the darkness.[2] Hotere's and Wendt's black rainbow can be interpreted in
terms of sorrow for the present world as a site of loss and damage. But it
also illuminates hope, referencing peoples' struggles in everyday practices,
social movements, political institutions, and artistic projects to survive,
halt, and recover from nuclear weapons. The black rainbow evokes both
hope and sorrow, not because these are the same phenomena but because they exist in the same world. Such a perspective breaks with literary
works and other archives that reveal hope by situating the Pacific as a good
world beyond that in which people usually live. In countless artistic, academic, and corporate archives, at least from the sixteenth century onward,
the Pacific Islands are figured as promising spaces to which people can
escape from the exhaustions, boredoms, or losses that they face in their
ordinary worlds. To draw from an advertisement for tourism in Samoa,
this is "a destination that remains uncluttered by tourists where just after
your first day on holiday, your senses are stimulated, your mind, body and
soul begin to recharge and you start to feel refreshed and relaxed" (Samoa
Tourism Authority 2011, n.p.). The motif of escape from everyday life also
formally structures utopian literary narratives, which usually encompass
a narrator's travels to, around, and from a strange, utopian place (Vieira
2010, 7). Immersed in these unfamiliar worlds, people might gain a critical
distance on their own worlds (Ahmad 2009, 5; Suvin 1972).

What if writers associate hope with the everyday worlds in which
human and nonhuman beings live? And what if these places evoke not
only hope but also loss and many other experiences? Much, if not most,
contemporary cultural production by Indigenous and settler peoples describes the ocean as a place of ordinary, and at times extraordinary, daily
life rather than as an otherworldly retreat. In this chapter, I explore hope
through literary writings that engage the histories of nuclear weapons use
in the Republic of the Marshall Islands and in the Tuamotu Archipelago,

French Polynesia, after the Second World War. In *Black Rainbow,* Wendt makes oblique linkages between French nuclear tests at Moruroa Atoll and a socially and economically marginalized group of people who live in a utopia in Auckland city, while in *Meḷaḷ: A Novel of the Pacific* (2002) Hawai'i writer Robert Barclay imagines a family who live in the context of U.S. military activities in the Marshall Islands. Although these novels are different in many ways, both firmly connect hope to places where human and nonhuman beings have faced and still live with immense and unusual processes of loss, including of life, health, home, economic viability, and political autonomy.

In associating hope with such places, these writers come up against ethical concerns that can more easily be avoided by those writers who reveal hope by creating entirely other, promising worlds. What are the relationships between hope and loss? Is hope an attempt to deny or redeem the horror of nuclear weapons? Is sorrow an experience that destroys hope? It may be tempting to view hope as strongly allied with other types of "good feeling," in Sara Ahmed's words, such as happiness or love (2010, 30). Hope might be understood as combative with, or separable from, experiences such as fear, sorrow, anger, despair, and hurt. Yet, all the literary works that I engage in this book are just as much about such experiences as they are about hope. In particular, they sketch out deeply messy relationships between hope and loss. Theorists of hope, too, almost always work on hope in times and places where people face heightened loss, hurt, and danger, as well as what Australian novelist Richard Flanagan calls "the mud of the mundane" (2001, 14).[3] In a famous account of Paul Klee's *Angel of History,* who is blown into the future in a storm named "progress" while facing the past and unable to stop and repair the damage piling up there, Walter Benjamin sees hope not in turning back away from that damage toward the future but only in engagement with the bleak topologies of the past. The historian might connect with and enliven hopes that have been stopped in their tracks, fanning "the spark of hope in the past" (Benjamin 1969, 255). Many scholars have built on Benjamin's observation, suggesting that hope may overreach the places where it was historically interrupted as people died, livelihoods were destroyed, and futures were eliminated. Barclay and Wendt do not write only about hope that may be destroyed or survive in a world marked by excesses of violence, however. They also negotiate histories in which militarized states elided such violence by associating nuclear weapons with sparkling futures involving global peace and well-being. Rather than imaginatively marginalizing loss by evoking promising futures, in their novels Barclay and Wendt offer hope through their imaginings of efforts to address loss and violence. That such hope exists in this world is a source of sorrow. As such, Barclay and Wendt emphasize the intimacies between hope and other modes of engagement.

World of a Black Rainbow

In September 1995, when France detonated another nuclear bomb at Moruroa Atoll, hundreds of people in Papeete, Tahiti, bombarded and set fire to the international airport, cars, and French government buildings. They smashed shop windows and attempted to break into the French High Commission. France used tear gas and stun grenades to stop the protests. A journalist recalls a demonstrator saying, "This is only the beginning. France must take its nuclear bombs and blow them up in France, not here. This is our life" (Milliken 1995, n.p.).[4]

This fiery ocean draws us far away from early explorers' aspirations for a French Pacific variously characterized by scientific discovery and progress, a possible return to the Golden Age of Antiquity, and love and sexual freedom in a state of nature.[5] In 1768, French explorer Louis-Antoine de Bougainville came to Tahiti while searching the South Sea for new lands. He named the island *Nouvelle Cythère*, after the Greek Island where the goddess Aphrodite washed up (Salmond 2009, 20). In his journal, Bougainville describes the local people as enjoying health and happiness and inhabiting nature: "These people breathe only rest and sensual pleasures" (Bougainville 2002, 63). On leaving Tahiti, he writes, "Farewell happy and wise people, may you always remain what you are. I shall never recall without a sense of delight the brief time I spent among you and, as long as I live, I shall celebrate the happy island of Cythera. It is the true Utopia" (2002, 74). Nouvelle Cythère would join the unsettled, sometimes utopian, imaginative spaces that Europeans were making of the ocean—vivid spaces populated by people living nobly or savagely in a state of nature. Pacific intellectuals have long struggled to complicate or overturn these accounts of the ocean.[6]

Bougainville's story about Tahiti may appear to have come unmoored from the actual world, from the looming project of French imperialism in the Pacific and from both French and Tahitian peoples' experiences at that time. The story about Nouvelle Cythère is not simply a French story, however, and it is not just a fantasy. Historian Anne Salmond has painstakingly reconstructed the context for this story, observing that it reflects the collision of French and Tahitian peoples' histories and imaginings. She tells a story of a young Tahitian woman who boarded Bougainville's ship *Boudeuse* and stripped to her waist as the French arrived in Tahiti (2009, 19–20). Bougainville associated the woman's actions with sexual desire and freedom, describing her by evoking the goddess of love, Aphrodite, as well as Enlightenment ideas about a state of nature. Salmond observes that from the perspective of Tahitian history and thought, however, the woman's actions did not so much reflect sexual availability or freedom as a ritual performed in the company of gods and high chiefs (19). Prior to the arrival of French explorers in Tahiti, the *marae* or stone temple of 'Oro, the god of fertility and war, had been desecrated in a battle, and the priest Vaita prophesized that this momentous event had disturbed the divide between the world of people and the world of ancestors: "Something extraordinary would burst through, and according to Vaita, these strange beings would have bodies different from the islanders" (458). Salmond suggests that Tahitians initially associated the Europeans with this prophecy, with ancestral power, and with the possibility of restoring *mana* to the marae of 'Oro. Their sexually explicit performances reflected this association: "In Tahiti, it was as though the ancestors summoned the Europeans to work their will" (461).

If Bougainville does position Tahitians—in their sensuality, inhabitation of nature, and connection to a golden age lost to Europeans—as imbuing his world with the possibility of a way of life different from that at home, such a claim on hope reflects not a flight from but an interaction with that world, albeit this interaction clearly involved misinterpretation. Indeed, many scholars suggest that hope is not well understood as denial or disengagement, arguing that hope involves attunement to the ordinary worlds in which people live.[7] Although Bougainville's story of Tahiti as a utopia may reflect his interpretation of a traceable place and time, however, this interpretation not only involves mistakes but is highly selective. In his journal, Bougainville does not engage the question of what French and other European nations' imperial interests in the Pacific might mean for the idea of Nouvelle Cythère, the "true Utopia," at that time or in the future (2002, 74).[8] Bougainville does not simply ignore the conflicts, upheavals, and indeed the imperialism meant by the French arrival in Tahiti. His journal moves between effusive descriptions of Tahiti as a utopia and discrepant descriptions of the daily interactions between the French and

Tahitians, including accounts of women and children fleeing the area after French soldiers' violence and comments regarding the Tahitians stealing from the French: "I am afraid that we might in the end be forced to kill a few as examples to others" (66). His description of "the happy island of Cythera" and call for its people to "always remain what you are" is followed immediately by a "Copy of the Act taking possession of the Island of Cythera," which asserts that the French took possession of the archipelago in 1768 and emphasizes its favorable conditions for cultivation as compared to other colonies as well as the amiability of its people (74). Bougainville simply refuses or is unable to bring into dialogue the narrative of the colonial project and that of the utopia of Nouvelle Cythère.

In consequence, little in Bougainville's descriptions of Tahiti as the true utopia could prepare one for the desolation evident in more recent archives of French and other militarized states' presence in the Pacific. Between 1966 and 1996, France carried out approximately 193 nuclear tests at Moruroa and Fangataufa atolls in the Tuamotu Archipelago.[9] In this vast expanse of sea and coral islands, people were exposed to high levels of radiation over many years, permanently changing their lives and futures. Radioactive fallout from the program was measured in other places, including in the Cook Islands, Fiji, New Zealand, Niue, Samoa, Tokelau, and Tonga (Danielsson 1990, 25; Ministry of Foreign Affairs 1973, 11). France drilled into the narrow and porous base of Moruroa Atoll, detonating underground bombs that blasted chasms and cracks in the atoll fabric and that released an unmeasured amount of radioactive material into the sea. Storms picked up waste that France spilled on the reef, including plutonium, washing it into the water (Danielsson 1990). France has resisted peoples' efforts to carry out or access reliable research on health and ecology in this part of the world. But over the years, stories and data that point toward the existence of severe radiation-related health problems in French Polynesia have steadily found their way past France's denials and secrecy (Danielsson 1990, 27–28; Greenpeace International 1990; Vincent 2005).

Many Pacific peoples live in close physical and imaginative relation to the places most directly damaged by nuclear bombs. This point is not easy to grasp in narratives of nuclear histories as either utopian *or* apocalyptic, if the latter implies the complete elimination of life, as it does in English Australian writer Nevil Shute's *On the Beach,* a story of global destruction brought about by nuclear war (2010 [1957]). Utopian and apocalyptic narratives elide the continued pain and loss that surrounds nuclear weapons, peoples' hard-fought struggles for survival, justice, and repair, and the moments or spaces of relative well-being that they have been able to create. In a *Los Angeles Times* review of Robert Stone's *Radio Bikini* (1987), a documentary film based on footage of the U.S. nuclear program in the Marshall Islands, Leonard Klady notes, "The viewer will be awe-struck by images of a goat that survived the blast placed in sharp contrast to the expectations of officials who anticipated something apocalyptic" (1988, n.p.). Putting aside Klady's suggestion that someone will feel awe on seeing a goat tied to a ship and filmed during the blast of a nearby nuclear bomb, and even questioning whether such scientific research is in fact not well described as apocalyptic, one of the most important points here is the continuation of the goat's life and the question of what might follow. In other words, there is need to negotiate this world of hurt and responsibility that in important although very limited ways is still maneuverable.

The two works that I discuss here—*Black Rainbow* and *Mejaļ*—engage the nuclear histories in very different ways, but they both evoke hope through engagement with worlds that have been heavily altered by nuclear weapons. They consequently navigate perilous relationships among hope, loss, and many other experiences. Barclay's and Wendt's insistence on grounding hope in lived worlds, where all is not well and all cannot be repaired, perhaps traverses a line that is perilously close to naiveté or to a sick kind of affirmation. Wendt directly engages this concern in the novel *Black Rainbow*, describing complicated relationships between hope and loss in the context of a utopia enabled by nuclear weapons testing. Born in Apia, Samoa (then Western Samoa), in 1939, Wendt has lived in varied parts of the Pacific, once describing himself as "a pelagic fish on permanent migration—or is it seasonal migration?" (1990, 59). He is important in Pacific studies for his essays, art, poetry, novels, plays, and films.[10] In *Black Rainbow*, Wendt traces Eric Mailei Foster's pathways around a utopia named the Tribunal. The story unfolds primarily in Auckland, but the utopia involves a globally sprawling network of nation-states, corporations, and citizens. The Tribunal collects extensive knowledge about its citizens through interrogation sessions over many years. Eric completes these sessions, and the Tribunal declares that it now holds his complete history. Soon Eric's wife and children disappear, and the Tribunal sends him in search for them. The remainder of the novel tracks Eric's interactions with varied inhabitants of the utopia as he tries to find his family.

The utopians claim to have constructed their world in the wake of three

global wars, sickness, and nuclear disasters: "We are one with the Earth /
at peace forever / We have outlawed war strife / hunger poverty and dis-
ease" (73). Wendt quickly undermines such narratives, revealing the violence that has underpinned the utopia's emergence and survival. In the
course of *Black Rainbow*, Eric loses his family as well as his familiar understanding of the world in which he lives. He realizes that the Tribunal has
biologically remade him several times over the years and that it was literally built on top of other ecosystems and Indigenous peoples' life worlds.
By the end of the novel, he has become aware of processes of deprivation
that have heavily affected his family, including ancestors, and ecology: "I
wept into the open sky and the atua. I had become the sum total of what
I had lost. That loss defined me, confined me" (196).

To see loss is to apprehend some measure of difference between what
has been and what exists now, not only in terms of what no longer exists
but also in terms of altered configurations, such as a decline in someone's
well-being. Environmental activists are often preoccupied with entities
that have been changed or have become absent. In the face of those people
and institutions who do not want to hear another story about a vanished
species or ecosystem, and in conditions where there are often few traces
to work with, they insist on searching for and imaginatively reanimating
the missing. The affective worlds of loss are often disorienting, haunting,
and dominating in their archives. As I discussed in chapter 1, some environmental activists have been criticized for longing for a former world that
was more simple and natural, as well as for finding Indigenous peoples to
be the remaining, threatened representatives of such a world.[11]

While attempting to maintain a distance from these specific narratives
of environmental loss—which among the ways in which they are unhelp-
ful, do not always recognize that Indigenous peoples move in time—it
would be impossible and inaccurate not to see many of the land and sea-
scapes of the Pacific as places where people and nonhuman beings have
faced, and live with, immense and unusual loss: a runway placed over the
top of food gardens; a baby buried in an unmarked grave, born dead to
parents who were exposed to radioactive fallout. Life is never still, and loss
is a relentless dimension of life. But experiences of loss reflect the contingent worlds in which human and nonhuman beings live, including economic inequality and colonial histories, processes that do not affect every
person, community, ecosystem, or nonhuman being in the same way.

Telling stories of loss has been made difficult in some parts of the

Pacific, as military powers have sought to block apprehension of what lies buried in soil, is submerged in the water, or has moved into and altered bodies. An interviewer at work on the Greenpeace book *Testimonies: Witnesses to French Nuclear Testing in the South Pacific* was expelled by France from Tahiti for speaking with people living or working on or near Moruroa and Fangataufa Atolls, for example (Greenpeace International 1990, 4). In *Consequential Damages of Nuclear War: The Rongelap Report,* Barbara Rose Johnston and Holly M. Barker detail how American scientific research related to nuclear testing in the Marshall Islands was kept secret, particularly until the 1990s, making meaningful discussions of justice impossible because the Marshallese government could not know the full extent of the damage (2008, 23–31). They note that between 2001 and 2003, a number of previously declassified military documents related to the Marshall Islands once again became inaccessible (33).[12]

It is not surprising that Margaret acquires one of Ralph Hotere's *Black Rainbow* lithographs early in Wendt's novel but that she and Eric remain completely unaware of its historical relationship with nuclear weapons. Indeed, the utopia in which they live has been stamped with an environmental pedigree: according to the utopians' anthem, they are *"one with the Earth"* (73). The utopians' recurrent, possessive references to the Earth lead us in the direction of the struggles of powerful institutions, including governments, international organizations, and corporations, to enable or at least to circulate their visions of environmental repair. As Arturo Escobar writes in tracing disparate contemporary politics of concern for the survival of nature, not limited to activists but also including governments, nongovernmental organizations (NGOs), and corporations, "After two centuries of systematic destruction of nature and life, and through a dialectical process set in motion by capitalism and modernity, the survival of biological life has emerged as a crucial question in the global landscape of capital and science" (1997, 202). Focusing on the Pacific Coast of Colombia, Escobar argues that government, NGOs, and international organizations such as the World Bank seek not simply the exhaustive extraction of the rainforest but also the survival of biodiversity through conservation and sustainable development. He observes that such struggles to sustain nature are interlocked with sometimes unacknowledged efforts to secure or implement particular economic, social, and political forms of life.[13] In *Black Rainbow,* indeed, the claim that the utopians are "one with the Earth" situates their forms of life—from imperial history to market economy to modes of social control such as surveillance—as important, even as necessary, for biological survival (73). Such claims exert a legitimating force for the utopia, making it difficult to see the environmental losses that characterize its world.

Wendt responds to the utopians' claims regarding environmental well-being by situating the present world as excessive to what such claims recognize. In the first pages of *Black Rainbow*, he traces a conversation between Eric and Margaret, describing the light fading, summer ending, Margaret's desire to return home before winter, and the Indigenous peoples who once inhabited Maungakiekie in Auckland (9–10). When we try to settle on a person, moment, or place in these lines, we are drawn away, toward other times, places, or inhabitants. At the end of the novel, Wendt again describes the world in terms of ungraspable excess. After being captured and put on trial by the Tribunal, Eric is made to select among several sentences, opting for death. We learn that the Tribunal dreamed up and created his character, arranged his search for his family, and screened the search to the nation as a reality television show. While registering the prying, brutal control that the Tribunal has had over his life, Foster insists that he is more than what the Tribunal has known him to be, more even than what he has grasped: "I am of the worlds of the Tangata Maori and Tangata Moni and the abandoned Patimaori and his family and circumstances; of the highly trained assassin Supremo Jones and his adopted parents, the President and the Tribunal; of the timid loyal citizen Eric Mailei Foster, who through his courageous wife and children learned the meaning of love, adventure and courage. I am all that and more" (264).

In exploring modes of being that are excessive to the utopians' definitions of the existing world, Wendt evokes extensive environmental loss, which is shaped particularly by the military activities that secure the utopia's survival. It is difficult to apprehend such loss, because the utopia eliminated, rather than simply altered, many ecosystems. While searching for his family, Eric encounters a "road that was a river" and native forest that was "a careful replacement" (200). The utopian state forbids the memories and histories that might link people to vanished ecosystems and that would consequently provide a critical perspective on the ecology of the utopia. Wendt reveals histories of environmental loss primarily through the language of *Black Rainbow*, because the utopians have not been able to eliminate names and words as quickly as they have been able to wipe out places and life forms. Gravel on the streets of Auckland city crunches "like dry fish bones" (11). Trucks pass by "like whales groping through limestone seas" (36). The city is "a forest of high-rise apartment buildings" (75). Darkness creeps over the city, "like a black-furred sea" (135). Traffic surges "like metallic sea creatures" (141). Dawn washes away the darkness "like a school of white jellyfish, over the city" (155). Wendt takes language that we might expect to designate the sea and its life and applies it to the city. Directed onto something unexpected, the language is disorienting, characterizing not only the city but also drawing attention to ecosystems that are missing.

Many of *Black Rainbow*'s references to environmental loss orient readers from the city toward the sea and sea animals, as do Eric's recurring dreams of water and of drowning. Early in the novel, he dreams of watching as his body absorbs "luminous water. . . . Up to my knees, then belly button, chest, as heavy as mercury" (24). Another dream, where whales "bled under a sun that didn't move across the sky," evokes the visual effects of a nuclear bomb blast (152). Eric's dreams call up oceanic histories of militarization and environmental activism, including the Greenpeace ship *Rainbow Warrior*'s multiple campaigns against whaling and the drowning of photographer Fernando Pereira when French government agents detonated bombs on the ship in Auckland in 1985. In repeatedly referencing hurt or missing sea creatures, Wendt evokes the impacts of nuclear weapons on the human and nonhuman life of the ocean. Most of the beings who inhabited the sites blasted by nuclear weapons were not human. In addition to destroying corals, fish, trees, and entire land forms, the United States used thousands of nonhuman beings as test subjects, including pigs, rats, goats, mice, and guinea pigs. These beings were used to make scientifically sensible the process of being destroyed by a nuclear bomb.

As well as hinting at environmental loss in the utopia's oceanic hinterlands, Wendt draws us toward people whose lives have been marginalized in the thick of the utopia. He archaeologically excavates the city of Auckland to find the Tangata Moni, a dispersed class of people who exist in infrastructures beneath the buildings. The Tangata Moni formed when Māori connected with other people from the Pacific Islands and with a number of "Pakeha/palagi," who saw injustice in the utopia (158). They speak a mixture of English, Polynesian, and Street Pidgin. Befriending several Tangata Moni, Eric learns about unseen dimensions of the city:

"Sewage systems, tunnels, communication and power links and lines, forgotten byways and drains, nooks and crannies they used as home, as safehouses. A city underneath a city, holding it up. 'A city is layers of maps and geographies, layers of them, centuries of it. We were the first, our ancestors, no matter what lies the Tribunal says. . . .'" (134). Sheltering in the infrastructures that transport water, sewage, electricity, and communications, the Tangata Moni maintain relative difference from the Tribunal.

The processes of loss that haunt the utopia—from the marginalization of the Tangata Moni deep beneath the city, to apparently vanished oceanic species and ecosystems—reveal the militarized, colonial histories through which the utopia came into existence, as well as continued conflict. The utopia places immense pressure on the land in order to maintain a capitalist, techno-scientific way of life. Observing the seas of grass and cities that have replaced forests, Eric tells the Tribunal, "Your country is all grass which you turn into meat" (16). The Tribunal consequently maintains a combative relationship with those people who make other claims on this land. Early in the novel, Eric and Margaret run onto the volcano Maungakiekie, where they observe a memorial to the Māori people who once lived in the area. Margaret suggests that the "original people" are "still here, aren't they? The Pakeha have changed even the vegetation but *they're* still here" (12). She interprets the existing world differently than the utopian government, emphasizing Indigenous peoples' continuity in a way that calls into question the legitimacy of the utopians' occupation and use of the land. Shortly after this scene, Eric wakes up to find that Margaret has vanished. We later find out that she was taken by the Tribunal.

As people continue to live in ways that are distinct from the modes of life authorized by the utopian state, and because these people might undermine the utopians' claims to the land and its life, the utopia's violence continues, taking forms such as disappearance, surveillance, torture, and biological manipulation. The utopians attempt to secure their world by disturbing or destroying the lives, and indeed the ecological and political worlds, of others. Among the many literary references that we brush up against and usually pass over quickly in *Black Rainbow*, Wendt repeatedly engages *Faces in the Water*, a novel by European New Zealand writer Janet Frame (2005). In this 1961 novel, which likely evokes New Zealand in the 1940s and 1950s, Frame traces the lives of psychiatric patients as well as of those who care for them, "our Red Cross who will provide us with ointment and bandages for our wounds and remove the foreign ideas the glass

beads of fantasy the bent hairpins of unreason embedded in our minds"
(31). Frame was born in 1924 and spent almost a decade in psychiatric institutions undergoing electric shock treatment. She was scheduled to have
a leucotomy, but it was canceled at the last minute when she won a literary
prize for *The Lagoon and Other Stories* (Gordon 2005, 17–18). A nurse from
Faces in the Water appears in *Black Rainbow* and tortures Eric for informa-
tion about his family (56–62). *Faces in the Water* and *Black Rainbow* both
engage state efforts to make particular forms of human being. In *Faces in
the Water,* Frame describes institutional attempts to position psychiatric
patients within certain interpretations of health and affective life: "You
learned with earnest dedication to 'fit in'; you learned not to cry in company but to smile and pronounce yourself pleased" (2005, 57–58). In *Black
Rainbow,* the Tribunal places the Tangata Moni in "reordinarination cen-
tres," where they will be biologically remade into nonresistant "citizens,"
because the Tribunal "doesn't want us as we are" (143, 144). Both writers
observe state, and more broadly social, efforts to eliminate the difference
and unpredictability of singular people or social groups, "the foreign ideas
the glass beads of fantasy the bent hairpins of unreason" (Frame 2005, 31).
In *Faces in the Water,* Istina Mavet is told that electric shock treatment is
for her own good. "'For your own good',' observes Frame, "is a persua-
sive argument that will eventually make man agree to his own destruction"
(2005, 84). All manner of life forms fall into the perilous, often unsurviv-
able chasm between what is and what ought to be.

The Tribunal's conflicts with those who live differently are not simply
located in the spaces of institutions but are broadly economic and militarized. Wendt's oblique references to nuclear weapons testing—which
include Eric's dreams of drowning, the language that associates the city
with the ocean, and Hotere's *Black Rainbow* lithograph—can be understood in this context. The utopian government exerts physical power to
secure land and resources and to hold back opposition, so the utopia is not
possible without the suffering that takes form in weapons development.
But Eric is unable or unwilling to apprehend the military activities that
shape his experiences of security and economy. Wendt's references to the
nuclear testing programs mark a structural fault in the utopia, the impossibility of all people or nonhumans ever reaching it despite its supposedly
global reach, since the hurt of peoples in some sites underlies the possibilities of wealth and national security in other sites. Beneath the rapidly
moving and changing surface of *Black Rainbow,* then, we find a tenacious

confrontation with loss. Wendt traces loss in the thick of the utopia's most celebrated spaces as well as in the imaginatively marginalized ocean. He also suggests that such loss is likely to continue. The utopians eliminate or injure those human and nonhuman beings who are physically in their way or whose disagreement, hurt, and pain reveals faults in the story of this world as a utopia.

Hope in a Place of Loss

Perhaps a story in which the present world is without loss—the story promoted by utopian institutions in *Black Rainbow*—would allow for hope, an awareness of a promising, open future. Certainly, some commentators suggest that hope equates to blindness to the environmental damage that characterizes existing life and heavily inhabits projected futures.[14] Yet, if the world were experienced as entirely without realities of damage and loss, it is hard to see why hope would exist. In *Black Rainbow,* Wendt suggests that the narrative of Eric's world as a completed utopia undermines people's ability to engage not only loss but inseparably also to hope. He associates hope with people's efforts to repair damaged ecosystems, to remember and care for the dead, and to confront social injustices. Such efforts imply that this world is not finished, countering official utopian narratives that define current conditions—peace and oneness with Earth—as "forever" (73). The term *forever* imaginatively eliminates the potential for a future that is different from the present, because the future is already known and, indeed, has already been realized. Hope, in contrast, requires awareness that the future is a site of openness, or is not yet fully determined.[15]

In interviews and essays, Wendt argues that European and U.S. utopian thought about the Pacific elides hope. He describes Margaret Mead as "part of that escapist tradition which began with the Papalagi's search for El Dorado and the Noble Savage; a utopian mirror she was holding up to industrialised societies' ills" (1990, 70). Mead was a U.S. anthropologist who arrived in Samoa during the 1920s, a time when ethnographers and documentary filmmakers sought to archive Pacific cultures. Their efforts were inflected with ideas of emergency drawn from nineteenth-century fatal impact narratives, which said that Pacific places and peoples were not surviving the arrival of the modern (Geiger 2007, 133–36).[16] Mead framed ethnography as an American rescue project directed at cultures said to everywhere be vanishing in the face of the advancement of the West (Geiger 2007, 133–134). Her book, *Coming of Age in Samoa* (1943 [1928]), famously associates Samoan girls with a sexual freedom thought to be absent in the United States. In the words of contemporary Samoan writer Sia Figiel, *Coming of Age in Samoa* is "a book on Samoan girls doing 'it' a lot . . . and they were loving and loved 'it' too" (1999 [1996], 209). Wendt argues that his own creative work is "contrary to Mead's attractive but superficial stereotyped paradise" and engages "a Samoa with all the emotions, problems, hopes, and so on, common to humanity" (qtd. in Sharrard 2003, 26). He suggests that utopian narratives elide hope as a mode of engagement in Samoa. Rather than suggesting that such hope exists because Samoa is an alternative world, Wendt insists that Samoans are part of humanity and that hope coexists with other modes of being.

If we turn from Wendt's theorization of hope back to *Black Rainbow,* we may find that the novel evokes a partly promising, open future through engagement with the troubled world in which Eric lives rather than through recourse to an alternative world. It is difficult to miss the fact that the early European utopias of the Pacific are crafted to provoke thought about promising futures. But concern to allow for hope may be formally and thematically difficult to apprehend if it is tightly woven into a literary world focused on representing some of the most extreme forms of imperial, capitalist, and militaristic violence. In *Black Rainbow,* hope may be illuminated in a narrative also crafted in terms of rage, despair, and sorrow.

In exploring this possibility, we might begin with the black rainbow that names Wendt's novel. In an interview, Wendt describes black and darkness as bearing "very racist meanings in the English language, so we must decolonize the language too. . . . When I studied art, I was told by my art teacher not to use too much black in my painting because it kills the other colours. Ralph Hotere has reversed all that . . . we were not living in Darkness as defined by the missionaries, we were living in the Darkness of Creation and Possibility! (qtd. in Sharrard 2003, 207). He describes his own paintings and drawings as "using form and color, to explore the pōuliuli, the darkness. I love black. But I think the way I use black is not threatening, but elegant and fertile" (qtd. in Hereniko 2006, 63).

Hotere's black rainbow lithograph evokes possibility in referencing the nuclear-free and decolonization struggles that raged in the Pacific during the 1970s–90s and that spanned governments, local organizations, individuals, and transnational entities such as Greenpeace.[17] The people involved in these struggles were not always able to stop the horrors that they addressed, but their achievements are multiple and still shape life in the ocean today. It would be impossible here to convey their detail and scope. A significant organization, the ATOM (Against Tests on Moruroa [Mururoa]) Committee of Suva, Fiji, took form after a public meeting about French nuclear testing. The meeting was held in 1970 and sponsored by the Fiji Young Women's Christian Association, the Fiji Council of Churches, and the University of the South Pacific Students Association. ATOM produced pamphlets, press releases, and a newsletter, liaised with nuclear-free organizations, supported protest events, circulated scientific research on the impacts of exposure to radiation, and advocated for Pacific governmental responses, seeking to shape action on nuclear weapons at the level of the United Nations and the International Court of Justice (Johnson and Tupouniua 1976, 213–15). They organized a 1975 Conference for a Nuclear-Free Pacific, which was attended by about eighty-five organizations from the ocean (Johnson and Tupouniua 1976, 213, 216). The Nuclear-Free and Independent Pacific (NFIP) movement, an expansive oceanic coalition involving environmentalists, trade-union members, churches, aid organizations, and women's groups, emerged through ATOM's activities (Firth 2005, 361–62; Teaiwa 1994, 99–100). Stewart Firth argues that one of the long-term achievements of the NFIP movement "was to legitimize the idea of a nuclear-free Pacific, so that independent governments of the region had no alternative but to endorse it. . . . A simple but powerful idea had become the property of ordinary people throughout the region" (2005, 361–62). The meanings of a nuclear-free Pacific were, and are, multiple. An entangled concern in the archives of ATOM and the NFIP movements is that Pacific peoples be able to shape their oceanic home and its futures on their own terms. Such a concern pulls together nuclear-free struggles with decolonization and Indigenous peoples' rights.

Among the many achievements of these turbulent decades came the world's first nuclear-free constitution, created in Palau (Belau) in 1979 and democratically adopted in 1981. The United States aggressively undermined the nuclear-free dimensions of Palau's constitution, seeking continued nuclear presence in Palau through the Compact of Free Association, which defines the relationship between the United States and Palau in the wake of the United States' administration of Palau as part of a United Nations Trust Territory. Palauan intellectual Richard N. Salvador writes of the compact, "This is the treaty that the United States was adamant in compelling Belau to adopt, and which after 15 years and seven attempts to say NO to it, was finally 'approved' in 1993. The treaty has essentially laid to rest the nuclear-free provisions of Belau's Constitution for 50 years; the US, in return, will give Belau some economic assistance only for 15 years" (1999 n.p.).[18] The highly recognizable archive of a nuclear-free constitution, while tremendously significant, can barely take us beneath the surface of the painstaking and often undocumented ways in which people have interacted with the violence of nuclear weapons in the Pacific. Barbara Rose Johnston and Holly M. Barker's *The Rongelap Report: Consequential Damages of Nuclear War* (2008), which is based on archives, oral histories, and ethnography drawn from collaborative research with Marshallese people, provides some sense of peoples' ordinary and extraordinary struggles to survive and to advocate for justice in relation to nuclear weapons.

To return to Hotere's lithograph and Wendt's novel, we might understand the blackening of the rainbow to evoke not only the violence of nuclear weapons but also the creativity that emerged or survived in everyday worlds deeply affected by these weapons. In *Black Rainbow*, Wendt brings this insight—that realities of loss and violence might in complicated ways be a site of creativity and potential, and might include hope, among other modes of engagement—to bear on his story about a different, although connected, context of environmental loss in Auckland city. He associates hope with efforts to engage that loss, and so necessarily with the human and nonhuman beings that exist in the present world, suggesting that they evoke a future that is partially open and promising.

Until Eric interacts with the Tangata Moni, the people who live in subterranean urban infrastructures, he is largely oblivious to heterogeneity and conflict in the utopia. The Tangata Moni exist differently than the utopians in speaking of historical and present injustices and in cultivating a critical and wary outlook instead of seeing the world as completed. Wendt does not romanticize the implications of their alternative way of life. They were born in exile from the possibility of easily inhabiting the utopia, and they face police brutality and economic hardship as they struggle to survive on the streets or in welfare homes. Manu and Fantail, who befriend Eric, were raised by their aunt and saw her "waste away with the long slog and sorrow and poverty. . . . She suffered more when we refused to become 'good' law-abiding kids. How could we? This society, yeah, the President's heaven-on-earth, doesn't want us as we are" (144). The relationship between the Tangata Moni and the utopia is always ambiguous. Wendt goes so far as to evoke the possibility that the state has programmed the Tangata Moni's resistance as a form of entertainment and as a threat that justifies extreme security measures (238–39). The state's far-reaching powers to shape biological life remind Eric of the animated world of Disney: "The world of Toon Town and its cartoon characters, created since Walt Disney invented the form, are an everyday part of our lives, and we and our world are a part of theirs. . . . And it is frightening because it was the reality the Tribunal had created and in which I was just one of its cartoon characters which it could erase or dissolve in turpentine" (214). *Who Framed Roger Rabbit?*, Wendt suggests, is "a complex and profound statement about reality" (214). These observations resonate with a 1931 fragment titled "Mickey Mouse" in which Walter Benjamin sees the Disney cartoons as "unsymbolically" and "unatmospherically" speaking about existing life (1999a, 545). Benjamin argues that workers can apprehend themselves in the mouse, which illuminates capitalist property relations that extend to the body: "Property relations in Mickey Mouse cartoons: here we see for the first time that it is possible to have one's own arm, even one's own body, stolen" (1999, 545). In *Black Rainbow,* Eric recognizes himself, and specifically the manipulation of his body, in a Disney cartoon: "it is frightening because it was the reality the Tribunal had created and in which I was just one of its cartoon characters which it could erase or dissolve in turpentine" (214).

Although the utopian state exerts brutal, prying forms of power, in order to do so it must draw on a world that it did not alone make, as is evident in the colonial histories through which it accumulated land and inhabitants. It continues to come up against agents that survive its manipulations in excessive, unpredictable ways. If people exceed its plans, acting in ways that it did not program, the Tribunal describes them as "reverting," situating them as heading backward and as of the past (227). But such people alter the present world and its potential futures. The Tangata Moni, in particular, embody an actually and potentially very different way of living with others, one that is critical and wary of institutions, that involves politics of social difference, and that engages history and associated injustice. They remember the dead and colonial history, disagree with the utopians' present ways of life, and are able to alter the perspectives of utopians such as Eric. The Tangata Moni's ways of life never become hegemonic in *Black Rainbow.* But they embody an unsettling uncertainty regarding what exists in this world and the futures it might shape, clearly exceeding the utopian claims that this world constitutes peace and well-being and "is forever" (70). As Eric puts it, "The Tribunal tries to rule out all uncertainty and chaos. So we scare them because, by living deliberately outside their Rules, we are some of that uncertainty" (236). Such uncertainty is not simply imaginable in terms of a variety of bleak futures in *Black Rainbow;* Wendt faintly but unmistakably associates promise with the Tangata Moni's insistence on politics of difference and of memory.

Wendt also sees possibility in how people live, and might live, with nonhuman beings. Eric apprehends the world in terms of myriad sentient beings. Toward the end of the novel, he retreats to a lake, climbing through a forest where he is watched by a pigeon and feels that it "seemed to return my greeting" (190). He sits with it and the "silence was long and sad," evoking the profound marginalization of this being through the environmental transformations of the colonial history (190). While uncertain, Eric describes an interaction in which the pigeon observes, rather than simply is observed. He finds sentient beings throughout the utopia, suggesting that as the city grows dark, "night was walking across the water and stretching up into the heavens" (40). Buildings, too, are alive: "Around us the forest of cloned apartments held up the dark with its millions of eyes" (79). Eric acts on this awareness of coexistence partly through his conspicuous vegetarianism. When asked by the Tribunal to reflect on his vegetarianism, Eric ponders the transformation of the archipelago into farmland, reminding the utopians of their colonial history (16). Although Eric's vegetarianism does not otherwise particularly disturb the utopians, his way of understanding suggests that the concerns of nonhuman beings could shape the political life of the utopia. The utopia elides and materially undermines such a potential, however. For example, the utopians do not permit any vegetation in their headquarters, implying that nonhumans' modes of being are in no way to define utopian politics (69).

Nonhuman beings never recover in *Black Rainbow,* just as the Tangata Moni do not overthrow the hegemonic economic and military infrastructures of the utopia. Wendt simply evokes the possibility that the Tangata Moni, the *Black Rainbow* lithograph, and some marginalized nonhuman beings will survive, and that their survival bodes an uncertain, partly good future. In one of the book's possible endings, Eric is put on trial by the Tribunal. Before his execution, he asks the Tribunal to leave his Tangata Moni friends alone (267). He also buries the lithograph, and it continues to make a ticking sound, suggesting that it too may persist and one day may again call up memories of the ocean and nuclear weapons (243). The utopia, as Wendt situates it in *Black Rainbow,* is shadowed by past environmental loss. It is also haunted by the heterogeneous realities of its inhabitants and the varied futures that they evoke. Wendt reveals future promise and openness in writing of people's efforts and abilities to recognize the utopia's violence and to live differently. The utopians' effort to forbid people from seeing and addressing such violence is a way of denying hope. Hope is not a means of ignoring or affirming the damage brought by nuclear weapons and other forms of aggression. It emerges in efforts to engage the existing world and its pasts and is consequently closely allied to awareness of loss and responses such as sorrow. Indeed, because the Tangata Moni live differently and so suggest openness, or room for maneuverability, in the futures that the present might shape, they become subject to further violence from the utopian state. In *Black Rainbow,* hope involves an engagement with loss but poignantly such an effort also catalyzes further violence. Wendt insists on awareness of multivalent, dynamic relationships between hope and other modes of engagement. He illuminates hope through a narrative that places emphasis on loss, horror, and destruction rather than on a world in which all has been made right.

Unrealistic Hope

In conditions of environmental violence that has extended over decades and that in many ways is irreversible, hope may come into focus not simply for its precarious relationships with loss, but also as a failure to engage the world in a more realistic way. Early in Hawai'i-based writer Robert Barclay's *Meļaļ: A Novel of the Pacific* (2002), Ņoniep, a little person of the jungle and the spirit world, "dreams of a plan, a hope, a small and unrealistic chance of stopping what looms like a monstrous wave risen to a precarious height" (14). In what kind of place might a person experience their hope as about to be violently crushed? What would make hope realistic, and what are the implications of such a way of addressing hope? In *Meļaļ,* Barclay engages the places of nuclear weapons testing more directly than does Wendt in *Black Rainbow.* Barclay traces the lives of Rujen Keju and his sons, Jebro and Nuke, across Good Friday 1981 on Ebeye Island in the stressed environmental context of a military occupation. Barclay spent some of his childhood at the U.S. military base on Kwajalein Island in Kwajalein

Atoll (Kiste 2004, 208). People have lived in this part of the Earth for about 2,000 years, facing multiple, interlocked imperialisms from Spain, Germany, Japan, and the United States (Republic of the Marshall Islands et al. 2007, 1.1.1). Invading the Marshall Islands in 1944 and ending the Japanese occupation, the United States administered the Marshall Islands as part of a United Nations trust territory. Between 1946 and 1958, the U.S. government conducted sixty-seven nuclear weapons tests at Bikini Atoll and Enewetak (Eniwetok) Atoll, exposing thousands of Marshallese people to radioactive fallout and contaminating, blasting, or entirely vaporizing marine and terrestrial ecosystems (Johnston and Barker 2008, 17, 43). Today, the U.S. military uses Kwajalein Atoll in testing long-range missiles that are launched from California. These missiles are in development for deployment in more recognizable sites of war elsewhere.

   After using nuclear weapons to kill hundreds of thousands of people at Hiroshima and Nagasaki, the U.S. government worked to counter opposition to these weapons' continued deployment, associating them with a magical capacity to bring global peace and well-being (Cordle 2008, 11–12; Nilsen 2011, 87). In 1946, the U.S. military governor of the Marshall Islands reportedly told the people of Bikini Atoll that they needed to be relocated so that a new bomb could be tested for "the good of mankind and to end all world wars" and "for the welfare of all men" (qtd. in Alexander 1994, 21). He likened the Bikini Islanders to "the Children of Israel whom the Lord had saved from their enemy and led into the Promised Land" (qtd. in Alexander 1994, 21). Although the military governor's story of peace and welfare evokes a promising future, it cannot well be understood as a story that allows for hope. In picturing devastating war as the sole alternative to nuclear weapons development, it is designed to allow people very little or no awareness of openness in their futures. Michel Foucault observes that atomic weapons work to lock the world into just one means of reaching a promising future: "The power to expose a whole population to death is the underside of the power to guarantee an individual's continued existence" (1978, 137).

   The U.S. military governor's abstract story of a global future also lures us far away from the lived and differential consequences of nuclear weapons, the human and nonhuman beings irreversibly falling away from its luminous world of peace. Barclay begins Me̗ḷa̗ḷ with an epigraph from a 1968 petition that was signed by displaced Marshallese people who request permission to return to their homes. The petition speaks to the association that the U.S. military made between nuclear weapons and peace: "We believe in peace and love, not in the display of power to destroy mankind. If maintaining peace means killing and destruction of the fruits of man's efforts to build himself a better world, we desire no part of it" (1). Moving away from an abstract imaginary of a future that is dissociated from concerns about present reality, the petition engages what peace means in contingent contexts. In the opening scenes of *Meļaļ*, Barclay likewise turns attention toward the profound impacts of nuclear weapons and other military activities on lived contexts. He sketches Ebeye Island as a place where it is difficult to hold things together. Rujen Keju awakens to a blackout, sewage coming up through the sink, and the debris of commodities such as plastic flowers in vases made of Pepsi cans (3–5). "German roaches" scuttle around the house, like the Pepsi cans reflecting the force exerted by layered imperial histories on this material world (4). As Rujen walks across Ebeye to the boat that will take him to Kwajalein Island, where he works in the sewage treatment plant at the military base, we are drawn from image to image of environmental damage. The reef is "strewn with rusting twisted piles of cars and trucks and heavy machinery, some of it looking to be the remains of bulldozers and a crane, all of it blistered and fusing together in different shades of orange and black and casting long jagged shadows" (9). Many things run together in this long sentence, which formally reflects its themes of fusion, heat, and meltdown, evoking the virtually unimaginable force exerted by nuclear bombs in the Marshall Islands: "These tests unleashed the equivalent power of 1.7 Hiroshima bombs every day for twelve years" (Kahn 2009, 402). Barclay captures the long-term, everyday, and spatially diffuse violence of the bombs in linking them to Ebeye Island, which was not the direct target of any bomb.[19] We learn that Rujen's family came to Ebeye after being displaced from Tar-Wōj in 1965 (23). After the Second World War, the United States opened up space for military activities by relocating varied Marshallese peoples to Ebeye Island. These people formed a labor source for the nearby military base. As their population rapidly grew, infrastructures such as housing, schools, sewage and freshwater systems, and medical facilities became inadequate. Barclay describes Ebeye as a place where blackouts and the discharge of raw sewage into the lagoon are common, and where there is no adequate hospital, even though its people bear many radiation-related injuries. He also tells us that Rujen's wife Iia was coated by radioactive fallout from Bravo shot while living on Rongelap Atoll, and that she later died during a miscarriage. As Bravo exploded on March 1, 1954, it melted coral atoll and blasted it into the atmosphere, combining it with radiation and then dropping it on atolls and islands, including on Rongelap, Ailinginae, Ailuk, Bikar, Likiep, Rongerik, Taka, Wotho, Utrik, Jemo, and Mejit, as well as on U.S. military personnel and a Japanese fishing boat (Alexander 1994, 28; Johnston and Barker 2008, 17). The people of Rongelap played in the fallout and drank contaminated water. They face severe health difficulties, including miscarriages and the birth of badly injured children, as well as cancers and other diseases (Alexander 1994, 29–31; Johnston and Barker 2008).

For some people, this world and the futures that it promises are unbearable. Barclay observes the high occurrence of suicide among young, unemployed men of Ebeye Island. The Marshallese community provides them with food, clothing, and shelter, but they have nothing to occupy their energy and time: "Nobody relied on them, nobody could make any use of them, nobody asked for their advice, and as if by some design, their idle minds found troubled thoughts, while their idle hands found rope and learned to tie a noose" (93). Jebro suggests that they experience their lives as without meaningful content, momentum, or potential, as "full of nothing" and with "no reason to keep living, nothing to look forward to" (129). These young people's experiences evoke the unusual economic context of the U.S. occupation, which centered on the damage of sites for weapons development. Such a regime has little use for the local people, beyond those people who work in military facilities or whose damaged bodies have been used in U.S. scientific research on human exposure to radioactive fallout.[20] Ebeye Island, writes Barclay, is a place of "souls seething in a pile in the middle of the dump" (283).

It is not that Barclay sees this place as without pleasures, peace, or happiness. Meļaļ is striking in its expressions of love, playfulness, and humor, which characterize many interactions between people, nonhuman beings, and the mischievous inhabitants of the spirit world: "The gentle people of Ebeye, their tiny island barren as a sand spit, more filthy and more crowded than almost any other place on Earth, have managed to live in peace, to find happiness at times despite their plague of demons" (283). Some of Barclay's characters also see in this world the capacities for the care of the hurt, displaced, and dead. Ņoniep, in particular, seeks to defeat the demons that torment the living of Ebeye Island. He experiences his hope as "small and unrealistic" (14).

It is perhaps tempting to dismiss hope as a mistaken assessment of reality, or more troublingly, as no assessment of reality at all, a willful turn
away from conditions that could be more accurately felt in terms of despair.[21] Utopia is often similarly framed as a delusional mode of existence,
having become a derogatory adjective for any way (at all) of imagining a
good state of being that transgresses what someone feels is realistic and
grounded.[22] Making claims on reality, including on damages and potentials, is vital in the Pacific, where foreign governments have been reluctant to survey the damage that their weapons have created, even in using
their own methods, as well as to ensure environmental remediation and
to support effective health care and education. Such concerns also mark
ecocriticism at this time when powerful institutions undermine scientific and other explanations of environmental change. Greg Garrard ends
Ecocriticism: The New Critical Idiom in affirming the Eden Project—an as-
semblage of biomes and socioecological projects in Cornwall, England—
because it is "a great-souled vision with its feet planted solidly on the
ground" (2004, 182).

The question of whether hope is grounded and realistic, and whether
or not this matters, cannot be settled in an absolute, abstract way. It should
be addressed in relation to specific contexts and with concern for whose
claim on reality is being privileged. In *Meḷaḷ*, it quickly becomes clear that
while Ṇoniep experiences his hope as "unrealistic," this hope is not unrealistic in the context of the broader, collective potentials of the world in
which Ṇoniep lives. In parallel with Ṇoniep's struggle to defeat the demons
on Ebeye Island, Barclay tells a story in which three boys from the U.S.
base capsize Jebro and Nuke's boat and then flee the scene, leaving Jebro
and Nuke adrift in the ocean. As Jebro and Nuke fight to hold onto life, the
Americans eventually rethink their actions and return, helping them from
the water, and negotiating terms with them regarding the provision of a
new boat. Barclay not-so-subtly connects this story to his broader insistence that the United States acknowledge responsibility for its role in the
conditions of life on Ebeye Island and support the Marshallese peoples'
recovery. He tells us that the name Ebeye is drawn from the ancient word
epjā, "short for *epliklik jā*: Mostly capsized" (92). Just before this line, he
outlines several mundane, concrete pathways to more viable conditions
on Ebeye Island: "More than anything," there is need for a decent hospital,
new sewage and freshwater systems, power plant repairs, and a causeway
to increase living space by connecting Ebeye to other islands (92).[23]

Barclay offers hope in making a claim on limited, concrete potential to maneuver in the world in which his characters live, rather than in imagining an abstract, detached future. It is hard to imagine how he could do otherwise, since his characters bear the irreversible marks of the military histories in their bodies, in their memories of the dead, and in their ways of imagining, such that Rujen and Iia name their son Nuke.[24] He ends *Meḷaḷ* with an uncertain claim that one day the living and the dead might be able to grieve and better thrive in their world, rather than with a vision of complete repair. Ṇoniep overcomes the demons who have settled on Ebeye, and then collects the souls piled at a dump site and takes them to Ewerōk, an "eternal paradise for the souls of the dead" (297). Once they arrive at Ewerōk, the spirit Ḷōrōk tells Ṇoniep that this place where souls "want for nothing, need nothing" is not a happy place, because here the souls "have no use for themselves" (298). Ḷōrōk suggests that Ṇoniep take the souls back to their ancestral islands and ocean, where they can cause mischief among the people (298–99). Barclay associates a promising future with a restless world that is not entirely free from sorrow or conflict rather than with eternal perfection. After following Ḷōrōk's advice, Ṇoniep is finally left with the souls of the jellyfish babies, or the souls of the Marshallese children who were born in unlivable forms because their parents were exposed to radioactive fallout. In the last lines of the book, he pairs whale souls with jellyfish baby souls, "so that over time, with love, they might stop their squalling and maybe even learn to sing" (300). The dead are embodied, renewed, and remembered in the living. Over time, such relationships may make some of the hurt, confusion, and sorrow felt by the dead less alive and less violent. Such a possibility emerges not from forgetting but from addressing the hurt faced by the dead. Their loss can never be reversed, but that does not mean there are no potentials for healing left in this world.

Critiques of hope that focus on its blindness to more realistic ways of interacting with the world may risk eliding the power dynamics that shape what someone feels is realistic as well as the remaining potentials for maneuvering in conditions of severe environmental damage. They also conflate an assessment of hope's productivity with an idea about the content that informs it. Hope is not simply reducible to someone's effort or ability to realize an imaginary of the future. For example, as a boy, Rujen collected magazines, catalogs, and other materials that contained images of the world beyond Kwajalein Atoll. He "saved those pages he would need later to guide him around the Earth" (57). He hid the materials in a safe place, holding onto an awareness of future possibility in the context of severely curtailed geographical mobility inside the Marshall Islands, let alone beyond. Rujen remembers the travel materials as he walks into an elementary school on Kwajalein Island, a privileged space that might allow him to experience global travel but from which he is excluded. He then recalls his earliest memory, in which he sees an airplane flying over his home island and stretches toward it "with his hand as the plane banked toward Kwajalein and flew out of sight" (57). In aspiring to touch the world of the airplane, Rujen reaches toward potentials that presumably have become compelling partly through the U.S. military presence in the Marshall Islands but that remain out of reach. The future that Rujen imagines in relation to the visible infrastructures of international mobility is not well understood as unrealistic. He can see the airplanes and schools that would enable him to realize such mobility, but his access to these infrastructures is blocked by political, social, and economic contingencies. Rujen does not ever travel internationally in Mȩla̧l, but his hope has a different creativity. His tenuous dream of one day visiting selected places around the world adds a little more pleasure and interest to daily life: "What he really liked was looking through magazines. . . . At times, when he had the maps spread out, he would pretend that he was looking down from an airplane, bringing the maps close to his face as he dived in for a closer look" (57–58). Hope is important as a lived mode of engagement, rather than simply for any future toward which it might, or might not, contribute.[25] For Rujen, imaginaries of travel provide a small moment of pleasure in a life often characterized by exhaustion and loss.

Rujen's imaginary of flying draws on a model of economic success and personal social mobility conditioned by the U.S. military presence in the Marshall Islands. Compared to the sharp resistance undertaken by nuclear-free and decolonization movements, or even the structural critiques made in utopian literatures, a dream of flying, and the promising, open futures such a dream inspires, might appear to be a weak mode of engagement. But such a reading of Rujen's hope, with its implicit desire for hope to be drawn from practices that in a straightforward way resist the military occupation, would risk naivety regarding the economic and political duress that shapes Rujen's modes of engagement. We see such pressure when Rujen reacts to Jebro's plans to take Nuke to their home island, Tar-Wōj. Such a visit would be illegal from the perspective of the

U.S. military, and Rujen expresses fear that if the Americans catch Jebro at Tar-Wōj, Jebro will lose his opportunity to work at the military base's sewage plant (10). Having a job matters, because food cannot be caught or grown on Ebeye: "On Ebeye, the land did not support very much life, boasted no crops, few pigs, no ground water, no jungle, no grass, no stands of fruit-bearing trees. The people's lives were sustained not by the land but by money flowing in and then out like the tide" (79).[26] Rujen experiences physical hurt and endangerment when he is not able to meet the basic economic needs of this life. When his work boots disappear, he is unable to quickly replace them. Barclay repeatedly describes Rujen's pain on wearing old, borrowed boots that do not fit well, as well as the danger that his injured feet will get infected: "His ankles were raw, one of his toes was badly swollen by a spider bite, dried blood caked another toe where he had stubbed it while walking to work, and the bottoms of his feet were so badly blistered they looked as though they might have been held over a fire" (113). Rujen thinks of the people of Ebeye who "neglected their sores, some losing limbs or dying from blood poisoning" (114).

While Barclay insists on the immense legitimacy of the hope allowed for by materialistic dreams in this place, he also suggests that hope can have multivalent and sometimes unpredicted relationships with the dominant forms of life in which it seems trapped and that make it continuously precarious. Rujen's imaginary of global travel contributes to his emerging, critical understanding of socioeconomic injustices in the Marshall Islands. On recalling how much he liked to collect maps, Rujen suddenly feels that his life has no meaning and that he will simply disappear (58). Later, he again remembers the maps, wondering where he hid them and "feeling strangely uncomfortable" (112). Rujen's discomfort in relation to his memory of the maps joins his broader sense of "some distress, some mystery, which it seemed he didn't have either the ability or the will to face" (121). His barely understood feeling of unease and distress builds, and eventually he is able to articulate it around the injustice of a conflict between Americans and Marshallese regarding two dolphins that swim into the lagoon. Several people catch the dolphins and place them in the turtle pond on Kwajalein Island, with the intent of later killing them in accordance with the Marshallese understanding that to refuse this gift would bring bad luck (120). One of Rujen's American coworkers tells him that it is illegal to kill the dolphins. When Rujen responds that he has never heard about such a rule, except in relation to Marshallese restrictions on specific catches at times such as breeding season, his colleague replies, "U.S. law" (97). Following several more incidents in which Americans ignore or malign Marshallese perspectives, Rujen approaches the turtle pond and kills one of the dolphins. As Jebro puts it, too often "American *justice*" prevails in the home of the Marshallese people (220). In this small instance, Rujen asserts the survival of Marshallese ecological practices and their primacy in the Marshall Islands. His hope of flying does not transform into an attempt to find a way to travel internationally, but it does contribute to his critical awareness of the injustice inherent in the difficulty of realizing dreams that are drawn from observations of ways of life made particularly visible by the U.S. military presence. His hope is creative in ways that are not visible simply in terms of the content that he initially attributed to it.

In *Meḷaḷ*, then, Barclay imagines and offers hope in a place where hope seems impossible or unrealistic, given conditions of severe, long-term violence. Rujen's and Ṇoniep's hope draws from and supports their efforts to address their community's hurt and loss. It involves apprehending a world that is open to questioning and maneuverability, where potential exists for creativity. Such potentials are not always realized in *Meḷaḷ*. Barclay suggests that hope's force in the lived moment and beyond is not entirely predictable, however. It entails pleasure in everyday life or critical perspectives on the configurations of power in which important potentials come to be blocked and diminished.

Hope in a Dark Ecology

Timothy Morton uses the concept of dark ecology to characterize a time "somewhere in the future" when thought will grasp the "mesh of interconnected things" or each being's entanglements with never entirely knowable others (2010, 3, 15). The affects to which such an ecology would give life include "anger, compassion, confusion, curiosity, depression, disgust, doubt, grief, helplessness, honesty, humiliation, humility, openness, sadness, shame, and tenderness" (125). Despair is particularly prevalent in this future. "Dark ecology," Morton writes, "oozes through despair. Being realistic is always refreshing. Depression is the most accurate way of experiencing the current ecological disaster. It's better than wishful thinking" (95). In European cultures, hope has often been linked with the light, as in the phrase "there is light at the end of the tunnel." Noting the association between light and hope in Ernst Bloch's writings, for example, Neville

Plaice, Stephen Plaice, and Paul Knight write, "Bloch holds up a light-meter to history to test its utopian content" (1986, xxxi). It is likely that in this cosmology, despair belongs to the darkness. Hope, in turn, might evoke wishful thinking rather than dark ecology. It may involve interacting with environmental crisis through optimism against the evidence. Darkness bears different meanings in literature and art from the Pacific. As Paula Savage writes, "Hotere's work encapsulates a specifically Pacific darkness" (2011, 8). For Hotere and Wendt, a black rainbow marks nuclear histories that destroyed vital, heterogeneous life. As such, it calls up responses such as rage, grief, and despair. But the black rainbow motif situates such modes and forces of engagement in an ambiguous, troubling relationship with hope, making a claim on the potential and creativity that exists in the same world as the loss and violence wrought by nuclear weapons.[27] It evokes people's efforts to stop nuclear weapons and to care for the dead and the living. The reduction of life over the years of nuclear bombs and other forms of militarism does not provide hope. But Hotere and Wendt, as well as Barclay in *Meļaļ*, offer hope through a reading of efforts and capacities to address the loss that has attended these histories. Perhaps such hope might make such loss less alive, at least for a time, as Barclay suggests in tracing the pleasure that Rujen experiences in imagining future possibilities. In my estimation, however, hope, as an awareness of the promise and openness of the future, could never entirely erase the losses that have made indelible marks on life in the ocean. Instead of reading hope as escapism or as wishful thinking, we might understand it as a mode of attunement to a world that is characterized by both damage and potential. The existence of such hope is a source of sorrow, not only of hope, a point suggested by the evocation of both in the black rainbow.

An Unsettling Ocean

Hope and Climate Change

Unpacified
This ocean
Still
Has much to teach me

Teresia K. Teaiwa, "L(o)osing the Edge"

ACCORDING TO MANY SCIENTISTS' STORIES, the Hawaiian Islands took form through the past 80 million years as magma flowed up through the ocean floor from a hotspot in the mantle below the Pacific plate. As the tectonic plate moves, another mountain in the chain may be growing and could eventually emerge from the ocean. Three thousand feet below the ocean surface and 20 miles from the southern coast of Hawai'i, a volcano named Lō'ihi is emerging and may become the next island in the Hawaiian chain. John L. Culliney writes that during the 1990s sensors such as thermometers and listening devices were attached to Lō'ihi: "Among the spectrum of signals from Lō'ihi the most evocative have been its sounds. Until it was retrieved in 2002 for refurbishing, the geological stethoscope moored far out on the seamount's summit transmitted the creaks, crackles, and rumbles of splitting, grinding, and rolling rocks that voice the growing pains of this embryonic Hawaiian terrain" (2006, 6).

In discussing the sounds that Lō'ihi makes in its entanglement with scientific technologies, Culliney comes close to situating the seamount as a sentient being, an unusual moment in his mainly European cultural approach to ecology in Hawai'i, perhaps bringing him closer to Native Hawaiian approaches that recognize the liveliness of mountains, rocks, and other beings.[1] Lō'ihi is "evocative," in Culliney's terms, because it is a marginal presence, here right now, perhaps surprising our understanding of the world in which we live and bringing to mind an island that is yet to emerge, a possible ecology, reconfiguring our sense of the future (Culliney 2006, 6). And, as Culliney's brief account makes clear, Lōʻihi is already well entangled in politics, technologies, and histories. Ten thousand to one hundred thousand years before its projected moment of surfacing, the seamount is imagined as a potential island of Hawaiʻi.

If recognition of Lōʻihi's presence and potential emergence from the ocean does provoke, for a moment, awareness of a promising and open future, such awareness emerges through imaginative engagement with immense durations of time that well exceed contingent human lives. Lōʻihi is a reminder that hope involves attunement to the entanglements of human and nonhuman beings. In and around the Pacific Ocean, people live in geologically active areas with histories of devastating earthquakes, tsunamis, volcanic eruptions, and other disasters. Most of the planet's earthquakes and volcanic eruptions occur on the Pacific Ring of Fire, where the Pacific tectonic plate is interacting with other tectonic plates. As I was writing this book, the ordinary material worlds in which people lived suddenly and catastrophically shifted during the Christchurch earthquake of February 2011, followed by the earthquake and tsunami in Japan in March 2011. As an awareness of the openness of the future, hope involves attunement to the unexpected, whether that unfolds as emergency or emergence, in Anna Lowenhaupt Tsing's words (2005, 269). Hope cannot exist without temporal awareness of an undetermined future, an abyss into which may seep apprehensions of promising pathways but also of losses and pain yet to come. Yet, hope is sometimes described as disengagement from the realities of living on and with the Earth: "Hope," writes Fredric Jameson, "being after all also the principle of the cruelest confidence games and of hucksterism as a fine art" (Jameson 2005, 3).[2]

I began this book with the possibility that hope is a mode of engagement that is more closely attuned to this unsettled world, and to the long durations in which people have sought to live within it, than is recognized in such critiques. *Hope* as a term first caught my attention in literary works that speak about environmental loss in a rapidly changing ocean. The presence of the term *hope* in such archives made me wonder whether hope really is necessarily or well understood as misleading, weak, or disengagement. Throughout this book, I understood hope as an awareness of the openness and promise of the future, in which thoughts, feelings, and practices are connected. In the literary works engaged here, the importance of hope lies in the relationship it forges with a future that is open, or that is a site of possibility rather than is locked into one trajectory. Literary writers evoke promising futures through their stories of an unsettling present world ocean. They make claims on existing struggles, commitments, and imaginaries and the specific pathways into the future that these might allow. Such a hope is a mode of engagement in the present world, an active attunement to individuals' and communities' hard-fought struggles across decades and even centuries for a viable environmental life. Such attunement can further give meaning to such struggles, because it suggests that not all is given.

In this book, I have explored how literary works are crafted to allow for hope as they work to create an unsettling relationship with the ocean, putting words to its loss and damage as well as to the marginalized struggles and dreams that might take it in still-promising directions. They also contribute to this ocean their stories about what could or should be, imagining possible oceans, rivers, cities, and forests. But hope is not inevitably "good." It is a multivalent, partly personal mode of engagement that always has implications for others. In this book, I sought to create a reflexive relationship with hope, reflecting on how the term is mobilized, including on what in this world is said to offer hope. Each chapter of this book elaborated a different concern related to hope. In the first chapter, I explored how literary writers animate hope in an imperial context where transformation, new worlds, and improvement came to mean the devaluation and even the destruction of existing peoples, nonhumans, and ecosystems. Such writings evoke future promise and openness through stories of certain continuities between the present and the future. Rather than affirm or condemn everything that exists, they undertake the difficult, imperfect, political work of navigating appreciable and unacceptable forms of life. This chapter opened up this book toward an exploration of hope through a variety of literary forms that are not based on imaginaries of an alternative world.

Hope is often understood as a human experience, and in some traditions, as an interior, personal state. The literary writings engaged in this book offer hope through stories of people's coexistence with other life forms and forces. For example, in Cathy Song's poetry in *Picture Bride* (1983), water, in shape-shifting between and through bodies, is a reminder that people too exceed predetermined, seemingly unmovable gendered and nationalistic forms of categorization. As such a reminder, water animates a relationship with the present world and future that includes awareness of possibility, or of the capacity to go in multiple, partly promising directions. Although hope relies on environmental relations, it cannot be conflated with the experience of everyone. Rather, it brings us up against differences and the difficulties of communal life. The three middle chapters of this book engaged literary works that suggest how communal life can allow for and make impossible hope, situating water, fish, and aluminum as agents that can support or diminish someone's relationship with a promising, open future. In the final chapter, I explored the complex ways in which literary writers offer hope through confrontation with, rather than denial of, environmental loss. They evoke promising futures—often faint and cast alongside other potential futures—through claims on limited but concrete potentials for repair, revitalization, grieving, and responsibility in this world too often characterized by brutal exertions of power and blatant illegalities. My archives are never simply about hope, and within them hope is never far from sorrow, anger, or despair. They reveal the turbulent and somewhat molten relationships between different modes of engagement in ecology. Someone who lives with hope does not believe that the present world or its futures are all sunshine.

The literary works engaged in this book cannot be equated with any person's or social group's actual experience of hope, of course. They make claims on what hope may have been. Resituated through my own critical work in this book, however, they are also accounts about what hope could be: the forms of life that could give hope, the work in which hope might be involved. As Hirokazu Miyazaki observes, there is a temporal disagreement between the prospective momentum of hope and a critical effort to capture what hope has been. He suggests that we recognize and cultivate not only the hope that we engage, but the hope entailed in the critical work (2004, 8). We might understand literary criticism as engaging its archives partly with an eye toward the future, toward ideas and imaginaries that they may support and that are only just emerging. And neither literary fictions nor criticisms are blueprints for environmental life. Their critical and creative imaginings cast the present world as unsettling in the ways in which it might shape the future, and so might encourage thought about what exists now and where life might go.

As I was working on this book, the term *hope* was thrown about in political discourse, further heightening my concerns regarding the relationships among hope, environmental change, and action. It will always be important to view hope with wariness. But universalizing critiques of hope ignore the differences of what hope may mean for an individual or more broadly for a social struggle. Such critiques undermine people's claims on present realities that disrupt business as usual in terms of environmental damage. As Anna Lowenhaupt Tsing writes, "Hope is most important when things are going badly in the world; in the face of almost certain destruction, hope is a Gramscian optimism of the will. Such 'unrealistic' hope begins in considering the possibility that tiny cracks might yet break open the dam; contingent openings are sites of unexpected force—for better or worse" (2005, 267).

In concluding, I address once more the question of why hope matters, turning to climate change, which is reshaping life in the ocean in severe and frightening ways. The intergovernmental organization SPREP or Secretariat of the Pacific Regional Environmental Programme observes that Pacific Island peoples currently contribute under 0.03 percent of global greenhouse gas emissions. Yet climate change is "disproportionally affecting," and will increasingly affect, the people of this ocean (SPREP n.d). Average global sea level and water temperature are rising as a result of increased atmospheric carbon dioxide (Hoegh-Guldberg et al. 2007, 1737). Changes in water temperature affect marine life, including coral bleaching and changes in the distribution and abundance of fish populations (Donner 2009; Perry et al. 2005). The ocean also absorbs large amounts of the carbon dioxide from the atmosphere, and as the carbon dioxide interacts with the water, it creates carbonic acid. Ocean acidification affects all marine organisms, particularly those who use carbonate minerals in their skeletons and shells (Wood, Spicer, and Widdicombe 2008, 1767). For peoples living on islands in the Pacific, the changes engulfing the ocean may also mean stress on agriculture, water supplies, coastal ecosystems, fisheries, and social dynamics (SPREP n.d).

Disappearing Pacific islands have grabbed hold of international media attention in recent years. A large number of documentary filmmakers have sought to publicize climate change by evoking the future submersion of islands into the ocean.[3] In opening *The Disappearing of Tuvalu: Trouble in Paradise* (2005) U.S. director Christopher Horner visualizes a watery future. The camera is half-submerged, water rinsing up and down against the lens and at moments coming close to breaking over the top. On the screen appear words spoken by Saufatu Sopoanga, then prime minister of Tuvalu, to the United Nations General Assembly of September 2003: "We live in constant fear of the adverse impacts of climate change. The threat is real and serious, and is of no difference to a slow and insidious form of terrorism against us." Just before we leave this shot, the water washes up and engulfs the camera, suggesting that the sea will eventually rise over Tuvalu, anticipating a future in the first moments of the film. Horner and Sopoanga both recognize the reality and gravity of climate change, but the opening scene of *The Disappearing of Tuvalu* is marked by a discrepancy between Horner's imagery of the future submersion of Tuvalu and Sopoanga's insistence that climate change is a "slow and insidious form of terrorism against us." Sopoanga firmly directs attention to the present world, but he also implicitly makes a different, although not incompatible, claim on the future than does Horner's footage of water flooding the camera lens. In describing climate change as "terrorism," Sopoanga insists on seeing responsibility and maneuverability in the present entanglement of climate, economy, and sociopolitical life. Such openness lies in reducing greenhouse gas emissions and in contesting the social and economic injustices that will make migration difficult, for example. In the full transcript of the presentation to the UN, Sopoanga describes Tuvalu's active engagement in the UN Framework Convention on Climate Change and the Kyoto Protocol and his dismay regarding certain industrialized nations' lack of action regarding climate change: "We believe all nations must take positive steps to mitigate their greenhouse gas emissions, but in saying this we also believe the industrialized world must act first. It is their historical emissions that are creating the problems of today. Steps must be taken to account for and redress the emissions of the past. We implore all nations to ratify the Kyoto Protocol, as this is the only appropriate process that will bring about effective collective action to resolve this growing threat" (Sopoanga 2003, n.p.). Sopoanga insists that the present world reveals openness to maneuver in partly promising ways in relation to climate change. He makes this suggestion not by offering "happy" images but in sharp, bleak, and far-reaching claims that people should and can make a difference in difficult realities. Such a relationship with the future relies heavily on the actions of other people and more broadly institutions such as governments. Yet it does not, and could not, mark a passive relationship with present life and its futures. It reflects the immense effort it took an individual and countless others to reach the point of standing up at such a forum, and everything that lies beyond, in the shadows of such a moment. Climate change is reshaping existing life and futures in profound ways that are not fully understood, but that does not mean that people see no capacities in this world to help those who are being hurt and disrupted inhabit more livable and secure ground. These people ask that the countries, peoples, and institutions that are most responsible significantly change their ways of coexisting with others, including by cutting their greenhouse gas emissions and providing reparations.

When such potentials are articulated in the context of climate change, they are not always welcomed. Discussing the heavy focus on the Pacific Islands and on the figure of the climate refugee in the media and in other institutions, Carol Farbotko and Heather Lazrus argue that such narratives often position Pacific peoples as victims and as evidence of global climate change, rather than engage their concerns, support their wellbeing, and ask what survival means in their histories (2012, 386–87). They describe a meeting of climate activists in Australia in 2008, at which representatives of Friends of the Earth framed their struggle as one of saving climate refugees. The group then "received with utter dismay a statement made by President Tong, of Kiribati (a Pacific atoll-state facing significant sea level rise). He stated on Australian national radio that the people of Kiribati do not want to leave their homeland as environmental refugees. Instead, they wanted training to become skilled migrants" (383). The people of Kiribati could migrate as peoples who are well able to establish lives in different places. To do so, they would require significant hospitality and reparation from those people who are making their homes difficult to inhabit.[4]

In my estimation, hope matters in these difficult contexts because it is a way of apprehending the existing world both in terms of appreciation and of sorrow; it is also a claim on that world as unsettling in the directions it might head, as in Sopoanga's claim that industrialized nations *can* reduce their emissions. Hope involves attunement to present world efforts and capacities to address environmental diminishment. It may inspire a political commentary on how such efforts are made precarious. It is a way of brushing up against and complicating narratives that situate the future as already given.

The complicated theorizations of hope in literary writings from the Pacific might speak to the many environmental writers who are drawn to the ocean at this time, searching for hope and yet wary of finding it. In a 2003 article in *National Geographic*, journalist Michael Parfit goes to Fiji, "looking for doves and hope" (2003, 114). This article, "Islands of the Pacific," is part of *National Geographic*'s "Hotspots: Preserving Pieces of a Fragile Biosphere" series, about the Micronesia-Fiji-Polynesia biodiversity hotspot.

In the Marquesas Islands, Parfit visits a grove of mango trees where the "air was dreamy with ripeness from laden branches and rot underfoot" (116). Even amid the decay of the forest, the dreaminess of such places remains. Parfit searches throughout the article for the *biib,* a fruit dove from Palau, longing to finally see it: "She was as elusive as hope but just as real. She was there, but maybe she was actually here" (125).

Hope can seem fleeting and ghostly against the backdrop of a world that often feels very bleak, as Parfit suggests. Hope is most vividly illuminated in the small moment in Richard Flanagan's *Gould's Book of Fish* when an ordinary, deeply hurt Indigenous person of Tasmania, Tracker Marks, reaches out and touches the convict William Buelow Gould, creating for a moment a different social reality than the violence that often marks such relationships in the penal colony. Or, it is revealed in the image of a family of people, *mo'o* (lizards, water spirits), and cows at the end of the Gary Pak's "Language of the Geckos," all around them water, pooling at the site of a long-destroyed pond of spiritual and material significance to Hawaiians.

Yet, these scenes do not simply emerge out of thin air. We might recognize that hope is ecological by asking what is temporally or spatially entangled with its most intensely vibrant moments. Pak's image of water's return to a Hawaiian family at the end of "Language of the Geckos," for example, is drawn from the long-term struggles of local and Hawaiian communities for justice in relation to the removal of water from rivers for sugar plantations. Hope, once imaginatively reconnected with the world in which it exists, seems less naïve and less passive, but also more troubled, exposed in its complicated relationships with economy, colonial histories, and environmental change. We can follow writers' stories to and beyond the places where hope flashes up, like the glow of bioluminescence, streaming for a moment through the ocean.

Acknowledgments

I RECEIVED GENEROUS SUPPORT from teachers, colleagues, friends, and family while writing *Hope at Sea*. This book began life as a dissertation at Duke University. Special thanks to my advisor, Michael Hardt, whose commitment to thinking and deep generosity has been sustaining ever since I arrived in the United States. I worked with many other inspiring teachers at Duke, including my committee members Leo Ching, Fredric Jameson, Ralph Litzinger, and Kenneth Surin, as well as Toril Moi and Tomiko Yoda. Brian Opie, who supervised my MA thesis at Victoria University of Wellington, has continued to provide generous encouragement ever since. I thank all my colleagues in the English Department at the University of California, Santa Barbara for bringing me back to the Pacific and creating an energetic space for work in the environmental humanities. Bishnupriya Ghosh read part of the book early on and again offered crucial insights at the end of the process. She has provided much caring mentorship over the years. Stephanie LeMenager also read part of the manuscript and has been an inspiring mentor and friend.

Many additional people offered vital advice and support during the research and writing process. I particularly thank my book writing group: ann-elise lewallen, Mhoze Chikowero, Xiaorong Li, and Christina McMahon. I also received helpful feedback from Erin Post, Corina Stan, Richard Hardack, and Richard Watts. In the last stretches of writing, I benefited greatly from UC Santa Barbara's Mellon Sawyer Seminar on "Sea Change" and particularly from the collegiality of Peter Alagona, David Lopez-Carr, and Jennifer Martin. Charles Dawson and James Beattie have been inspiring in creating an environmental humanities network in New Zealand. I remember Geoff Park here for an energizing meeting and for such graceful writing on ecology and history in New Zealand. For their engagement, thank you to my graduate students Marcel Brousseau, Elizabeth Callaway, Leah Fry, Andrew Kalaidjian, Stefani Overman-Tsai, Sharon Tang-Quan, and Christopher Walker, as well as to all my undergraduate students in my classes on literature and the environment, water, and literatures of the Pacific. Two anonymous readers for the University of Minnesota Press provided crucial feedback that helped to make this a stronger book. It is a pleasure to thank Richard Morrison, Jason Weidemann, Erin Warholm-Wohlenhaus, and the team at the University of Minnesota Press for their support, encouragement, and professionalism in the publication process.

I received financial support for this book from the Graduate School, the Program in Literature, the Mellon Dissertation Working Group, and the Kenan Institute for Ethics, all at Duke University. The Interdisciplinary Humanities Center and the Regents Junior Faculty Fellowship at UC Santa Barbara provided valuable release time. The Hellman Family Faculty Fellowship at UC Santa Barbara allowed me to complete international archival research. Dean David Marshall of UC Santa Barbara provided research funding and a leave to complete the book. Lydia Wevers and the Stout Research Centre at Victoria University of Wellington generously offered a peaceful and productive place to write during fall 2011.

I could not have completed *Hope at Sea* without the wonderful company of friends over the years in Durham and Santa Barbara. My warmest thanks, in particular, to Natasha Naus, Erin Post, Yanoula Athanassakis, Christina McMahon, Heather Blurton, Brian Donnelly, Andrew Griffin, ann-elise lewallen, Esron Gates, Richard Neher, Ribhu Kaul, Jean Kim, Corina Stan, Alison Carpenter, Renato Ramos da Silva, Ferdinand Schober, Neda Podergajs, and Philip and Sarah Steer.

My deepest appreciation goes to my family. They have been with me through all the ups and downs of these years. I thank my parents, Kaye and Rob, and siblings, Ben and Tamie. I am also grateful to Natalia, Kobe, Ella, Ruby, and everyone else in the family. In memory of Lois and Elaine, who provided a down-to-earth attitude and much humor in the early years of this project.

Notes

Introduction

1. Goldberg-Hiller and Silva (2011) and Wilson (2000, 191–213) discuss Hawaiian cultural and political life involving sharks.

2. David Harvey observes that corporate discourses relentlessly push the message that there are no alternatives to the free market (2000, 154). See also Paulo Freire, who observes, "We are surrounded by a pragmatic discourse that would have us adapt to the facts of reality. *Dreams*, and *utopia*, are called not only useless, but positively impeding" (1994, 1).

3. Jayna Brown argues that struggles for alternatives to exploitation would not be possible without a collective, utopian sense of potential (2010, 128).

4. Rozwadowski (2005) and Corbin (1994) provide useful histories of European cultures of the ocean.

5. The ocean was named *Mare Pacificum* by sixteenth-century Portuguese explorer Ferdinand Magellan. For accounts of European explorations and imaginative histories of the Pacific Ocean, see Keown (2007); Matsuda (2005); Smith (1985); and Wedde (2005a).

6. I use the terms *ecology* and *environment* interchangeably in this book, but I am aware that many critics, for varied reasons, differentiate these terms. Arturo Escobar critically explores the uptake of the term *environment* in institutions such as the World Bank during the late twentieth century. As the concept of the environment replaced that of nature, the world was resituated as a resource rather than as a site of heterogeneous sources of life, agency, and imagination (1995, 196). The concept of ecology emerged in the transnational networks of European imperialism, as Peder Anker shows in his analysis of the development and expansion of ecology within and beyond biology during the twentieth century (2001). I also draw on the concept of the nonhuman in this book, emphasizing the many entities, beings, and processes with which humans coexist, but I never imagine these entities as without politics or as fully distinct from the equally provisional concept of the human. Many research projects entangle concern for the human and the nonhuman, showing the provisionality of such terms. See, for example, Haraway (1991); Harvey (1996); Latour (2004); Morton (2010); and Raffles (2002).

7. Not every apprehension of a "good" future, particularly those involving

claims on inevitability, can be conflated with hope. I am drawing on Arjun Appadurai's description of hope as involving a relationship with possibility but not with probability (2007, 30).

8. Sophia A. McClennen argues that hope involves exchanges between reason and emotion: "It requires their collaboration to exist" (2010, 63). See also Kathy Rudy's use of the concept of affect to understand the love shared by humans and nonhuman beings. She argues that affect not only evokes the connections with others that shape someone's experiences, but also linkages between emotion and reason (2011, xvi).

9. Critiques of hope may extend at least back to early Greek writers, who may have positioned hope as a blind form of optimism or as relying on mutability and futurity in ways that conflict with fate, the constant, and the unchanging (Eliott 2005, 5). In conversation with Mary Zournazi, Michael Taussig suggests that perhaps Western intellectual work "correlates lack of hope with being smart, or lack of hope with profundity" (Taussig and Zournazi 2002, 44). Utopian thought has also attracted controversy. Critics have heavily diminished utopian writers for building a "castle in the clouds," in Bloch's terms (Bloch and Adorno 1988, 2). Fredric Jameson observes that during the Cold War utopia was associated with "a program which neglected human frailty and original sin, and betrayed a will to uniformity and the ideal purity of a perfect system that always had to be imposed by force on its imperfect and reluctant subjects" (2005, xi).

10. I do not intend to suggest that imagining a radically different world, as if this were any way possible, is inevitably a way of devaluing the existing world. It is important to remember that classical utopias may not work through an expectation that the reader will feel they should make the utopian world as given. They may be designed to enable the reader to see her or his own world through strange eyes and so to reflect critically on it, exploring what matters and what should change. As Fredric Jameson writes, "Utopia's deepest subject, and the source of all that is most vibrantly political about it, is precisely our inability to conceive it, our incapacity to produce it as a vision, our failure to project the Other of what is, a failure that, as with fireworks dissolving back into the night sky, must once again leave us alone with *this* history" (1988, 101).

11. As Michael Hardt observes, ecology movements often focus on the singularity and finitude of the Earth: "The World Social Forum motto, 'Another world is possible,' might translate in the context of the climate changes movements into something like, 'This world is still possible, maybe'" (2010, 271). Dipesh Chakrabarty also argues that in thinking about desirable forms of being, such as freedom, we must recognize parameters on survival, such as climate (2009, 218).

12. I am drawing this discussion of endurance from the work of Elizabeth A. Povinelli, which I discuss in more depth in chapter 1 (Povinelli 2011a).

13. Many theorists at work in the Pacific emphasize the importance of ties

among the present, the future, and the past within their cultures, negotiating continuity and change in ways that benefit life and well-being (Hau'ofa 2008b; Wilson 2000). In the Austronesian languages, including in Hawaiian and Māori, the word for the past is that for in front, while the word for the future is that for behind. The past is situated ahead, a source of orientation as people move into the future (Hau'ofa 2008b, 67).

14. Jennifer Wenzel argues that sites of catastrophe are places of pain and despair but also of incomplete dreams that the living may enliven (2009). Sumathi Ramaswamy suggests that cultivating a sense of loss can sometimes produce hope. She argues against "a dominant diagnosis of the modern preoccupation with loss as inevitably and unequivocally regressive or reactionary" (2004, 8).

15. A number of scholars have discussed hope's entanglement with other forms of experience. Angus Fletcher discusses the entanglement of hope and despair: "despair mates with hope in a twin relationship, and neither will be present without the threat or promise of the other" (1999, 521). Christopher Nelson describes connections between experiences of possibility, loss, and horror in postwar Okinawa (2008, 5).

16. See, for example, Matt K. Matsuda's discussion of the imaginative linkages between the Pacific Ocean and love (2005).

17. For example, Elizabeth Grosz seeks a temporal understanding that is not dominated by the present and that is open to a future that we do not know (2005). Anna Lowenhaupt Tsing also frames her work as seeking to make space for a sense of the future in which all possibility, wonder, and surprise has not been washed out (2005, 269).

18. For a discussion of the abrupt, late twentieth-century emergence of concern for marine environmental crisis in U.S. archives, see Buell (2001, 200–201).

19. See Goldberg-Hiller and Silva (2011); Hau'ofa (2008a); Park (1995); Teaiwa (1994); and Wilson (2000).

20. See DeLoughrey and Handley (2011); Huggan and Tiffin (2010); Mukherjee (2010); Nixon (2011). This book is not a broad overview of the convergence between postcolonial studies and environmental studies, a project already undertaken by Cilano and DeLoughrey (2007); DeLoughrey and Handley (2011); Huggan and Tiffin (2010); and Nixon (2005). The book joins a number of recently published articles and book chapters about postcolonial and Indigenous peoples' writings on marine environmental change, most notably Graham Huggan and Helen Tiffin's discussion of literary thought about nuclear colonialism and tourism (2010) and Elizabeth DeLoughrey's work on solar ecologies and nuclear militarization in Indigenous Pacific writing (2009).

21. Linda Tuhiwai Smith (1999) and Selina Tusitala Marsh (1999) explore how colonialism involved the devaluation of Indigenous peoples' perspectives.

22. Epeli Hau'ofa discusses how scholars and institutions have framed the contemporary Pacific as a place without hope (2008a, 29–30).

23. For example, Dana Phillips challenges ecocritics who suggest that "the presence and reality of the natural world" is available in literature (2003, 7).

1. Endurance, Ecology, Empire

1. See Darko Suvin (1972) on science fiction as a literature of cognitive estrangement that provides a reflective and transformative mirror on readers' own worlds. He distinguishes this concern from nonfictional utopianism, presumably because this is directed toward realizing imagined utopias rather than creating an estranging viewpoint on the existing world (373). Fredric Jameson characterizes utopian writers' concerns for the difference of their utopias as crucial and distinctive: "Utopian form is itself a representational meditation on radical difference, radical otherness, and on the systemic nature of the social totality" (2005, xii).

2. Drawing from Henri Marcuse by way of Baruch Spinoza, Hage apprehends a kind of hope that involves "saving and deferring gratification" (Hage and Zournazi 2002, 151). He suggests that capitalist social and imaginative worlds encourage, but do not evenly distribute, this type of hope, because they cast pain felt now in the context of a better life later, even though that life rarely eventuates. Although I agree with Hage's argument that encouraging someone to defer their joy and well-being can be a tactic of power, a life oriented toward having what is immediately graspable and likeable, without thought or engagement in a longer term time frame, can also be environmentally destructive and unjust.

3. Imagining a radically new world may reflect care for certain aspects of, rather than devaluation of everything in, the existing world. This interpretation of utopia is certainly possible if we conceive it as designed to enable people to reflect on their own worlds from an estranged vantage point. As imperial administrators and settlers attempted to make utopias, they moved beyond the concerns of the classical utopian literary form, with its impossible attempt at a new but only imagined world that could provoke critical perspectives and aspirations.

4. The New Zealand Company framed Māori as new migrants to New Zealand, so total were their aspirations to make a new world of the archipelago. As John Beecham observes of the New Zealand Company's plans, "The recently-discovered method of transplanting a full-grown tree, without injury, from one soil to another, is used as a simile to represent the introduction of the New Zealanders [Māori], with their national peculiarities and usages, into the British Colony" (Beecham 1838, 34).

5. Compared to the term *endurance,* the term *survival* places sharper emphasis on the living, as evident in its etymology. Survival is shaped by *vivere* (to live) and endurance by *durare* (to harden).

6. Elizabeth Grosz wonders, for example, whether ecology does, and could, value a future that is not the same as the present: "If an ecology that values not only the living—the present—but also the future could be possible, it would be very close to the (non)moral ontology of Darwinism, which mourns no particular extinction and which waits, with surprise, to see what takes the place of the extinct" (2005, 221). Critiques of environmentalist preoccupations with stability often revolve around the pastoral literary form. "At the root of pastoral," observes Greg Garrard, "is the idea of nature as a stable, enduring counterpoint to the disruptive energy and change of human societies" (2004, 56).

7. Numerous scholars have traced linkages among European exploration, imperialism, and utopia. Dohra Ahmad observes how Thomas More, Francis Bacon, and others drew on exploration narratives in the sixteenth and seventeenth centuries (2009, 6). Fredric Jameson suggests that utopianism drew interests in tribal societies, climatalogical determinism, exotic travel narratives, and primitivism from European geographical exploration (2005, 18–19).

8. In discussing New Zealand ("Maoriland") writing of 1872–1914, Jane Stafford and Mark Williams observe that "one of the requirements of settlement is the ability to ignore the land's indigenous occupants," noting that this is a troubled rather than straightforward concern in their archives (2006, 59). They describe varying and sometimes conflicted ways in which European writers situate the land as "maiden" or "fallow," associate land appropriation with progress, and represent Māori as primitive (59, 59, 59–63).

9. In 1838 John Beecham, secretary of the Wesleyan Missionary Society, writes in *Colonization Being Remarks on Colonization in General, with an Examination of the Proposals of the Association which has been formed for Colonizing New Zealand*: "The 'Parliamentary Select Committee on Aborigines' advert, in their Report, to the very latest Act that has been passed for founding a Colony, in which an immense tract of country is disposed of as 'waste lands,' on which a single habitation of man was not to be found, and whose soil was not imprinted with a human footstep; while the Company themselves, in whose favour the Act was framed, state that 'great numbers of natives have been seen along that part of the coast' where they are commencing operations" (1838, 4). Beecham had his own agenda, which was to push the New Zealand Association for financial support of missionaries.

10. For accounts of the King Movement, see Adams and Meredith (2009) and Marr (1996).

11. Historian David Young documents varied nineteenth-century New Zealand archives that express concern regarding the environmental consequences of the colonial economy, including on whales, seals, forest, climate, and birds (2004, 61–72).

12. See Elizabeth Povinelli's observations about the conditions in which radical

environmental activists in the United States and Indigenous groups in Australia actually live, and hold the potential to live, otherwise (2011a, 101–30).

13. As New Zealand ecologist Geoff Park notes, "Our environmental literature tends to marginalise people as wreckers of a mythical, ancient world that had no need of them" (1995, 15). Anna Lowenhaupt Tsing also observes that some environmentalists situate people as "amassed atoms whose sheer density and undifferentiated drive to consumption destroys everything around them" (2005, 249).

14. See Latour (2004) and Morton (2010) on how nature has been positioned as a sphere separate from human life.

15. On some of the ways in which Māori historically altered the ecology of the archipelago, see Park (1995) and Young (2004, particularly 37–56).

16. I am drawing on Sue Zemka's discussion of how *Erewhon* reveals anxiety regarding the uncontrollable and unforeseen environmental and social implications of utopian dreaming (2002, 447).

17. On Stead and *The Bone People,* see Najita (2006, 126) and DeLoughrey (2007, 187).

18. Susan Y. Najita writes about other ways in which Kerewin seeks to separate from the capitalist market, including in rejecting marriage (2006).

19. See also Taonui (2011).

20. Greg Garrard discusses how the classical form of pastoral has sometimes romanticized the past and elided issues of economy and class (2004). See also Rob Nixon's discussion of pastoral in United States cultural histories (2005).

21. See Nigel Clark on this history (2004).

22. David Harvey discusses connections between environmentalism and exclusionary forms of social life (1996, 169–72).

23. Geoff Park notes that Māori hunters "revered" kahikatea (1995, 36; see also, 35–38; 47). David Young suggests that Māori historically used kahikatea in varied ways, including as a source of fruit. They kept kahikatea forest intact partly because it supported "special birds" like the wood pigeon (2004, 47). See also Knight (2010).

24. Elizabeth Povinelli suggests that endurance involves "the temporality of continuance, a denotation of continuous action without any reference to its beginning or end" (2011a, 32).

25. See Harvey (1996, 187–88) and Garrard (2004, 120–35).

26. Bernard Smith discusses a duality that took form in European imagination of Pacific peoples between 1773 and 1784: "The first depicted the Pacific, particularly its islands, as a southern Arcadia or paradise, as the lands of free love and easy living, where life could be lived without toil and labour. The other depicted these same islands as the abode of savages who performed ghastly rites in the fear of their pagan gods" (1992, 188). He understands this imagery through the cultural legacies of classical antiquity and medieval Christianity.

27. This imaginative status is evident in parts of Johnston's article: "It's too inhuman around here. Way too eerie. Time has stood still—we've arrived at the very end, in Westland" (2004, n.p.).

2. In Search of Rain

1. For example, Frantz Fanon situates the land as vital to anticolonial struggles: "For a colonized people, the most essential value, because the most concrete, is first and foremost the land: the land which will bring them bread and, above all, dignity" (1963, 44). Edward W. Said also writes that the main contest in imperialism is over the land, that "everything about human history is rooted in the earth," and that at most basic "imperialism means thinking about, settling on, controlling land that you do not possess, that is distant, that is lived on and owned by others" (1994 [1993], 7).

2. In varied parts of the world, settlers diverted water out of existing hydrological regimes and into infrastructures like dams and pipelines, feeding it into processes such as capitalist agriculture and settler imaginaries of conservation and belonging. For discussions of the ties among fresh water, cultural production, and imperialism, see Dudoit (1997), Hughes (2006), Linton (2006), and Watts (2007).

3. Another scholar of water, Christopher Connery, notes of Euro-American thinking that "liquid is always the problem element—shapeless but not abstract; temporal; changeable" (1996, 290). Michel Foucault also suggests that people historically have experienced water as unaccountable and troubling, discussing the conceptual links between water and madness in European imagination (1988, 7–13).

4. As Anna Lowenhaupt Tsing writes of subterranean ecosystems, "One of the many extinctions our development projects aim to produce is the cosmopolitanism of the underground city. And almost no one notices, because so few humans even know of the existence of that city" (2011, n.p.).

5. See the Maunalua Fishpond Heritage Center website (maunaluafishpond .org/).

6. The Hawaiian language is rich with terms and phrases for water. Shawn Malia Kana'iaupuni and Nolan Malone note that there are thousands of Hawaiian names for rain (2006, 292). John Culliney writes, "At Hilo there was the rain that 'makes the *lehua* blossom quiver,' and at Hāna, Maui, the 'rain of the low-lying heavens.' Also on Maui (at Waiehu) came the 'rain that pricks the skin'; and 'the fine mist of Waihe'e'; and at Kaupō, there was 'the rain that drives one to the rocks for shelter'" (2006, 200).

7. Water is associated with loss and memory in varied cultural contexts. Gaston Bachelard poignantly suggests that water offers "a daily tomb to everything that dies within us each day" (1983, 55). This is because water bears things

away: "The first to be dissolved is a landscape in the rain; lines and forms melt away. But little by little the whole world is brought together again in its water" (91–92). Water, he argues, is the element "which remembers the dead" (56).

8. Such a story of time is distinct from early European archives in which Europeans lead Hawaiian peoples to leave behind a primitive past and blast into a civilized future. Rob Wilson observes such a story in Reverend Sheldon Dibble's 1843 *History of the Sandwich Islands,* where the displacement of Native Hawaiians is framed in a teleological story of progress in which backward Indigenous ways are overcome (2000, 194–95). But in different places of loss, some European theorists of time have sought to invoke a more complex dynamic between retrospection and anticipation. Working against the notion of progress, or the idea that the working class is naturally drifting in prevailing currents toward a better future, Walter Benjamin and Ernst Bloch both frame hope as "unclosed both backwards and forwards" (Bloch 1986, 9). Benjamin imagines the historian "fanning the spark of hope in the past," connecting with uncompleted dreams in ways that might interrupt the dangerous pathways on which the present is moving (1969, 255). For Bloch, too, "unbecome future becomes visible in the past, avenged and inherited, mediated and fulfilled past in the future" (1986, 9).

9. In Hawaiʻi, the term *local* can be controversial: local status may evoke racial categories, how long one has been in Hawaiʻi, working-class background, language (particularly use of pidgin), or behavior (Kwon 1999, 6). The relationship between local politics and Hawaiian sovereignty politics has sometimes been troubled.

10. Elizabeth M. DeLoughrey suggests that attending to water evokes transnational spaces, emphasizing the entanglement of land with the sea as a way to challenge ideas that islands are isolated and outside of history (2007). Hugh Raffles grapples with the complex spaces and social life of water in his discussion of rivers in the Amazon: "It is by transgressing the conventions of human space that rivers reveal the poverty of scalar categories" (2002, 181). These "*immanently translocal*" entities always promise to be on their way to somewhere else (182).

11. For extended readings of "The Valley of the Dead Air," see Najita (2006) and Kwon (1999).

12. In some European cultures, the sea has long been imagined as a site beyond history and civilization. Alain Corbin writes of how biblical texts frame the sea as an enigmatic threat to human life: "There is no sea in the Garden of Eden. There is no place within the enclosed landscape of Paradise for the watery horizon whose surface extends as far as the eye can see" (1994, 2). Philip E. Steinberg also describes how the sea has been framed in developmental, geopolitical, and legal discourses as refractive of civilization, territorial claims, and social order, while Elizabeth M. DeLoughrey observes that in British colonial contexts the sea was narrated as unmarked, feminine, and atemporal (DeLoughrey 2007, 22; Steinberg 2001, 35).

13. For example, Alice Yun Chai observes the historical invisibility of elderly Asian working-class women who came to Hawai'i as picture brides in the early twentieth century (1988, 52). Kathi Weeks discusses feminist theoretical debates regarding whether domestic labor is situated within or beyond capitalist production (2007).

14. A number of literary writers and artists have drawn water and women together in order to evoke femininity, purity, and maternity. Gaston Bachelard observes that numerous European male poets have attributed maternal and feminine characteristics to water, noting the frequent appearance of the figure of the woman at her bath: she "must be white and young; she must be nude" (1983, 33). The water enables gender ideologies to appear as part of a natural, inevitable order: "Water evokes *natural* nudity, a nudity that can keep its innocence" (33).

15. Stefan Helmreich describes the controversies that converge on the identification of "invasive" and "native" species in the fluid ecosystems of water in Hawai'i (2005).

16. Greg Garrard observes that everyday spaces are highly relevant in understanding how people imagine and shape the environment, but that environmentalists often overlook them in focusing on spaces conceived in terms of wilderness or nature (2004, 71).

17. As Hugh Raffles observes, drawing on Wittgenstein, water illuminates the relative invisibility of what is vital and very familiar to us (2002, 181). Fiona Allon notes that water was crucial to early twentieth century national economies, capital expansion, urbanization, and sanitation, in conjunction with the development of massive infrastructures such as reservoirs, sewage treatment plants, and pipelines (2006). Through these very processes, though, water became difficult to apprehend as a site of history, politics, power, or even importance: "flows of water became so *naturalised, commonplace* and *everyday* in domestic urban environments that water, harnessed by technology, was seen as constantly available, an abundant, never ending supply accessed simply by the turn of a tap" (n.p.).

18. Sonali Perera also writes about the ethical potential of everyday practices, in the context of working-class women's writing from Sri Lanka and the United States. She argues that such writings cannot be recognized in terms of the eventful templates that often mark working-class histories. Rather, their unfinished forms situate working-class history within the temporalities of the everyday rather than of revolutionary, arresting events: "They remind us that measures of chronology—important dates, periods, and 'events' in labor history—do not let us into quiet moments that are 'too late' or 'too early,' into secret places where chance meetings and haphazard alignments take place" (2008, 2). The everyday is an important site of struggle because it involves the "lasting ethical transformation that can alone secure the political" (2). See also Leela Gandhi's discussion of South Asians and Europeans who forged politics of friendship that fled from

the orderly imperial hierarchies of race, species, genders, and classes in the late nineteenth century. Their politics never gained the influence of imperial projects but nevertheless quietly reworked the ethical, epistemological, and political potentials of the societies with which they were engaged (2006, 188).

3. Hope in the Poetry of a Fractured Ocean

1. On sooty shearwater restoration projects following the *Command* oil spill, see NOAA (n.d) and Oikonos (2006). There may be a correlation between a decline in sooty shearwater numbers and the oceanic and atmospheric processes involved in climatic fluctuations (El Niño events), which impact on prey abundance and distribution (Lyver, Moller, and Thompson 1999, 244). On the impact of overfishing on sooty shearwater, as well as on sooty shearwater as bycatch in certain fisheries, see Lyver et al. (245).

2. See, for example, the many shots of and across water in Briar March's *There Once Was an Island—Te Henua e Nnoho* (2010), a documentary film about the impact of sea-level rise on peoples living on Takuu, an atoll that is part of the Autonomous Region of Bougainville in Papua New Guinea.

3. Ian Wedde suggests that European New Zealand nationalist discourses associate the ocean horizon with the divides and losses attending migration: "The ocean horizon is distance, it's the out-of-reach finitude of longing that also, given the paradoxical nature of voluntary unrequital and exile, folds away infinitely, forever receding, forever drawing out that minor chord of hopeless desire. The ocean horizon is distance and loss: it's also a kind of celibacy" (2005c, 29).

4. Focusing particularly on the awareness of risk that imbues American literature, art, and other media works that seek to enfold or otherwise engage the global, Ursula K. Heise argues for greater attention in ecocriticism to the socioculturally textured ways in which literary writers and others may have imagined global connections (2008). See also Garrard (2004, 160–82), Morton (2010), and Nixon (2011).

5. For example, Herman Melville plays up but also critically engages stories of the isolated native in *Typee: A Peep at Polynesian Life* (1996 [1846]). Melville simply places our narrator Tommo's recountings of such popular narratives of the Marquesan's status as "undisturbed for years" alongside references to their experience in trade, their attempts to manipulate and shape their political relationships with France and the United States and to retain their sovereignty at a time of imperialism, and their physical competence in water (5).

6. Mary Zournazi also explores the collective life through which hope takes form, arguing that in Australian politics hope is often framed in terms of national security and comfort in ways that ignores the suffering of others: "The major political parties, and democratic politics in general, are failing to provide other possibilities for hope based on compassion, sensitivity and care" (2002, 16).

7. The profound importance of the island in the cultural history of utopia can be partly understood in the context of powerful European cultural trajectories that situated the ocean as an external space beyond the borders of human civilization and so as the ideal buffer for an alternative world. On such imaginative histories of the ocean, see Corbin (1994) and Steinberg (2001).

8. I am drawing from *Madness and Civilization: A History of Insanity in the Age of Reason,* where Michel Foucault traces Renaissance imaginings in which ships of people perceived to be mad are set adrift on rivers and the sea (1988, 7). Today, many human rights activists and environmentalists sift in and across the murky borderlands of land-oriented socio-spatial templates, searching the waters for the secrets of violence and disappearance. There have been many instances of people driven by political and economic violence into the ocean in the Pacific Rim. The term "boat people"—still commonly used in the Pacific Rim today—poignantly reflects people's oceanic status of exile from a place of refuge or belonging.

9. The island of Bensalem in Francis Bacon's *New Atlantis* is likewise quite porous within limits determined by the utopians. Bacon's utopians secretly travel the world to accumulate scientific knowledge and yet can retain control over their borders with that world. They are dedicated to studying "Works and Creatures of God" within a scientific institution known as Salomon's House (Bacon 1999, 167). Their king banned them from sailing beyond his dominion, but he also ruled that every twelve years two ships would carry fellows from Salomon's House out into the world, where they would collect knowledge, books, and instruments related to the affairs and state of particular countries, focusing on "the sciences, arts, manufactures, and inventions of all the world" (167). Such activities are carried out covertly and, as such, the utopians have devised a way of "preserving the good which cometh by communicating with strangers, and avoiding the hurt" (166–67).

10. Elizabeth M. DeLoughrey observes that imperial projects were sometimes mapped onto the ocean rather than simply onto islands. In the nineteenth century, in the context of empire, the ocean was situated in some writings as a "natural home" for English men (qtd. in DeLoughrey 2007, 27). Matt K. Matsuda writes that the French Pacific was imagined through the language of love for and against empire (2005). During the Meiji and Taishō periods in Japan, the South Seas became an imaginative site of paradise, adventure, and imperial desire shaped by the Japanese navy's advocacy for the southward advance that would justify its existence and expansion (Schencking 1999). On the narratives of the American Pacific, see Wilson (2000).

11. For an introduction to Wedde, see Ricketts (1986).

12. For a description of New Zealand as "100% Pure," see Tourism New Zealand (2011, n.p).

13. An early linkage between green and environmental loss is made in 1925 in New Zealand poet William Pember Reeves's "The Passing of the Forest," which describes the transformation of hills from "green old age" to "fire's black smirch"

(1997, 499). Reeves does not simply see the forest as green, however, noting the yellow of kōwhai and crimson of rātā blossoms (1997, 499).

14. For example, "the green revolution" came to name varied projects and discourses that were mobilized and framed at least partly around the aspiration of economically and technologically "modernizing" agriculture, especially from the end of the Second World War to the 1970s and in the Global South. The administrator of USAID, William S. Gaud, coined the name in 1968: "Developments in the field of agriculture contain the makings of a new revolution. It is not a violent Red Revolution like that of the Soviets, nor is it a White Revolution like that of the Shah of Iran. I call it the Green Revolution" (qtd. in Hesser 2006, 100). Heavily incorporating fertilizers, pesticides, and other technologies in agriculture, the green revolution was supposed to cheapen food and labor forces (Escobar 1995, 126–31). For a critical, historically informed perspective on the green revolution, see Escobar (1995).

15. In some environmental forums, there may be a particular sense of entitlement to speak on behalf of the entire planet—ideally, if not in reality, without regard for the interests that local peoples or the state might bring to environmental politics—because of connections that shape the realities and potentials of life across borders and because biodiversity is understood as global heritage that "belongs to no one" (Litzinger 2006, 69). I am drawing from Ralph Litzinger's work on narratives and activities associated with the Critical Ecosystem Partnership Fund, a global project that channels conservation funding to civil society groups—defined, in these particular circumstances, as groups autonomous from the state—and that is funded partly by the World Bank, Conservation International, and the Global Environment Facility. Although its publicity archives suggest it may aspire to intervene in environmental life in China regardless of the claims of people living in targeted areas and the state, such an aspiration does not simply coincide with unfolding realities (69).

16. See, for example, Geoff Park's discussions of the extractive economy of dairy farming in New Zealand and the ecology that it shapes (1995, 23–24).

17. On the histories of New Zealand's floodplain forests, see Park (1995).

18. On Māori thought regarding forests, see Taonui (2009b). For a discussion of the relationships between Te Roroa and the forest more specifically, see Waitangi Tribunal (1992).

19. I am drawing on Gordon H. Brown's detailed discussion of McCahon's *Necessary Protection* works (1984, 154–76).

20. On the imaginative histories that figure Pacific peoples as living in isolation, see D'Arcy (2006, 5–6) and DeLoughrey (2007, 6–20). For a discussion of the anthropological history that takes Pacific cultures as a site for salvage from European influences, see Geiger (2007, 133–36).

21. For further background on Tuwhare's life, see Hunt (2011).

2

22. On the controversial Nugget Point marine reserve proposal processes, see Royal Society (2005).

23. Several scholars explore people's understandings of landscape entities that listen, respond, or otherwise act in the world. See Julie Cruikshank's discussion of Athapaskan and Tlingit oral traditions of glaciers that listen in northwestern North America (2005). Jonathan Goldberg-Hiller and Noenoe K. Silva observe that in Native Hawaiian thought, "humans are part of a vast family that includes celestial bodies, plants, animals, landforms, and deities. Sentient beings that interact with humans include pigs, sharks, stones, and forests" (2011, 436).

24. Many important temporal concepts in ecocriticism involve recognition that the future is uncertain in some measure, from Ursula K. Heise's scholarship on risk (2008), to Timothy Morton's interests in openness (2010), to Rob Nixon's concept of slow violence (2011).

25. For an extensive discussion of the artistic dialogues between Hotere and McQueen, see O'Brien (1997, 103–15).

26. See also Elizabeth Povinelli's description of an environmental activist's project of transforming deep-fry oil into fuel. She argues that this project enables beings and ecological-social relationships that are excessive to capital (2011a, 124).

27. As Gregory O'Brien observes of Hotere's works, "The beauty of such 'vernacular' materials as old iron, busted-up wood and lead-head nails inadvertently states the argument against the pristine operational machinery of progress and capitalism" (1997, 101).

28. On Ōkārito and Pureora, among other forests, see Young (2004, 179–89).

29. I am drawing from Damon Ieremia Salesa's discussion of the traceability and specificity of networks in the British Empire: "These networks were cultural artefacts, historically situated and spatially and socially variegated. They did not indiscriminately connect" (2011, 9).

4. In a Strange Ocean

1. Butler does express some anxiety regarding animal testing activities in *New Atlantis*. He tells us that the utopians' experiments do not work "by chance" because they "know beforehand of what matter and commixture what kind of those creatures will arise" (1999, 179).

2. Numerous monographs engage endangered species of the Pacific, including Mark Jerome Walters's account of the *'alalā*, or Hawaiian crow (2006), Paul Alan Cox's discussion of the flying foxes of Savai'i, Samoa (1997), and Alison Ballance's book on the *kākāpō*, a New Zealand parrot (2010).

3. Angus Fletcher argues that a "new geography of hope and despair" emerged in sixteenth-century European thought (1999, 524). Hope and despair shifted from their "place" in a transcendental source (despair in hell, hope in heaven) to

a secularized, psychological place, which was both interiorized and linked to the "outward" dimensions of everyday working-class life (1999, 526).

4. Political controversy surrounds the spatial definitions of these waters. In international political archives, Tasmania is sometimes situated at the meeting point of the Pacific and the Indian Oceans, with the borders of the Southern Ocean much further to the south. The Australian government, in contrast, recognizes the Southern Ocean as flowing right up from Antarctica to southern Australia and so as intersecting Tasmania and the southern coasts of the mainland. In this story of the oceans, Tasmania lies on the border of the Pacific and the Southern Oceans (Darby 2003, n.p.).

5. For example, William Buelow Gould was born in England and transported to Hobart Town for stealing clothing. He was eventually sent to the penal station on Sarah Island in Macquarie Harbour. Gould was freed in 1835 and his fish paintings are housed in the Allport Library in Tasmania. On Gould's biography, see Tasmanian Government (n.d.) and Bogue (2010).

6. Flanagan's insistence that the registry creates an alternative world reflects historical accounts of Van Diemen's Land. The lieutenant-governor of Tasmania, George Arthur, described Van Diemen's Land to the Colonial Office as a place of success incomparable to "any former instance of Colonization" and as moving into a state "of absolute wealth" (qtd. in Reynolds 2012, 89). Likewise, George Augustus Robinson, who was appointed by Arthur to negotiate the removal of Indigenous peoples from Tasmania, sent Arthur "highly optimistic but essentially fanciful reports about progress on Flinders Island" (Reynolds 2012, 84).

7. I am drawing from Cristina Vatulescu's work on the creativity of police files in Romania and Russia. These files were not simply reflective. A person might find his life to be in tension with the life described in the police file, but he would be forced to admit and take on the file's account of himself (2004, 249). Damon Ieremia Salesa also discusses the productivities of colonial archives, describing how they shaped policy, arranged space and people, and defined the illicit or licit (2011, 11–12).

8. Olsen (2010) and Hooker (2004, 11–12) discuss natural history in the European settlement of Australia. Ritvo (1997) and Raffles (2002, 114–49) more broadly describe the uncertainty, contestations, and heterogeneity of taxonomic practices of classifying animals in eighteenth- and nineteenth-century Britain and in colonial networks.

9. On Europeans' imaginative placement of Australia's Indigenous peoples within classificatory orders, see Reynolds (2012, 30–31). On the connections between nineteenth-century practices of classification, race, imperialism, and space more broadly, see Raffles 2002 (116–23). As many scholars observe of Tasmania and of other colonial contexts, European brutality against Indigenous peoples was connected with imaginaries of nonhuman animals. But while nineteenth-

century Europeans often described Australian Indigenous peoples as animals, defined as a lower being than the human, there was no seamless correlation between Europeans' relationships with Indigenous peoples and with nonhuman animals. For example, Caroline Jordon observes that during the nineteenth century some upper-class European women artists critiqued the heavy killing of animals and landscape upheaval in the settlement. But these critiques did not extend to settler violence against Indigenous peoples. Rather, these women imaginatively situated Indigenous peoples as a vanishing race of the past or even sought to justify violence against them (Jordon 2002, 352–56).

10. On transportation as a technology of power, see Reynolds 2012 (160–61).

11. An archive from 1839, *The Penal Settlements of Van Diemen's Land, Macquarie Harbour, Maria Island, and Tasman's Peninsula*, written by Thomas James Lempriere, magistrate for Van Diemen's Land, reveals the importance and the disruptive force of water in administrators' efforts to control the convicts. Sarah Island, Lempriere writes, was selected as a place of confinement because the "lonely locality" would block escape (1954, 10). The most badly behaved convicts were sent to an island half a mile off Sarah Island. This island was just large enough for one building composed of two rooms and a small cookhouse: "In bad weather the surf often broke over it with great violence. In these cases the jetty would be covered with water and the unfortunate prisoners, perhaps after a hard day's work, had, on their landing, to wade to their middles, without a change of raiment" (30). Lempriere also describes murders on the island, including someone "deprived of life by having his head held under water until he was drowned" (31). Not all of the water-related incidents noted in Lempriere's text favor the penal settlement administrators. He writes that in 1822 the first commandant, Lieutenant Cuthbertson, drowned after his boat overturned while navigating through heavy surf to Sarah Island (11).

12. For example, whalers from Van Diemen's Land caught about 1,000 right whales in 1839, but less than 300 in 1841 and twenty-six in 1847 (Lawrence 2008, 28). From 1810 to 1830 on Macquarie Island, around 1500 kilometers to the south of Tasmania, "the resident fur seals were exterminated and the elephant seal population declined by 70 per cent" (Nash 2003, 55). In *The Penal Settlements of Van Diemen's Land, Macquarie Harbour, Maria Island, and Tasman's Peninsula*, Thomas James Lempriere describes Sarah Island as "thickly wooded when first occupied and to a person who had seen it at that period and at the time of its evacuation, the change would appear surprising. Save one venerable fern tree near the new sawpits and a few small trees, not a vestige remained of the dense forest which once covered its surface" (1954, 28). He refers to the years from 1821 to 1834, at which point the settlement was abandoned. Many of these trees were Huon Pine, which was considered a valuable source for timber and was felled by convict laborers (Lempriere 1954, 9–10). In 1824, G. T. W. B. Boyes, colonial auditor in Hobart,

wrote in a diary, "I soon found occasion to lament the unfeeling spirit that urged the settlers to give so many noble trees so wantonly to the axe and the flame" (qtd. in Jordon 2002, 341). Caroline Jordon discusses a "counter-picturesque" aesthetic in diaries, amateur artworks, and poems of nineteenth-century Tasmania, arguing that it reveals a "brutal landscape-in-progress" (341, 342).

13. Rob Wilson describes U.S. cultural archives that demonize oceanic creatures, particularly whales and sharks. He suggests that sharks have been positioned as spiritually offensive and as economically obstructive of U.S. efforts to dominate the Earth as a commodity (2000, 203). Some Indigenous peoples of the Pacific, in contrast, view social and political life as extending among humans and fish, among other beings, and recognize the porosity of all beings. Jonathan Goldberg-Hiller and Noenoe K. Silva write that within Hawaiian cosmology *manō* or sharks are powerful agents in political life that extends among humans and nonhumans, the borders of which are dynamic and were not defined by the concept of the animal before the arrival of Europeans in Hawaiʻi (2011).

14. For example, see scientists' account of the visual capacities of squid, or of how the California Spiny Lobster communicates to deter predators through sounds named rasps (Patek, Shipp, and Staaterman 2009; Sweeney et al. 2007).

15. As Donna J. Haraway observes, the categories of the human and the animal may elide continuities among life forms, such as language and tool use, social behavior, and biology (1991, 151–52).

16. Kathy Rudy provides a theoretical perspective on social life between humans and nonhumans, focusing on love between people and dogs (2011). She observes that such love does not simply mean positive experiences but also positions us to recognize the loss and violence that often shape these relationships: "An affective approach is one that takes responsibility for all kinds of losses because the life it shares with other species is the foundation of everything that is good, everything that has value" (2011, 215). I have also drawn on her argument that rather than simply try to reform institutions like capitalism and racism in search of a way to enable animal welfare, we must challenge the structures that underlie the suffering of animals (2011, 10–11).

17. William Buelow Gould's painting is of a weedy seadragon, but at some point it was mislabeled as a leafy seadragon, either by Gould or someone else (Cranston 2003, 38).

18. In the documentary film *Sharkwater* (2006), for example, Canadian director Rob Stewart tracks the decimation of shark species within the shark fin industry. He represents illegal shark fishers in fragmentary moments of brutality, as they haul sharks over the sides of boats, cut the fins off these still-living beings, and toss them back into the water to die. He does not engage their stories, but we are given a glimpse of the immense economic duress under which they must work when we learn of the precariousness of their lives within illegal fishing industries.

Stewart speaks with several men who are illegally collecting sea cucumbers in the Galapagos Islands. Several of the divers who work off their boat are sick with the bends, but the men do not want to go for help because they still have to finish twelve days of fishing. Noting that the "cucumbers were worth more than the lives of the fishermen," Stewart does not explain whether or not the divers survive or show the film crew offering to take them to shore for treatment. He does not address the possibility that these fisher people need to bring home money at the end of their fishing trips nor the ways in which the geoeconomic dynamics of industrial fishing may undermine the livelihood of local fishers.

19. See Zach Weir for an in depth discussion of narrative inconsistencies in *Gould's Book of Fish* (2005, n.p.).

20. For example, see the May 2010 edition of the journal *PMLA,* which includes a section on oceanic studies.

21. Theorists such as Epeli Hauʻofa and Albert Wendt address the European tendency to isolate the land from the sea, using the term *Oceania* to connect the sea, islands, and all their life (Hauʻofa 2008a; Wendt 1982).

22. Flanagan experienced a personal attack from representatives of the Tasmanian State Government. After he criticized the government's logging and gambling policies, a politician described him as a "traitor to Tasmania" and Paul Lennon, then premier of Tasmania, stated that Flanagan and his writings are unwelcome in the "new Tasmania" (qtd. in Moss 2007, n.p.). "I realised then," says Flanagan in an interview, "that what was happening in a very small way to me was happening in a much larger, more horrific way to people around the world . . . and when it happens to you it is a really shocking thing. A number of people say to me, 'Of course they're going to do it and you shouldn't worry about it,' but it is a terribly disturbing thing to have happen to you, and you do feel something fundamental has been taken from you" (qtd. in Moss 2007, n.p.).

23. See Eben Kirksey's account of the massacre by Indonesian soldiers and police officers of protestors in Biak, West Papua, in 1998, in which some people were shot and others, still alive, were taken out to sea and dumped (2012, 42–50). "Names without Graves, Graves without Names" is the title of rights organization Elsham's report on the Biak massacre (Kirksey 2012, 50).

5. Utopia Haunted

1. On Hotere's gift to Wendt, see Sharrard (2003, 206). For a discussion of the black rainbow, see DeLoughrey (2011, 242).

2. Wendt associates the black in Hotere's works with Māori, and more broadly Pacific, creation genealogies that link darkness and potential (Sharrard 2003, 207). Ranginui Walker describes *Te Pō*, "the darkness" and the second stage of being

from the beginning of the universe through to the creation of humans, as "preg-nant with potential" (1987, 42).

3. For example, see Sumathi Ramaswamy's work on the affective worlds of the lost continent Lemuria (2004); Jennifer Wenzel's engagement with hope in the afterlives of the Xhosa cattle killing (2009); Jonathan Lear's research on hope at the time when the Crow nation lost its land as well as attendant frameworks for making sense of the world and its futures (2006); and Hirokazu Miyazaki's research on Suvavou people's long-standing hope to recover ancestral land from the Fijian government (2004).

4. For journalists' accounts of the 1995 protests in Tahiti, see Milliken (1995) and Shenon (1995).

5. Salmond (2009) and Matsuda (2005) provide detailed historical accounts of early French thought about the Pacific.

6. Smith (1992), Wendt (1990), and Vaai (1999) observe early European uto-pian thought about differing Pacific sites.

7. Mary Zournazi advocates that we "explore hope through the societies we live in: the alienations that affect us in individual and collective ways; the grief, despair and loneliness; and the new social, ethnic and class relations that come out of these alienations" (2002, 16). She suggests that in Australia, individual eco-nomic success and national security are among the powerful contemporary sto-ries that shape hope (15).

8. Ian Wedde argues that European artists of the exploring expeditions in the Pacific often prefer to simply leave out the present in their narratives, avoiding thinking about hope in relation to Indigenous people's perspectives as well as the conflicts and upheavals associated with European imperialism (2005a).

9. The statistics on the numbers of nuclear bomb tests detonated in the Pacific Islands sometimes vary from account to account, but I am drawing this number from Chaumeau (2012). On the histories of French nuclear testing in the Pacific, see Danielsson (1990); Greenpeace International (1990); and Ministry of Foreign Affairs (1973).

10. Michelle Keown writes that Wendt is "the most prolific and influential In-digenous writer of the wider Pacific region" (2005, 16). He is known for poetry, novels, drama, short stories, art, political essays, and for editing major collections of Pacific fiction. Postcolonial critics have often overlooked Wendt as an anti-colonial theorist and fiction writer. Paul Sharrard associates Wendt's marginality with his enduring affirmation of nationalist identity politics, which contrasts with the decentered identities often privileged in postcolonial studies (2003, 12).

11. Hugh Raffles, for example, suggests that ecologists working in the con-text of deforestation in Amazonia strategically produce a narrative of Indigenous peoples as stewards of nature who are being tragically destroyed by civilization

and the modern, along with the forests and other natural habitats with which they are integrated (2002, 152).

12. Elizabeth DeLoughrey discusses the silences that mark nuclear weapons histories, focusing on discourses that naturalize radiation by linking it to the sun (2011).

13. For example, see Julianne A. Hazlewood's account of the seas of oil palms that are being established in the Global South to support climate change mitigation in the Global North (2012, 123). Numerous scholars discuss how individuals and institutions use claims about nature to undermine political life. See Haraway (1991), Latour (2004), and Morton (2007; 2010).

14. In *Sea Sick: The Global Ocean in Crisis*, Canadian journalist Alanna Mitchell wonders about the persistence of hope when "the evidence about the advanced illness of the global ocean and its enervated vital signs has seemed to build a terrifyingly strong case of incalculable disaster" (2010, 191).

15. In discussing relationships between hope and democracy, Arjun Appadurai suggests that hope involves engagement with possibilities not probability (2007, 30).

16. For example, in the documentary *Moana: A Romance of the Golden Age*, American filmmakers Robert Flaherty and Francis Hubbard Flaherty represent activities such as food gathering and tattoo in a village on Savai'i, Samoa, where "the people still retain the spirit and nobility of their great race" (Flaherty and Flaherty 1926). In 1929 Robert J. Flaherty called on the U.S. government to create "indigenous 'preserves'" to protect Indigenous Pacific peoples from extinction (Geiger 2007, 135).

17. Wendt has also suggested that Hotere created a lithograph in the *Black Rainbow* series each time France detonated a nuclear device at Mururoa Atoll (Sharrard 2003, 206).

18. Ronni Alexander discusses Palau's nuclear-free constitution and the Compact of Free Association (1994, 213–31).

19. Barclay's imagery describes the long term, open-ended, and chaotic temporal dynamics that Rob Nixon characterizes as slow violence (Nixon 2011).

20. After the people of Rongelap Atoll were exposed to heavy radioactive fallout in 1954, they were used in medical research carried out by the Brookhaven National Laboratory. A large amount of U.S. funding went toward advancing U.S. scientific interests rather than into health infrastructure in the Marshall Islands (Johnston and Barker 2008, 22).

21. Writing of the hope of Abu Saeed, a Palestinian refugee who lives in Lebanon in conditions of severe economic and political duress, Sylvain Perdigon notes, "The temptation is irresistible . . . to grasp hope as resignation ('necessity made a virtue', dear to social scientists), or as a mistake (a mistaken evaluation of

the state of the world), verging on psychotic madness (downright denial of one's condition)" (2008, n.p.).

22. Ernst Bloch describes "the slogan 'That's merely utopian thinking' reduced as depreciation to 'castle in the clouds,' to 'wishful thinking' without any possibility for completion, to imagining and dreaming things in a banal sense" (Bloch and Adorno 1988, 2).

23. Barclay perhaps here evokes tensions regarding the extent of the U.S. government's responsibilities in relation to the extensive damage in the Marshall Islands. The people of Bikini Atoll filed a lawsuit against the U.S. government in 2006, seeking enforcement of $561,036,320 of damages that were calculated on the basis of an original amount determined by the Nuclear Claims Tribunal, less payments and plus interest. The Tribunal was set up under the Compact of Free Association, which defines the Marshall Islands and United States relationship after the end of the trusteeship. The United States had paid just $2,279,000 of the amount awarded by the Tribunal, "or less than one-half of one percent" of the total (People of Bikini 2006, 2). Following years of back-and-forth legal clashes between the United States and the people of Bikini Atoll, in 2010 the U.S. Supreme Court denied the people of Bikini's petition (Supreme Court 2010).

24. As Graham Huggan and Helen Tiffin observe, "Meļaļ/Ebeye will continue to struggle with the human and environmental legacies of its nuclear past, with its residually colonised present, and with its marginal location in an unevenly developed world" (2010, 60).

25. I am drawing from Christopher Nelson's discussion of the importance of the present in Okinawan people's performances of the dance for the dead or the *eisā:* "I do not want to take away from the importance of the moment itself. It seems that practices are too often considered only to expose their reference to other situations, their relationship to other times and places" (2008, 214).

26. Rujen's financial dilemmas perhaps evoke broader dilemmas in the Marshallese relationship with the United States. The United States currently leases the military base land at Kwajalein Atoll. This funding, as well as other funding derived from the Marshallese–U.S. relationship, has annually provided the Marshall Islands with much more than 50 percent of gross domestic product (Republic of the Marshall Islands et al. 2007, 1.1.1).

27. As Christopher Nelson observes of Okinawan people's relationship with the everyday landscapes that provoke memories of Japanese colonialism, the Pacific war, and the American military occupation, these landscapes are "characterized by the powerful and unsettling ambiguity of horror and possibility" (2008, 5). In relation to these memories, hope and loss, among other experiences, tangle and conflict: "However carefully the narrative is crafted to emphasize one aspect, its counterpart remains just at the edge of perception" (2008, 5).

Conclusion

1. Jonathan Goldberg Hiller and Noenoe K. Silva discuss Hawaiian thought regarding the sentience of varied beings, including landforms (2011).

2. Jameson links hope to a "Utopian impulse" that infuses life and that might involve "liberal reforms and commercial pipedreams," in contrast with the Utopian program, with its systemic engagement directed at new societies (2005, 3).

3. Recent documentary films about climate change in the Pacific include Elizabeth Pollock's *Atlantis Approaching* (2006); Briar March's *There once was an Island: Te Henua e Nnoho* (2010); and Christopher Horner's *The Disappearing of Tuvalu: Trouble in Paradise* (2004).

4. Farbotko and Lazrus argue that Tuvaluans often frame the necessary responses to climate change as "extensive, immediate reductions in global greenhouse gas emissions, and significant legal and financial action to redress lost livelihoods and self-determination if emissions reduction is not achieved" (2012, 388). Focusing on civil society in Tuvalu, they describe ways of apprehending climate change that draw on existing material and cultural resources such as Tuvaluans' long histories of migration, as well as on potentials for adaptation to climate change, including global citizenship.

Bibliography

Adams, Tūhuatahi Tui, and Paul Meredith. 2009. "Ngāti Maniapoto—The Māori King Movement." *Te Ara: The Encyclopedia of New Zealand.* www.TeAra.govt .nz/en/ngati-maniapoto/4

Ahmad, Dohra. 2009. *Landscapes of Hope: Anti-Colonial Utopianism in America.* New York: Oxford University Press.

Ahmed, Sara. 2010. "Happy Objects." In *The Affect Theory Reader,* ed. Melissa Gregg and Gregory J. Seigworth, 29–51. Durham, N.C.: Duke University Press.

Ahuja, Neel. 2011. "Abu Zubaydah and the Caterpillar." *Social Text 106* 29, no. 1: 127–49.

Alexander, Ronni. 1994. *Putting the Earth First: Alternatives to Nuclear Security in Pacific Island States.* Honolulu: University of Hawai'i, Matsunaga Institute for Peace.

Alley, Elizabeth. 1992. "Keri Hulme." In *In the Same Room: Conversations with New Zealand Writers,* ed. Elizabeth Alley and Mark Williams, 141–56. Auckland, N.Z.: Auckland University Press.

Allon, Fiona. 2006. "Dams, Plants, Pipes, and Flows: From Big Water to Everyday Water." *Reconstruction: Studies in Contemporary Culture* 6, no. 3. reconstruction .eserver.org/063/contents.shtml.

Anker, Peder. 2001. *Imperial Ecology: Environmental Order in the British Empire, 1895–1945.* Cambridge, Mass.: Harvard University Press.

Appadurai, Arjun. 2007. "Hope and Democracy." *Public Culture* 19, no. 1: 29–34.

Australian Broadcasting Corporation. 2006. "Flanagan Novel Condemns Modern Australia." *ABC.* www.abc.net.au/7.30/content/2006/s1779192.htm.

Australian Marine Conservation Society. 2011. "Ningaloo Coast World Heritage Listing: A Victory for People Power and the Seas!" *Australian Marine Conservation Society.* www.amcs.org.au/MediaReleases-AMCS.asp?active_page_id =768.

Bachelard, Gaston. 1983. *Water and Dreams: An Essay on the Imagination of Matter.* Translated by Edith R. Farrell. Dallas, Tex.: Pegasus Foundation.

Bacon, Francis. 1999 [1627]. *New Atlantis.* In *Three Early Modern Utopias: Utopia, New Atlantis, and the Isle of Pines,* ed. Susan Bruce, 149–86. Oxford: Oxford University Press.

Balaz, Joe. 2003. "Da Last Squid." In *Whetu Moana: Contemporary Polynesian Poems in English,* ed. Albert Wendt, Reina Whaitiri, and Robert Sullivan, 8–10. Honolulu: University of Hawai'i Press.

Ballance, Alison. 2010. *Kakapo: Rescued from the Brink of Extinction.* Nelson, N.Z.: Craig Potton Publishing.

Barclay, Robert. 2002. *Meḻaḻ: A Novel of the Pacific.* Honolulu: University of Hawai'i Press.

Bayat, Asef. 2010. *Life as Politics: How Ordinary People Change the Middle East.* Stanford, Calif.: Stanford University Press.

Beecham, John. 1838. *Colonization Being Remarks on Colonization in General, with an Examination of the Proposals of the Association which has been formed for Colonizing New Zealand.* London: Hatchards, Piccadilly; Seeleys, Fleet Street; Hamilton, Adams & Co; and John Mason, Paternoster Row.

Benjamin, Walter. 1969. "Theses on the Philosophy of History." Translated by Harry Zohn. In *Illuminations: Walter Benjamin: Essays and Reflections,* ed. Hannah Arendt, 253–64. New York: Schocken Books.

———. 1999. "Mickey Mouse." Translated by Rodney Livingstone. In *Walter Benjamin: Selected Writings. Vol. 2, 1927–1934,* ed. Michael W. Jennings, Howard Eiland, and Gary Smith, 545. Cambridge, Mass.: Harvard University Press.

Bennett, Jane. 2010. *Vibrant Matter: A Political Ecology of Things.* Durham, N.C.: Duke University Press.

Berry, K. A. 2006. "Changing Narratives of Water Control in Hawai'i." In *A History of Water: The World of Water,* ed. T. Tvedt and T. Oestigaard, 38–48. London: I.B. Tauris & Co.

Binney, Judith. 1997. *Redemption Songs: A Life of the Nineteenth-Century Maori Leader Te Kooti Arikirangi Te Turuki.* Honolulu: University of Hawai'i Press.

Bloch, Ernst. 1986. *The Principle of Hope. Vol. 1.* Translated by Neville Plaice, Stephen Plaice, and Paul Knight. Cambridge, Mass.: MIT Press.

———. 1988. "Better Castles in the Sky at the Country Fair and Circus, in Fairy Tales and Colportage (1959)." *The Utopian Function of Art and Literature: Selected Essays,* 167–85. Translated by Jack Zipes and Frank Mecklenburg. Cambridge, Mass.: MIT Press.

Bloch, Ernst, and Theodor W. Adorno. 1988. "Something's Missing: A Discussion between Ernst Bloch and Theodor W. Adorno on the Contradictions of Utopian Longing (1964)." *The Utopian Function of Art and Literature: Selected Essays,* 1–17. Translated by Jack Zipes and Frank Mecklenburg. Cambridge, Mass.: MIT Press.

Bogue, Ronald. 2010. *Deleuzian Fabulation and the Scars of History.* Edinburgh, U.K.: Edinburgh University Press.

Bougainville, Louis-Antoine de. 2002. *The Pacific Journal of Louis-Antoine de Bougainville 1767–1768.* Translated by John Dunmore. London: Hakluyt Society.

Brand, Ian. 1984. *Sarah Island Penal Settlements 1822—1833 and 1846—1847.* Launceston, Aus.: Regal.

Brown, Gordon H. 1984. *Colin McCahon: Artist.* Wellington, N.Z.: A. H. & A. W. Reed Ltd.

Brown, Jayna. 2010. "Buzz and Rumble: Global Pop Music and Utopian Impulse." *Social Text 102* 28, no. 1: 125–46.

Brunner, Thomas. 1848. *Journal of an Expedition to Explore the Interior of the Middle Island of New Zealand.* Nelson, N.Z.: Examiner Office.

Buell, Lawrence. 2001. *Writing for an Endangered World: Literature, Culture, and Environment in the U.S. and Beyond.* Cambridge, Mass.: Harvard University Press.

Butler, Samuel. 1970 [1872]. *Erewhon.* London: Penguin.

Cameron, James. Dir. *Avatar.* 2009. Beverly Hills: Twentieth Century Fox Corporation and Dune Entertainment LLC.

Cameron, Patsy. 2005. "Aboriginal Life Pre-Invasion." In *The Companion to Tasmanian History,* ed. Alison Alexander, 3–6. Hobart, Aus.: University of Tasmania, Centre for Tasmanian Historical Studies.

Chai, Alice Yun. 1988. "Women's History in Public: 'Picture Brides' of Hawaii." *Women's Studies Quarterly* 16, no. 1/2: 51–62.

Chakrabarty, Dipesh. 2009. "The Climate of History: Four Theses." *Critical Inquiry* 35 (Winter): 197–222.

Chaumeau, Christine. 2012. "France Urged to Clean Up Deadly Waste from Its Nuclear Tests in Polynesia." *The Guardian,* February 7. www.guardian.com.

Cilano, Carla, and Elizabeth DeLoughrey. 2007. "Against Authenticity: Global Knowledges and Postcolonial Ecocriticism." *ISLE: Interdisciplinary Studies in Literature and Environment* 14, no. 1: 71–87.

Clark, Malcolm R., Owen F. Anderson, R. I. C. Chris Francis, and Dianne M. Tracey. 2000. "The Effects of Commercial Exploitation on Orange Roughy *(Hoplostethus Atlanticus)* from the Continental Slope of the Chatham Rise, New Zealand, from 1979 to 1997." *Fisheries Research* 45, no. 3: 217–38.

Clark, Nigel. 2004. "Cultural Studies for Shaky Islands." In *Cultural Studies in Aotearoa New Zealand: Identity, Space, and Place,* ed. Claudia Bell and Steve Matthewman, 3–18. Oxford: Oxford University Press.

Connery, Christopher. 1996. "The Oceanic Feeling and the Regional Imaginary." *Global/Local: Cultural Production and the Transnational Imaginary,* ed. Rob Wilson and Wimal Dissanayake, 284–311. Durham, N.C.: Duke University Press.

Corbin, Alain. 1994. *The Lure of the Sea: The Discovery of the Seaside in the Western World, 1750–1840.* Translated by Jocelyn Phelps. Berkeley: University of California Press.

Cordle, Daniel. 2008. *States of Suspense: The Nuclear Age, Postmodernism, and United States Fiction and Prose.* Manchester, U.K.: Manchester University Press.

Cousteau, Jacques-Yves. Dir. 2010 [1964]. *Le Monde sans Soleil*. Paris: TF1 Vidéo.

Cox, Paul Alan. 1997. *Nafanua: Saving the Samoan Rain Forest*. New York: W. H. Freeman and Company.

Cramer, Chris. 2011. "Maunalua Bay's Last Fishponds." *Maunalua Fishpond Heritage Center*. maunaluafishpond.org/talk-story/maunalua-bay-fishponds.

Cranston, C. A. 2003. "Rambling in Overdrive: Travelling through Tasmanian Literature." *Tasmanian Historical Studies* 8, no. 2: 28–39.

Cruikshank, Julie. 2005. *Do Glaciers Listen? Local Knowledge, Colonial Encounters, and Social Imagination*. Vancouver and Toronto: UBC Press.

Culliney, John L. 2006. *Islands in a Far Sea: The Fate of Nature in Hawaiʻi*. Honolulu: University of Hawaiʻi Press.

Danielsson, Bengt. 1990. "Poisoned Pacific: The Legacy of French Nuclear Testing." *The Bulletin of the Atomic Scientists* 46, no. 2: 22–31.

Darby, Andrew. 2003. "Canberra all at Sea over Position of Southern Ocean." *Fairfax Digital: theage.com.au* December 22. www.theage.com.au/articles/2003/12/21/1071941610556.html.

D'Arcy, Paul. 2006. *The People of the Sea: Environment, Identity, and History in Oceania*. Honolulu: University of Hawaiʻi Press.

Darwin, Charles. 2010. *The Voyage of the Beagle: Charles Darwin's Journal of Research*. Seattle: Pacific Publishing Studio.

DeLoughrey, Elizabeth M. 2007. *Routes and Roots: Navigating Caribbean and Pacific Island Literatures*. Honolulu: University of Hawaiʻi Press.

———. 2011. "Heliotropes: Solar Ecologies and Pacific Radiations." In *Postcolonial Ecologies: Literatures of the Environment*, ed. Elizabeth DeLoughrey and George B. Handley, 235–53. Oxford and New York: Oxford University Press.

DeLoughrey, Elizabeth M., and George B. Handley. 2011. *Postcolonial Ecologies: Literatures of the Environment*. Oxford: Oxford University Press.

Department of Conservation. 2011. *Rowi—The Rarest of Them All*. Hokitika, N.Z.: Department of Conservation Westland *Tai Poutini* Conservancy. www.doc.govt.nz/upload/documents/conservation/native-animals/birds/rowi-the-rarest-of-them-all.pdf.

———. n.d.a. "Special Forests: Okarito Kahikatea Forest." *Department of Conservation Te Papa Atawhai*. doc.govt.nz/getting-involved/events-and-awards/international-decade-of-biodiversity/international-year-of-forests-2011/new-zealands-native-forests/special-forests.

———. n.d.b. "Te Matua Ngahere Walk." *Department of Conservation Te Papa Atawhai*. Available: www.doc.govt.nz/parks-and-recreation/tracks-and-walks/northland/kauri-coast/te-matua-ngahere-walk.

Donner, Simon D. 2009. "Coping with Commitment: Projected Thermal Stress on Coral Reefs under Different Future Scenarios." *PLoS ONE* 4, no. 6: 1–10.

Dudoit, D. Māhealani. 1997. "Reservoir of Hope." *Mānoa* 9, no. 1: 161–63.

Edgar, Graham J., Cath R. Samson, and Neville S. Barrett. 2005. "Species Extinction in the Marine Environment: Tasmania as a Regional Example of Overlooked Losses in Biodiversity." *Conservation Biology* 19, no. 4: 1294–1300.

Eggleton, David. 2000. "From Absence to Presence." In *Ralph Hotere Black Light: Major Works Including Collaborations with Bill Culbert,* ed. Cilla McQueen, Priscilla Pitts, Mary Trewby, John Walsh, and Ian Wedde, 61–69. Wellington and Dunedin, N.Z.: Te Papa Press and Dunedin Public Art Gallery.

Eliott, Jaklin A. 2005. "What Have We Done with Hope? A Brief History." In *Interdisciplinary Perspectives on Hope,* ed. Jaklin A. Eliott, 3–45. Hauppauge, N.Y.: Nova Science Publishers.

Ellis, Richard. 2003. *The Empty Ocean: Plundering the World's Marine Life.* Washington, D.C.: Island Press.

Escobar, Arturo. 1995. *Encountering Development: The Making and Unmaking of the Third World.* Princeton: Princeton University Press.

———. 1997. "Cultural Politics and Biodiversity: State, Capital, and Social Movements in the Pacific Coast of Colombia." In *The Politics of Culture in the Shadow of Capital,* ed. Lisa Lowe and David Lloyd, 201–26. Durham, N.C.: Duke University Press.

———. 2012. Preface to the 2012 edition. In *Encountering Development: The Making and Unmaking of the Third World,* vii–xliii. Princeton: Princeton University Press.

Fahrenthold, David A. 2009. "Tastier Names Trouble for Seafood Stocks." *Washington Post,* July 31. articles.washingtonpost.com/2009-07-31/news/36862491 _1_seafood-study-familiar-fish-boris-worm.

Fanon, Frantz. 1963. *The Wretched of the Earth.* Translated by Constance Farrington. New York: Grove Press.

Farbotko, Carol, and Heather Lazrus. 2012. "The First Climate Refugees? Contesting Global Narratives of Climate Change in Tuvalu." *Global Environmental Change* 22, no. 2: 382–90.

Figiel, Sia. 1999 [1996]. *Where We Once Belonged.* New York: Kaya Press.

Firth, Stewart. 2005. "A Comment on 'The Nuclear Issue in the South Pacific.'" *Contemporary Pacific* 17, no. 2: 359–62.

Flaherty, Robert, and Francis Hubbard Flaherty. Dir. 1926. *Moana: A Romance of the South Seas.* Los Angeles: Paramount Pictures.

Flanagan, Richard. 2001. *Gould's Book of Fish.* New York: Grove Press.

———. 2006. *The Unknown Terrorist.* Sydney, Aus.: Picador.

Fletcher, Angus. 1999. "The Place of Despair and Hope." *Social Research* 66, no. 2: 521–29.

Foucault, Michel. 1978. *The History of Sexuality: An Introduction. Vol. 1.* Translated by Robert Hurley. New York: Random House.

————. 1988. *Madness and Civilization: A History of Insanity in the Age of Reason.* Translated by Richard Howard. New York: Vintage Books.

Fourier, Charles. 1996 [1808]. *The Theory of the Four Movements.* Translated by Ian Patterson. Cambridge: Cambridge University Press.

Frame, Janet. 2005 [1961]. *Faces in the Water and The Edge of the Alphabet.* Auckland, N.Z.: Random House.

Freire, Paulo. 1994. *Pedagogy of Hope: Reliving Pedagogy of the Oppressed.* Translated by Robert R. Barr. London: Continuum.

Fryd, Vivien Green. 2003. *Art and the Crisis of Marriage: Edward Hopper and Georgia O'Keeffe.* Chicago: University of Chicago Press.

Gandhi, Leela. 2006. *Affective Communities: Anticolonial Thought, Fin-de-Siècle Radicalism, and the Politics of Friendship.* Durham, N.C.: Duke University Press.

Garrard, Greg. 2004. *Ecocriticism: The New Critical Idiom.* London: Routledge.

Garrett, Rob. 2012. "Ralph Hotere: Towards Aramoana, 1982." *Rob Garrett Curator.* www.robgarrettcfa.com/content/2007/09/15/ralph-hotere.

Gauguin, Paul. 2005 [1919]. *Noa Noa: The Tahiti Journal of Paul Gauguin.* Translated by O. F Theis. San Francisco: Chronicle Books.

Geiger, Jeffrey. 2007. *Facing the Pacific: Polynesia and the U.S. Imperial Imagination.* Honolulu: University of Hawai'i Press.

George, James. 2006. *Ocean Roads.* Wellington, N.Z.: Huia Publishers.

Goldberg-Hiller, Jonathan, and Noenoe K. Silva. 2011. "Sharks and Pigs: Animating Hawaiian Sovereignty against the Anthropological Machine." *South Atlantic Quarterly* 110, no. 2: 429–46.

Gordon, Pamela. 2005. "Truth Is Indeed Stranger Than Fiction: A Biographical Sketch." In *Faces in the Water and The Edge of the Alphabet,* by Janet Frame, 17–21. Auckland, N.Z.: Random House.

"Gould William Buelow." n.d. In *Record Book of "Miscellaneous" Convicts Locally Convicted or Transported from Other Colonies. LINC Tasmania.* search.archives .tas.gov.au/ImageViewer/image_viewer.htm?CON37-1-3,404,228,C,80.

Gould, William Buelow. ca. 1832. *Sketchbook of Fishes. LINC Tasmania.* catalogue. statelibrary.tas.gov.au/item/?id=80818.

Greenpeace International. 1990. *Testimonies: Witnesses of French Nuclear Testing in the South Pacific.* Auckland, N.Z.: Greenpeace International.

Grosz, Elizabeth. 2005. *Time Travels: Feminism, Nature, Power.* Durham, N.C.: Duke University Press.

Hage, Ghassan, and Mary Zournazi. 2002. "'On the Side of Life'—Joy and the Capacity of Being." In *Hope: New Philosophies for Change,* by Mary Zournazi, 150–71. Annandale, NSW, Aus.: Pluto Press Australia.

Halliday, William R. 1998. "History and Status of the Moiliili Karst, Hawaii." *Journal of Cave and Karst Studies* 60, no. 3: 141–45.

Haraway, Donna J. 1991. *Simians, Cyborgs, and Women: The Reinvention of Nature.* New York: Routledge.

Hardt, Michael. 2010. "Two Faces of Apocalypse: A Letter from Copenhagen." *Polygraph* 22: 265–74.

Hardt, Michael, and Antonio Negri. 2004. *Multitude: War and Democracy in the Age of Empire.* New York: Penguin.

Harvey, David. 1996. *Justice, Nature and the Geography of Difference.* Malden, Mass.: Blackwell.

———. 2000. *Spaces of Hope.* Berkeley: University of California Press.

Hau'ofa, Epeli. 2008a. "Our Sea of Islands." *We Are the Ocean: Selected Works,* by Epeli Hau'ofa, 27–40. Honolulu: University of Hawai'i Press.

———. 2008b. "Pasts to Remember." *We are the Ocean: Selected Works,* by Epeli Hau'ofa, 60–79. Honolulu: University of Hawai'i Press.

———.2008c. "The Ocean in Us." *We Are the Ocean: Selected Works,* by Epeli Hau'ofa, 41–59. Honolulu: University of Hawai'i Press.

Hazlewood, Julianne A. 2012. "CO2lonialism and the 'Unintended Consequences' of Commoditizing Climate Change: Geographies of Hope Amid a Sea of Oil Palms in the Northwest Ecuadorian Pacific Region." *Journal of Sustainable Forestry* 31, nos. 1–2: 120–53.

Heise, Ursula K. 2008. *Sense of Place and Sense of Planet: The Environmental Imagination of the Global.* New York: Oxford University Press.

Helmreich, Stefan. 2005. "How Scientists Think; About 'Natives', For Example. A Problem of Taxonomy among Biologists of Alien Species in Hawaii." *Journal of the Royal Anthropological Institute* 11: 107–28.

———. 2009. *Alien Ocean: Anthropological Voyages in Microbial Seas.* Berkeley: University of California Press.

Hereniko, Vilsoni. 2006. "Interview with Albert Wendt: Art, Writing, and the Creative Process." *Contemporary Pacific* 18, no. 1: 59–69.

Hesser, Leon. 2006. *The Man Who Fed the World: Nobel Peace Prize Laureate Norman Borlaug and His Battle to End World Hunger: An Authorized Biography by Leon Hesser.* Dallas, Tex.: Durban House.

Hirschman, Albert O. 1971. *A Bias for Hope: Essays on Development and Latin America.* New Haven: Yale University Press.

Hoegh-Guldberg, O., et al. 2007. "Coral Reefs under Rapid Climate Change and Ocean Acidification." *Science* 318, no. 5857: 1737–42.

Hooker, Claire. 2004. *Irresistible Forces: Australian Women in Science.* Carlton, Aus.: Melbourne University Press.

Horner, Christopher. 2005. *The Disappearing of Tuvalu: Trouble in Paradise.* Watertown, Mass.: Documentary Educational Resources.

Huggan, Graham, and Helen Tiffin. 2010. *Postcolonial Ecocriticism: Literature, Animals, Environment.* New York: Routledge.

Hughes, David McDermott. 2006. "Hydrology of Hope: Farm Dams, Conservation, and Whiteness in Zimbabwe." *American Ethnologist* 33, no. 2: 269–87.

Hulme, Keri. 1986 [1984]. *The Bone People*. New York: Penguin.

Hunt, Janet. 2011. "Introduction." In *Hone Tuwhare: Small Holes in the Silence: Collected Works*, by Hone Tuwhare, 15–18. Auckland, N.Z.: Random House.

Huot, Nikolas. 2002. "Cathy Song (1955–)." In *Contemporary American Women
Poets: An A-to-Z Guide*, ed. Catherine Cucinella, 352–55. Westport, Conn.:
Greenwood Press.

Ibuse, Masuji. 1969. *Black Rain*. Translated by John Bester. Tokyo, Japan: Kodan-
sha International.

Ingram, Annie Merrill, Ian Marshall, Daniel J. Philippon, and Adam W. Sweeting.
2007. "Introduction: Thinking Our Life in Nature." In *Coming into Contact: Explorations in Ecocritical Theory and Practice*, ed. Annie Merrill Ingram, Ian Marshall,
Daniel J. Philippon, and Adam W. Sweeting, 1–14. Athens: University of Georgia
Press.

IUCN. 2006. "Phyllopteryx taeniolatus (Common Seadragon, Weedy Seadragon)."
IUCN Red List of Threatened Species. www.iucnredlist.org/details/17177/0.

Jackson, Peter. 2003. "Foreword." In *The Lord of the Rings Location Guidebook: Re-
vised Edition*, by Ian Brodie, 6–7. Auckland, N.Z.: HarperCollins Publishers
(N.Z.).

Jameson, Fredric. 1988. *The Ideologies of Theory: Essays 1971–1986, Vol. 2: Syntax of
History*, 75–102. Minneapolis: University of Minnesota Press.

———. 2005. *Archaeologies of the Future: The Desire Called Utopia and Other Science Fictions*. London, U.K., and New York: Verso.

Johnson, Walter, and Sione Tupouniua. 1976. "Current Developments in the Pacific: Against French Nuclear Testing: The A.T.O.M. Committee." *Journal of
Pacific History* 11, no. 4: 213–16.

Johnston, Barbara Rose, and Holly M. Barker. 2008. *The Rongelap Report: Consequential Damages of Nuclear War*. Walnut Creek, Calif.: Left Coast Press.

Johnston, Chris. 2004. "World's End." *FairfaxMedia:Theage.com.au*, August 13.
www.theage.com.au/articles/2004/08/13/1092340444210.html.

Jordon, Caroline. 2002. "Progress versus the Picturesque: White Women and the
Aesthetics of Environmentalism in Colonial Australia 1820–1860." *Art History*
25, no. 3: 341–57.

Kahn, Miriam. 2009. *"Consequential Damages of Nuclear War: The Rongelap Report, by Barbara Rose Johnston and Holly M Barker." Contemporary Pacific* 21,
no. 2: 401–4.

Kanaʻiaupuni, Shawn Malia, and Nolan Malone. 2006. "This Land Is My Land:
The Role of Place in Native Hawaiian Identity." In *Race, Ethnicity, and Place in
a Changing America*, ed. John W. Frazier and Eugene L. Tettey-Fio, 287–300.
Binghamton, N.Y.: Global Academic Pub.

Kawaharada, Dennis. 1999. *Storied Landscapes: Hawaiian Literature and Place.* Honolulu: Kalamakū Press.

Keane, Basil. 2009. "Kurī—Polynesian Dogs—What Is the Kurī?" *Te Ara: The Encyclopedia of New Zealand.* www.TeAra.govt.nz/en/kuri-polynesian-dogs/1.

Keown, Michelle. 2005. *Postcolonial Pacific Writing: Representations of the Body.* New York: Routledge.

————. 2007. *Pacific Islands Writing: The Postcolonial Literatures of Aotearoa/ New Zealand and Oceania.* Oxford, U.K.: Oxford University Press.

Kirksey, Eben. 2012. *Freedom in Entangled Worlds: West Papua and the Architecture of Global Power.* Durham, N.C.: Duke University Press.

Kiste, Robert C. 2004. "*Melal: A Novel of the Pacific* (review)." *Contemporary Pacific* 16, no. 1: 208–11.

Klady, Leonard. 1988. "Movie Review: 'Radio Bikini': Documentary with Fallout." *Los Angeles Times,* March 12. articles.latimes.com/1988-03-12/entertainment/ca-636_1_radio-bikini.

Knight, Catherine. 2010. "The Slewing of Our Kahikatea Forests: How Jurassic Giants Became Butter Boxes." *Envirohistory NZ,* October 31. envirohistorynz.wordpress.com.

Kohn, Eduardo. 2007. "How Dogs Dream: Amazonian Natures and the Politics of Transspecies Engagement." *American Ethnologist* 34, no. 1: 3–24.

Kolbert, Elizabeth. 2009. *Field Notes from a Catastrophe: Man, Nature, and Climate Change.* New York: Bloomsbury.

Koshin, Jillian. 2011. "Shifting Visions: Developmentalism and Environmentalism in Australian History." *Australian Studies* 3: 1–21.

Kwon, Brenda L. 1999. *Beyond Ke'eaumoku: Koreans, Nationalism, and Local Culture in Hawai'i.* New York: Garland Publishing.

Latour, Bruno. 2004. *Politics of Nature: How to Bring the Sciences into Democracy.* Translated by Catherine Porter. Cambridge, Mass.: Harvard University Press.

Lawrence, Susan. 2008. "A Maritime Empire: Archaeological Evidence for Van Diemen's Land Whaling in the Southern Oceans." *Tasmanian Historical Studies* 13: 15–33.

Lear, Jonathan. 2006. *Radical Hope: Ethics in the Face of Cultural Devastation.* Cambridge, Mass.: Harvard University Press.

Lem, Stanisław. 1970 [1961]. *Solaris.* Translated by Joanna Kilmartin and Steve Cox. New York: Berkeley Publishing Group.

Lempriere, Thomas James. 1954. *The Penal Settlements of Van Diemen's Land, Macquarie Harbour, Maria Island, and Tasman's Peninsula.* Launceston, Aus.: Royal Society of Tasmania (Northern Branch).

Linton, Jamie. 2006. "The Social Nature of Natural Resources: The Case of Water." *Reconstruction: Studies in Contemporary Culture* 6, no. 3. reconstruction.eserver.org/063/linton.shtml.

Litzinger, Ralph. 2006. "Contested Sovereignties and the Critical Ecosystem Partnership Fund." *PoLAR: Political and Legal Anthropology Review* 29, no. 1: 66–87.

Lyver P. O'B, H. Moller, and C. Thompson. 1999. "Changes in Sooty Shearwater *Puffinus griseus* Chick Production and Harvest Precede ENSO Events." *Marine Ecology Progress Series* 188 (November): 237–48.

Mane-Wheoki, Jonathan. 1997. "Hotere: Out the Black Window." *Landfall 194* (Spring): 233–40.

Manhire, Bill. 1988. "Ready to Move: Interview with Hone Tuwhare." *Landfall 167* 42, no. 3: 262–81.

March, Briar. 2010. *There Once Was an Island—Te Henua e Nnoho.* Auckland, N.Z.: On the Level Productions and New Day Films.

Marr, Cathy. 1996. "The Alienation of Maori Land in the Rohe Potae (Aotea Block), 1840–1920." *Waitangi Tribunal.* www.waitangi-tribunal.govt.nz/doclibrary/public/researchwhanui/district/08/pt1/District8(1)-RohePotae_1840–1920.pdf.

Marsh, Selina Tusitala. 1999. "Theory 'versus' Pacific Islands Writing: Towards a *Tama'ita'i* Criticism in the Works of Three Pacific Islands Woman Poets." In *Inside Out: Literature, Cultural Politics, and Identity in the New Pacific,* ed. Vilsoni Hereniko and Rob Wilson, 337–56. Lanham, Md.: Rowman & Littlefield.

Matsuda, Matt K. 2005. *Empire of Love: Histories of France and the Pacific.* New York: Oxford University Press.

Maunalua Fishpond Heritage Center. n.d. "History of Kanewai." maunaluafishpond .org/kanewai/history/.

Maxwell-Stewart, Hamish. 2010. "Convicts." In *The Companion to Tasmanian History,* ed. Alison Alexander, 415–19. Hobart, Aus.: Centre for Tasmanian Historical Studies, University of Tasmania.

McCahon, Colin. 1977. "Necessary Protection." *Art New Zealand* 7 (Spring). www .art-newzealand.com/Issues1to40/environcm.htm.

McClennen, Sophia A. 2010. *Ariel Dorfman: An Aesthetics of Hope.* Durham, N.C.: Duke University Press.

McGinnis, Michael V. 2011. "Straddling the Pacific Ocean: Wild Maritime Places in California and New Zealand." Unpublished manuscript.

McLintock, Alexander Hare. 2009 [1966]. "Dog, Maori." *Te Ara: The Encyclopedia of New Zealand.* www.TeAra.govt.nz/en/1966/dog-maori/1.

McPherson, Michael. 1998. "The Waking Stone." In *Growing Up Local: An Anthology of Poetry and Prose from Hawai'i,* ed. Eric Chock, James R. Harstad, Darrell H.Y. Lum, and Bill Teter, 318. Honolulu: Bamboo Ridge Press.

McQueen, Cilla. 2000a. "Dark Matter: Ralph Hotere and Language." In *Ralph Hotere Black Light: Major Works Including Collaborations with Bill Culbert,* ed. Cilla McQueen et al., 39–47. Wellington and Dunedin, N.Z.: Te Papa Press and Dunedin Public Art Gallery.

———. 2000b. *Markings.* Dunedin, N.Z.: University of Otago Press.

Mead, Margaret. 1943. *Coming of Age in Samoa*. Harmondsworth, Middlesex, U.K.: Penguin.

Melville, Herman. 1996 [1846]. *Typee: A Peep at Polynesian Life*. New York: Penguin.

Merry, Sally Engle. 2000. *Colonizing Hawai'i: The Cultural Power of Law*. Princeton: Princeton University Press.

Milliken, Robert. 1995. "Tahiti in Shock after 12 Hours Ablaze." *The Independent*, September 8. www.independent.co.uk/news/world/tahiti-in-shock-after-12 -hours-ablaze-1599999.html.

Ministry of Foreign Affairs, Wellington. 1973. *French Nuclear Testing in the Pacific: International Court of Justice. Nuclear Tests Case. New Zealand v. France*. Wellington, N.Z.: Ministry of Foreign Affairs.

Mitchell, Alanna. 2010. *Sea Sick: The Global Ocean in Crisis*. Millers Point, NSW, Aus.: Murdoch Books.

Miyazaki, Hirokazu. 2004. *The Method of Hope: Anthropology, Philosophy, and Fijian Knowledge*. Stanford, Calif.: Stanford University Press.

Moehu, Peter. 2010. "Oil and Gas for Maori too." *Taranaki Daily News Online*. www.stuff.co.nz/taranaki-daily-news/opinion/column-korero/3704483/Oil -and-Gas-for-Maori-too.

More, Thomas. *Utopia*. 1999 [1516]. Translated by Ralph Robinson. In *Three Early Modern Utopias: Utopia, New Atlantis, and The Isle of Pines*, ed. Susan Bruce, 1–148. Oxford, U.K.: Oxford University Press.

Morton, Timothy. 2007. *Ecology without Nature: Rethinking Environmental Aesthetics*. Cambridge, Mass.: Harvard University Press.

———. 2010. *The Ecological Thought*. Cambridge, Mass.: Harvard University Press.

Moss, Stephen. 2007. "The Art of Darkness." *The Guardian*, April 19. www.guardian .co.uk.

Mudford, Peter. 1970. Introduction to *Erewhon*, by Samuel Butler, 7-21. London: Penguin.

Mukherjee, Upamanyu Pablo. 2010. *Postcolonial Environments: Nature, Culture, and the Contemporary Indian Novel in English*. New York: Palgrave Macmillan.

Murayama, Milton. 1988 [1975]. *All I Asking for Is My Body*. Honolulu: University of Hawai'i Press.

Museum of New Zealand—Te Papa Tongarewa, TVNZ 7, and Vero. n.d. "Tales from Te Papa Episode 3: Kahu Kuri." www.youtube.com/watch?v =w8DXjad5ue8.

Nā Maka o ka 'Āina. 1996. *Stolen Waters*. Na'alehu: Nā Maka o ka 'Āina.

Najita, Susan Y. 2006. *Decolonizing Cultures in the Pacific: Reading History and Trauma in Contemporary Fiction*. New York: Routledge.

Nash, Michael. 2003. "The Tasmanian Maritime Heritage Program." *Bulletin of the Australasian Institute for Maritime Archaeology* 27: 43–58.

Navy.mil. 2006. "CPF Opens New Command Center." *Navy.mil,* June 16. www
.navy.mil/search/display.asp?story_id=24166.

Nelson, Christopher. 2008. *Dancing with the Dead: Memory, Performance, and
Everyday Life in Postwar Okinawa.* Durham, N.C.: Duke University Press.

Nilsen, Sarah. 2011. *Projecting America, 1958: Film and Cultural Diplomacy at the
Brussels World's Fair.* Jefferson, N.C.: McFarland.

Nixon, Rob. 2005. "Environmentalism and Postcolonialism." In *Postcolonial Studies and Beyond,* ed. Ania Loomba et al., 233–51. Durham, N.C.: Duke University
Press.

———. 2011. *Slow Violence and the Environmentalism of the Poor.* Cambridge,
Mass.: Harvard University Press.

NOAA. n.d. "Sooty Shearwater Restoration Project." *DARRP: Damage Assessment, Remediation, and Restoration Program.* www.darrp.noaa.gov/southwest/
command/sosh.html.

O'Brien, Gregory. 1997. *Hotere: Out the Black Window; Ralph Hotere's Work with
New Zealand Poets.* Auckland, N.Z.: Godwit Publishing Ltd and City Gallery,
Wellington.

Oikonos. 2006. "The Rakiura Titi Restoration Project: Mitigation of the *Command* Oil Spill Injury by Eradication of Rats from Sooty Shearwater Breeding
Colonies in New Zealand." www.oikonos.org/projects/titi.htm.

Olsen, Penny. 2010. *Upside Down World: Early European Impressions of Australia's
Curious Animals.* Canberra, Aus.: National Library of Australia.

Oxford Dictionaries. n.d. "Endurance." oxforddictionaries.com/definition/
endurance.

Pak, Gary. 1992. "The Valley of the Dead Air." In *The Watcher of Waipuna and Other
Stories,* by Gary Pak, 9–19. Honolulu: Bamboo Ridge Press.

———. 2004. *Children of a Fireland: A Novel.* Honolulu: University of Hawai'i
Press.

———. 2005a. "Language of the Geckos." In *Language of the Geckos and other
Stories,* by Gary Pak, 23–29. Seattle: University of Washington Press.

———. 2005b. "Living with Spirits, Writing as Activism: A Preface." In *Language of the Geckos and other Stories,* by Gary Pak, ix–xvi. Seattle: University
of Washington Press.

Parfit, Michael. 2003. "Islands of the Pacific." *National Geographic* 203, no. 3:
106–25.

Park, Geoff. 1995. *Ngā Uruora: The Groves of Life: Ecology and History in a New
Zealand Landscape.* Wellington, N.Z.: Victoria University Press.

———. 2006. *Theatre Country: Essays on Landscape and Whenua.* Wellington,
N.Z.: Victoria University Press.

Patek, S. N., L. E. Shipp, and E. R. Staaterman. 2009. "The Acoustics and Acoustic Behavior of the California Spiny Lobster *(Panulirus interruptus)."* *Journal of the Acoustical Society of America* 125, no. 5: 3434–43.

Peat, Neville. 2010. *The Tasman: Biography of an Ocean.* North Shore, N.Z.: Penguin.

Pemberton, Robert. 1985 [1854]. *The Happy Colony.* New York: Garland Publishers.

People of Bikini, by and through the Kili/Bikini/Ejit Local Government Council. 2006. "People of Bikini, by and through the Kili/Bikini/Ejit Local Government Council, Plaintiffs, v. United States of America, Defendant." *Bikini Atoll: U.S. Reparations for Damages.* www.bikiniatoll.com/2006%20Bikini%20vs.%20 US%20CFC.pdf.

Perdigon, Sylvain. 2008. "Yet Another Lesson in Pessoptimism—A Short Ethnography of Hope and Despair with One Palestinian Refugee in Lebanon." *Revue Asylon(s)* 5 (September). www.reseau-terra.eu/article805.html.

Perera, Sonali. 2008. "Rethinking Working-Class Literature: Feminism, Globalization, and Socialist Ethics." *Differences* 19, no. 1: 1–31.

Perry, Allison L., Paula J. Low, Jim R. Ellis, and John D. Reynolds. 2005. "Climate Change and Distribution Shifts in Marine Fishes." *Science* 308, no. 5730: 1912–15.

Perry, George. 1811. *Arcana, or, The museum of natural history: containing the most recent discovered objects: embellished with coloured plates, and corresponding descriptions: with extracts relating to animals, and remarks of celebrated travellers; combining a general survey of nature.* London: Printed by George Smeeton for James Stratford. *E Book and Texts Archive, Biodiversity Heritage Library.* archive .org/details/arcanaormuseumofooperr.

Phillips, Dana. 2003. *The Truth of Ecology: Nature, Culture, and Literature in America.* Oxford: Oxford University Press.

Piliāmoʻo and Vivien Lee. 1997. "A Portfolio of Photographs by Piliāmoʻo. Hoʻi ka Wai: The Waiāhole Stream Restoration." *Mānoa* 9, no. 1: 119–36.

Plaice, Neville, Stephen Plaice, and Paul Knight. 1986. "Translator's Introduction." In *The Principle of Hope, Vol. 1,* by Ernst Bloch, xix–xxxiii. Cambridge, Mass.: MIT Press.

Pollock, Elizabeth. 2006. *Atlantis Approaching.* Milwaukee, Wisc.: Blue Marble Productions.

Povinelli, Elizabeth A. 2011a. *Economies of Abandonment: Social Belonging and Endurance in Late Liberalism.* Durham, N.C.: Duke University Press.

———. 2011b. "The Persistence of Hope: Critical Theory and Enduring in Late Liberalism." In *Theory after 'Theory,'* ed. Jane Elliot and Derek Attridge, 105–19. New York: Routledge.

Raffles, Hugh. 2002. *In Amazonia: A Natural History.* Princeton: Princeton University Press.

Ramaswamy, Sumathi. 2004. *The Lost Land of Lemuria: Fabulous Geographies, Catastrophic Histories.* Berkeley: University of California Press.

Reeves, William Pember. 1997. "The Passing of the Forest." In *An Anthology of New Zealand Poetry in English,* ed. Jenny Bornholdt, Gregory O'Brien, and Mark Williams, 499–500. Auckland, N.Z.: Oxford University Press.

Republic of the Marshall Islands Economic Policy, Planning and Statistics Office, Secretariat of the Pacific Community, and Macro International. 2007. *Demographic and Health Survey 2007.* Noumea, New Caledonia: Secretariat of the Pacific Community. www.spc.int/prism/country/mh/stats/.

Reynolds, Henry. 2012. *A History of Tasmania.* New York: Cambridge University Press.

Ricketts, Harry. 1986. "Ian Wedde." In *Talking about Ourselves: Twelve New Zealand Poets in Conversation with Harry Ricketts,* by Harry Ricketts, 43–57. Wellington, N.Z.: Mallinson Rendel Publishers.

Ritvo, Harriet. 1997. *The Platypus and the Mermaid and Other Figments of the Classifying Imagination.* Cambridge, Mass.: Harvard University Press.

Royal, Te Ahukaramū Charles. 2009a. "Kaitiakitanga—Guardianship and Conservation—Kaitiaki—Guardians." *Te Ara: The Encyclopedia of New Zealand.* www.TeAra.govt.nz/en/kaitiakitanga-guardianship-and-conservation/4.

———. 2009b. "Tangaroa—The Sea—The Importance of the Sea." *Te Ara: The Encyclopedia of New Zealand.* www.TeAra.govt.nz/en/tangaroa-the-sea/1.

Royal Society. 2005. "More Heated Opposition to Marine Reserve Plan." *Royal Society of New Zealand: Te Apārangi.* www.royalsociety.org.nz.

Rozwadowski, Helen M. 2005. *Fathoming the Ocean: The Discovery and Exploration of the Deep Sea.* Cambridge, Mass.: Harvard University Press.

Rudy, Kathy. 2011. *Loving Animals: Toward a New Animal Advocacy.* Minneapolis: University of Minnesota Press.

Said, Edward. 1994. *Culture and Imperialism.* New York: Vintage Books.

Salesa, Damon Ieremia. 2011. *Racial Crossings: Race, Intermarriage, and the Victorian British Empire.* Oxford: Oxford University Press.

Salmond, Anne. 1997. *Between Worlds: Early Exchanges between Maori and Europeans, 1773–1815.* Honolulu: University of Hawai'i Press.

———. 2009. *Aphrodite's Island: The European Discovery of Tahiti.* Rosedale, North Shore, N.Z.: Penguin Group.

Salvador, Richard. 1999. "The Nuclear History of Micronesia and the Pacific by Richard N. Salvador, Republic of Belau, August 1999." *Nuclear Age Peace Foundation.* www.wagingpeace.org/articles/1999/08/00_salvador_micronesia.htm.

———. 2002. "NGO Presentation to the NPT Review Conference Preparatory Committee, New York, April 2002: Indigenous Perspective." *Reaching Critical Will.* www.reachingcriticalwill.org/images/documents/Disarmament-fora/npt/prepcom02/NGOpres2002/4.pdf.

Samoa Tourism Authority. 2011. "Your Samoan Holiday." *Samoa.* www.samoa.travel/about/a9/Your-Samoan-Holiday.

Sargent, Lyman Tower. 2010. "Colonial and Postcolonial Utopias." In *The Cambridge Companion to Utopian Literature,* ed. Gregory Claeys, 200–222. Cambridge: Cambridge University Press.

Sargisson, Lucy, and Lyman Tower Sargent. 2004. *Living in Utopia: New Zealand's Intentional Communities.* Aldershot, U.K.: Ashgate.

Savage, Paula. 2011. "Oceania: Imagining the Pacific." In *Oceania: Imagining the Pacific,* ed. Paula Savage, Gregory O'Brien, Reuben Friend, and Abby Cunnane, 8–13. Wellington, N.Z.: City Gallery Wellington.

Schencking, J. Charles. 1999. "The Imperial Japanese Navy and the Constructed Consciousness of a South Seas Destiny, 1872–1921." *Modern Asian Studies* 33, no. 4: 769–96.

Sharrard, Paul. 2003. *Albert Wendt and Pacific Literature: Circling the Void.* Manchester, U.K.: Manchester University Press.

Shaw, George. 1804. *General Zoology or Systematic Natural History. Vol. V. Part II. Pisces.* London: Printed for G. Kearsley Fleet Street.

Shenon, Philip. 1995. "Tahiti's Antinuclear Protests Turn Violent." *New York Times,* September 8. www.nytimes.com/1995/09/08/world/tahiti-s-antinuclear -protests-turn-violent.html?pagewanted=all&src=pm.

Shute, Nevil. 2010 [1957]. *On the Beach.* New York: Vintage.

Silva, Noenoe K. 2004. *Aloha Betrayed: Native Hawaiian Resistance to American Colonialism.* Durham, N.C.: Duke University Press.

Simpson, Peter. 1995. "Candles in a Dark Room: James K. Baxter and Colin McCahon." *Journal of New Zealand Literature: JNZL* 13: 157–188.

Smith, Bernard. 1985. *European Vision and the South Pacific.* New Haven and London: Yale University Press.

———. 1992. *Imagining the Pacific: In the Wake of the Cook Voyages.* New Haven: Yale University Press.

Song, Cathy. 1983. *Picture Bride.* New Haven: Yale University Press.

Sopoanga, Saufatu. 2003. "Statement by the Honourable Sopoanga OBE Prime Minister and Minister of Foreign Affairs of Tuvalu at the 58th United Nations General Assembly." United Nations. www.un.org/webcast/ga/58/statements/ tuvaeng030924.htm.

Sparrow, Giles. 1999. *The Elements: Iron.* Tarrytown, N.Y.: Marshall Cavendish.

SPREP. n.d. "Climate Change Overview." *SPREP: Secretariat of the Pacific Regional Environmental Programme.* www.sprep.org/Climate-Change/climate-change -overview.

Stafford, Jane, and Mark Williams. 2006. *Maoriland: New Zealand Literature, 1872–1914.* Wellington, N.Z.: Victoria University Press.

Stead, C. K. 1985. "Keri Hulme's 'The Bone People,' and the Pegasus Award for Maori Literature." *ARIEL: A Review of International English Literature* 16, no. 4: 101–8.

Steinberg, Philip E. 2001. *The Social Construction of the Ocean.* Cambridge: Cambridge University Press.

Sterling, Elspeth P., and Catherine C. Summers. 1978. *Sites of Oahu.* Honolulu: Bishop Museum.

Stewart, Frank. 1993. Introduction to *Deep River Talk: Collected Poems,* by Hone Tuwhare, 3–10. Auckland, N.Z.: Godwit Press.

Stewart, Rob. 2006. *Sharkwater.* Toronto: Alliance Films, Sharkwater Productions, and Diatribe Pictures.

Stone, Robert. 1987. *Radio Bikini.* Crossroads Film Project.

Sullivan, Robert. 1998. "Engaging all the Senses." *New Zealand Books* 8, no. 2: 6.

Supreme Court of the United States. 2010. "People of Bikini, Petitioner v. United States." *Bikini Atoll: U.S. Reparations for Damages.* www.bikiniatoll.com/SupremeCourtDenial.pdf.

Suvin, Darko. 1972. "On the Poetics of the Science Fiction Genre." *College English* 34, no. 3: 372–82.

Sweeney, Alison M., Steven H. D. Haddock, and Sönke Johnsen. 2007. "Comparative Visual Acuity of Coleoid Cephalopods." *Integrative and Comparative Biology* 47, no. 6: 808–14.

Takaki, Ronald. 1983. *Pau Hana: Plantation Life and Labor in Hawaii, 1835–1920.* Honolulu: University of Hawai'i Press.

Taonui, Rāwiri. 2009a. "Ngāpuhi—Early European Contact." *Te Ara: The Encyclopedia of New Zealand.* www.teara.govt.nz/en/ngapuhi/5?keys=hone+heke.

————. 2009b. "Te Ngahere—Forest Lore—Māori Relationship with the Forest." *Te Ara: The Encyclopedia of New Zealand.* www.TeAra.govt.nz/en/te-ngahere-forest-lore/1.

————. 2011. "Whakapapa—Genealogy—What is Whakapapa?" *Te Ara: The Encyclopedia of New Zealand.* www.TeAra.govt.nz/en/whakapapa-genealogy/1.

Tarkovsky, Andrei. 2002 [1972]. *Solaris.* Mosfilm Studios and The Criterion Collection.

Tasmanian Government. n.d. "[Sketchbook of Fishes]." *LINC Tasmania.* catalogue.statelibrary.tas.gov.au/item/?id=80818.

Tau, Te Maire. 2009. "Ngāi Tahu—The Ngāi Tahu claim." *Te Ara—The Encyclopedia of New Zealand.* www.TeAra.govt.nz/en/ngai-tahu/8.

Taussig, Michael, and Mary Zournazi. 2002. "Carnival of the Senses: A Conversation with Michael Taussig." In *Hope: New Philosophies for Change,* by Mary Zournazi, 42–63. Annandale, NSW, Aus.: Pluto Press Australia.

Teaiwa, Teresia K. 1994. "bikinis and other s/pacific n/oceans." *Contemporary Pacific* 6, no. 1: 87–109.

————. 2001. "L(o)osing the Edge." *Contemporary Pacific* 13, no. 2: 343–57.

Toer, Pramoedya Ananta. 2007. "Literature, Censorship, and the State: To What Extent Is a Novel Dangerous?" Translated by Alex G. Bardsley. literarystudies

.wordpress.com/2007/07/24/literature-censorship-and-the-state-to-what
-extent-is-a-novel-dangerous/.

Tourism New Zealand. 2011. "New Zealand 100% Pure. Official Travel Informa-
tion from Tourism New Zealand." *100% Pure New Zealand*. www.newzealand
.com/us.

Tourism Tasmania. 2010a. "Tasmania." *Tasmania*. www.discovertasmania.com.

———. 2010b. "Western Wilderness." *Tasmania*. www.discovertasmania.com/
western_wilderness/.

Tsing, Anna Lowenhaupt. 2005. *Friction: An Ethnography of Global Connection*.
Princeton: Princeton University Press.

———. 2011. "Arts of Inclusion, or, How to Love a Mushroom." *Australian Humanities Review* 50 (May). www.australianhumanitiesreview.org/archive/Issue
-May-2011/tsing.html

Tuhiwai Smith, Linda. 1999. *Decolonizing Methodologies: Research and Indigenous
Peoples*. London: Zed Books.

Tuwhare, Hone. 1964. *No Ordinary Sun*. Auckland and Hamilton, N.Z.: Blackwood
& Janet Paul Ltd.

———. 1997. *Shape-Shifter*. Wellington, N.Z.: Steele Roberts.

———. 2011. "Friend." In *Hone Tuwhare. Small Holes in the Silence. Collected Works*,
by Hone Tuwhare, 44. Auckland, N.Z.: Random House.

Union Steam Ship Company of New Zealand. 1889. *New Zealand: An Earthly
Paradise*. Dunedin, N.Z.: Union Steam Ship Company of New Zealand.

———. 1914. *The Islands of the Blest*. Dunedin, N.Z.: Union Steam Ship Company of New Zealand.

Updike, John. 2001. "Transparent Stratagems." In *Americana and Other Poems*,
by John Updike, 87–88. New York: Knopf.

Usui, Masami. 1995. "Women Disclosed: Cathy Song's Poetry and Kitagawa
Utamaro's *Ukiyoe*." *Ningen Bunka Kenkyu. Studies in Culture and the Humanities*
4: 1–19.

Vaai, Sina Mary Theresa. 1999. *Literary Representations in Western Polynesia: Colonialism and Indigeneity*. Apia, Samoa: National University of Samoa, Le
Papa-I-Galagala.

Vangioni, Peter. 2005. "The Lively Surface." In *Hotere: Empty of Shadows and
Making a Shadow: Lithographs by Ralph Hotere*, ed. Peter Vangioni and Jillian
Cassidy, 13–19. Christchurch, N.Z.: Christchurch Art Gallery.

Vatulescu, Cristina. 2004. "Arresting Biographies: The Secret Police File in the Soviet Union and Romania." *Comparative Literature* 56, no. 3: 243–61.

Vieira, Fátima. 2010. "The Concept of Utopia." In *The Cambridge Companion to
Utopian Literature*, ed. Gregory Claeys, 3–27. Cambridge: Cambridge University Press.

Vincent, Lindsay. 2005. "French accused of Pacific Nuclear Cover-up." *The*

Guardian, December 31. www.guardian.co.uk/world/2006/jan/01/france
.lindsayvincent.

Waitangi Tribunal. 1987. "Report of the Waitangi Tribunal on the Orakei Claim
(Wai-9)." *Waitangi Tribunal. Te Rōpū Whakamana I Te Tiriti O Waitangi.* www
.waitangi-tribunal.govt.nz.

———. 1991. "The Ngai Tahu Report 1991." *Waitangi Tribunal. Te Rōpū Whakamana I Te Tiriti O Waitangi.* www.waitangi-tribunal.govt.nz.

———. 1992. "The Te Roroa Report 1992." *Waitangi Tribunal. Te Rōpū Whakamana I Te Tiriti O Waitangi.* www.waitangi-tribunal.govt.nz.

———. 2004. "The Story of Te Kooti and the Whakarau." *Turanga Tangata
Turanga Whenua: The Report on the Turanganui a Kiwa Claims. Volume 1. Wai
814. Waitangi Tribunal. Te Rōpū Whakamana I Te Tiriti O Waitangi.* 169–252.
www.waitangi-tribunal.govt.nz.

Walker, Isaiah Helekunihi. 2008. "Hui Nalu, Beachboys, and the Surfing Boarder-
lands of Hawai'i." *Contemporary Pacific* 20, no. 1: 89–113.

Walker, Ranginui. 1987. "Maori Myth, Tradition and Philosophic Beliefs." In *Te
Whenua, Te Iwi: The Land and the People,* ed. Jock Phillips, 42–47. Wellington,
N.Z.: Allen & Unwin and Port Nicholson Press.

Wallace, Patricia. 1993. "Divided Loyalties: Literal and Literary in the Poetry of
Lorna Dee Cervantes, Cathy Song, and Rita Dove." *MELUS* 18, no. 3: 3–19.

Walters, Mark Jerome. 2006. *Seeking the Sacred Raven: Politics and Extinction on a
Hawaiian Island.* Washington, D.C.: Island Press.

Watts, Richard. 2007. "Contested Sources: Water as Commodity/Sign in French
Caribbean Literature." *Atlantic Studies* 4, no. 1: 87–101.

Wedde, Ian. 1973. "Ian Wedde." In *The Young New Zealand Poets,* ed. Arthur Baysting,
185–86. Auckland, N.Z.: Heinemann Educational Books.

———. 1975. *Pathway to the Sea.* Christchurch, N.Z.: Hawk Press.

———. 1997. "Where is the Art that does this?" Introduction to *Hotere: Out the
Black Window. Ralph Hotere's Work with New Zealand Poets,* by Gregory O'Brien,
8–11. Auckland and Wellington, N.Z.: Godwit and City Gallery Wellington.

———. 2005a. "Collecting Dreams: Art and Arcadia." In *Making Ends Meet: Essays and Talks, 1992–2004,* by Ian Wedde, 89–93. Wellington, N.Z.: Victoria
University Press.

———. 2005b. "Letter to Peter McLeavey: After Basho." In *Three Regrets and a
Hymn to Beauty,* by Ian Wedde, 40–67. Auckland, N.Z.: Auckland University
Press.

———. 2005c. "Lost at Sea: Drowning in New Zealand Literature." In *Making
Ends Meet: Essays and Talks, 1992–2004,* by Ian Wedde, 21–34. Wellington, N.Z.:
Victoria University Press.

Weeks, Kathi. 2007. "Life within and against Work: Affective Labor, Feminist Critique, and Post-Fordist Politics." *Ephemera: Theory and Politics in Organization*
7, no. 1: 233–49.

Weir, Zach. 2005. "Set Adrift: Identity and the Postcolonial Present in *Gould's Book of Fish.*" *Postcolonial Text* 1, no. 2. http://postcolonial.org/index.php/pct/article/viewArticle/345

Wendt, Albert. 1982. "Towards a New Oceania." In *Writers in East-West Encounter: New Cultural Bearings,* ed. Guy Amirthanayagam, 202–15. London: Macmillan.

———. 1990. "Pacific Maps and Fiction(s): A Personal Journey." In *Migration and New Zealand Society: Proceedings of the Stout Research Centre Sixth Annual Conference Victoria University of Wellington June 30-July 2 1989,* 59–81. Wellington, N.Z.: Stout Research Centre.

———. 1995a [1992]. *Black Rainbow.* Honolulu: University of Hawai'i Press.

———. 1995b. "Introduction." In *Nuanua: Pacific Writing in English since 1980,* ed. Albert Wendt, 1–8. Honolulu: University of Hawai'i Press.

Wenzel, Jennifer. 2009. *Bulletproof: Afterlives of Anticolonial Prophecy in South Africa and Beyond.* Chicago: University of Chicago Press.

Wigley, T. M. L. 2005. "The Climate Change Commitment." *Science* 307, no. 5716: 1766–69.

Wilcox, Carol. 1996. *Sugar Water: Hawaii's Plantation Ditches.* Honolulu: University of Hawai'i Press.

Williams, Mark. 1990. *Leaving the Highway: Six Contemporary New Zealand Novelists.* Auckland, N.Z.: Auckland University Press.

Williams, Raymond. 1973. *The Country and the City.* New York: Oxford University Press.

Wilson, Rob. 2000. *Reimagining the American Pacific: From South Pacific to Bamboo Ridge and Beyond.* Durham, N.C.: Duke University Press.

Winton, Tim. 2003. "Tim Winton's Ningaloo Reef Rally Speech." *Wilderness Society.* www.wilderness.org.au/campaigns/marine-coastal/tw_ning.

Wittmann, Livia Käthe. 2002. "Postmodern Ethnicity or Utopian Di-ethnia? Women's Multilingual/Multicultural Writing in Aotearoa/New Zealand." *Journal of Commonwealth Literature* 37, no. 1: 101–20.

Wood, Hannah L., John I. Spicer, and Stephen Widdicombe. 2008. "Ocean Acidification May Increase Calcification Rates, but at a Cost." *Proceedings of the Royal Society B* 275, no. 1644: 1767–73.

Yaeger, Patricia. 2010. "Editor's Column: Sea Trash, Dark Pools, and the Tragedy of the Commons." *PMLA* 125, no. 3: 523–45.

Young, David. 2004. *Our Islands, Our Selves: A History of Conservation in New Zealand.* Dunedin, N.Z.: University of Otago Press.

Zemka, Sue. 2002. "*Erewhon* and the End of Utopian Humanism." *ELH* 69, no. 2: 439–72.

Zournazi, Mary. 2002. *Hope: New Philosophies for Change.* Annandale, NSW, Aus.: Pluto Press Australia.

Index

activism, environmental: accounts of
oceans, 17; antinuclear, 21, 161–63,
172; engagement with loss, 154; of
New Zealand, 47–48, 111–12; on
stillness, 29; tactics of, 12–13; transnational actions of, 86–87; of U.S.,
191n12; water efforts of, 19–20, 59–60,
74. *See also* environmentalism
Afro-Ecuadorian peoples, hope
among, 10
Agamben, Giorgio, 52
Ahmad, Dohra, 191n7
Ahmed, Sara, 14, 149
Ahuja, Neel, 127
'alalā (endangered bird), 117, 199n2
Alexander, Ronni, 205n18
aluminum industry, transnational, 117;
environmental damage from, 88,
108–10; in New Zealand, 108–10, 111;
publicity material of, 107, 109, 110
animal welfare, nineteenth-century, 40
animism: Hawaiian, 102; in Oceanic
literatures, 10
Anker, Peder, 187n6
Aotearoa (New Zealand), hope for, 2
Appadurai, Arjun, 188n7, 205n15
art, colonial, 89, 95; of Kororāreka, 93;
of Tasmania, 202n12
Arthur, George, 120, 200n6
ATOM (Against Tests on Moruroa)
Committee (Fiji), 162

'aumākua (ancestral guardians), 1, 18
Australia: early Europeans on, 140;
hope for, 2; Indigenous peoples of,
124, 200n9; inequality in, 144–45;
marine ecosystems of, 140; politics
of national security, 196n6; social
ideals of, 10
Austronesian languages, past and
future in, 189n13
authors, Oceanic: social activism of, 21
Avatar (film): Indigenous people of,
53; oceanic setting of, 7
Awá people, hope among, 10

Bachelard, Gaston, 62, 193n7; on feminine aspects of water, 195n14
Bacon, Francis: use of exploration narratives, 191n7. *See also New Atlantis*
Balaz, Joe: "Da Last Squid," 116
Barclay, Robert: *Meḷaḷ*, 25, 149–50,
166, 206n24; creative potential in,
174; economic hardship in, 173,
206n26; hope in, 9–10, 169, 170–74;
imaginary of flying in, 172, 173, 174;
lived worlds of, 153; loss in, 171, 172;
nonhuman beings in, 169; nuclear
weapons in, 153, 167–68; spirit
world in, 9–10, 169, 171
Barker, Holly M.: *The Rongelap
Report: Consequential Damages of
Nuclear War*, 155, 163

Children of a Fireland (Pak), 67; U.S.
militarism in, 69
Christchurch earthquake (2011), 178
CIA, torture practices of, 127
classification, nineteenth-century,
123–24, 200nn8–9
climate change: documentary films
about, 181, 207n3; effect of capitalist
economy on, 16; effect on oceans, 16,
141; hope and, 25, 111; horizon in, 86;
Pacific, 181–83; reshaping of futures,
182; as terrorism, 182; uncertainty in,
15; understanding of time in, 15. See
also environmental change
colonialism: displacement through,
11; environmental destruction
under, 8, 31; hydrological regimes
in, 193n2; Indigenous peoples'
perspectives and, 189n21; Japanese, 206n27; nonurban spaces
in, 46; nuclear testing and, 17,
189n20; oceans in, 194n12; power
disparities in, 55; promising future
in, 60; relationship with hope, 184;
socioeconomic contradictions of,
46; utopianism in, 12, 28, 32, 33, 42,
190n3. See also imperialism
Command oil spill, 196n1; effect on tītī
birds, 85
Compact of Free Association, 162–63,
206n23
Conference for a Nuclear-Free Pacific
(1975), 162
Connery, Christopher, 193n3
Cook, James, 12
Corbin, Alain, 194n11
Cousteau, Jacques-Yves: Le Monde sans
Soleil, 7
Cramer, Chris, 64
creativity, environmental: everyday
practices in, 82; hope in, 83

Critical Ecosystem Partnership Fund,
198n15
Cruikshank, Julie, 199n23
Culbert, Bill: Pathway to the Sea,
105–6
Culliney, John, 65, 177
cultural production: across distances,
86; by Indigenous peoples, 148
culture, Māori, 49, 56–57; colors in, 90;
environment in, 53; sensitive sites
of, 55; taonga (treasures) of, 104
culture, Pacific: darkness in, 175; past
and future in, 189n13

Darwin, Charles: account of New
Zealand, 54–55
Darwinism, (non)moral ontology of,
191n6
deforestation, in New Zealand, 94–95,
112
DeLoughrey, Elizabeth M., 189n20,
194nn10,12; on imperialism, 197n10;
on nuclear weapons, 205n12
Dibble, Sheldon, 55; History of the
Sandwich Islands, 194n8
difference: dynamics of, 101; environmental, 87, 89–91; in environmental
hope, 180; in environmental life,
87, 97, 98, 101; in hope, 97, 106; in
Oceanic literature, 87; politics of,
165; social, 164
The Disappearing of Tuvalu (documentary), 181, 182
disconnection, politics of, 111–13
Disney cartoons, property relations
in, 164
distance: cultural production across,
86; in nonhuman relationships, 86
Dorfman, Ariel, 8
Dudoit, D. Māhealani: "Reservoir of
Hope," 19–20, 67

TERESA SHEWRY is associate professor of English at the University of California, Santa Barbara. Her research draws together Pacific and Pacific Rim literatures, environmental studies, water and the ocean, and hope and utopia. She is a coeditor of *Environmental Criticism for the Twenty-First Century*.